ANTHROPOLOGY OF TRANSFORMATION

Anthropology of Transformation

From Europe to Asia and Back

Edited by Juraj Buzalka
and Agnieszka Pasieka

OpenBook Publishers

ISBN Paperback: 9781800643628
ISBN Hardback: 9781800643635
ISBN Digital (PDF): 9781800643642
ISBN Digital ebook (EPUB): 9781800643659
ISBN Digital ebook (AZW3): 9781800643666
ISBN XML: 9781800643673
Digital ebook (HTML): 9781800649439
DOI: 10.11647/OBP.0282

Cover image: Lenin mural, House of Culture, Temirtau, Kazakhstan (2014). Photo by Tommaso Trevisani. Cover design by Katy Saunders.

Contents

Acknowledgements   vii

Contributor Biographies   ix

Introduction   xiii
Juraj Buzalka and Agnieszka Pasieka

1. Voiced versus Acted Trust: Managing Social Uncertainty and
   Marginalisation in Rural Southern Italy and
   Central Eastern Europe   1
Davide Torsello

2. Property Relations and Ethnic Conflict in Post-war Croatia:
   Reflections on Conceptual Approaches and Research Findings   25
Carolin Leutloff-Grandits

3. The 'Post' in Perspective: Revisiting the Post-socialist Religious
   Question in Central Asia and Central and Eastern Europe   51
Julie McBrien and Vlad Naumescu

4. "We Are Not Believers, We're Workers": The Synchrony of Work,
   Gender, and Religion in a Priestless Orthodox Community   81
Agata Ładykowska

5. The Moral Economy of Consensus and Informality in
   Uzbekistan   105
Tommaso Trevisani

6. The Moral Dimension of (Un)Employment: Work and
   Fairness in an Eastern German Town   131
Katerina Ivanova

7. Beyond Blue Eyes? Xenophobia on the Eastern Margins of the
   European Union   155
László Fosztó

8. Post-Peasant Progressivism: On Liberal Tendencies in the
   Slovak Countryside   179

Juraj Buzalka

9. Swimming against the Tide: Right-wing Populism, Post-socialism
and Beyond   205
Agnieszka Pasieka

10. *Transoceania*: Connecting the World beyond Eurasia   221
Edyta Roszko

Index   243

Acknowledgements

We would like to thank all those who helped us to make this volume a reality: the directors and staff of the Max Planck Institute for Social Anthropology, with special thanks to Bettina Mann and Anke Mayer; the four anonymous reviewers, whose comments and suggestions greatly improved the final chapters; our former colleagues Deema Kaneff and Kristen Endres, who edited their own volume dedicated to Chris Hann's work, *Explorations in Economic Anthropology: Key Issues and Critical Reflections* (Berghahn 2021), and encouraged and advised us to create our own 'doctoral students'' volume; Alessandra Tosi, Melissa Purkiss and Laura Rodríguez Pupo at Open Book Publishers, who assisted us with patience. Last but not least, we would like to thank all of our friends and colleagues—former doctoral students of Professor Chris Hann—who agreed to contribute to this volume and worked alongside us on it. Thank you for this truly collegial endeavour.

Contributor Biographies

Juraj Buzalka is Professor of Social Anthropology at the Faculty of Social and Economic Sciences of the Comenius University in Bratislava. His research includes the anthropology of social and political movements, politics of memory and religion, and the anthropology of wine. He recently published *The Cultural Economy of Protest in Post-Socialist European Union: Village Fascists and their Rivals* (2021). His first monograph was *Nation and Religion: The Politics of Commemoration in South-east Poland* (2007).

László Fosztó is a Senior Researcher at the Romanian Institute for Research on National Minorities, Cluj-Napoca, Romania. His main research interests include Romani studies, ethnicity and nationalism, anthropology of religion, migration and social networks. Most of his research has been carried out in ethnically mixed rural communities in Romania. He is the author of *Ritual Revitalisation after Socialism: Community, Personhood, and Conversion among Roma in a Transylvanian Village* (2009) and *Colecție de studii despre romii din România* [*Collected Studies on Roma in Romania*] (2009). He is the administrator of the European Academic Network on Romani Studies (http://romanistudies. eu/).

Katerina Ivanova is a postdoctoral scholar at the Faculty of Social and Economic Sciences of the Comenius University in Bratislava. Her research interests include industrial labour, post-socialism and ethnicity with a regional focus on Eastern Germany and Bulgaria.

Carolin Leutloff-Grandits is a senior researcher at the interdisciplinary Viadrina Center B/ORDERS IN MOTION at the European University Viadrina. Her research interests include migration, borders, temporality, social security, and family. She is particularly concerned with the countries of the former Yugoslavia. Selected publications include '"We are not Just the Border of Croatia; This is the Border of the European Union..." The Croatian Borderland as "Double Periphery"', *Journal of Borderlands Studies* (2022), and *Claiming Ownership in Post-War Croatia. The Dynamics of Property Relations and Ethnic Conflict in the Knin Region* (2006).

Agata Ładykowska is a research fellow at the Institute of Sociological Studies, Charles University, Prague. Her research interests include anthropology of religion and atheism, historical anthropology, anthropological theory, political anthropology, economic anthropology, anthropology of post-socialism/social change, and post-humanist and relational social sciences. Her publications include 'The shifts between: Multiple secularisms, multiple modernities and the post-Soviet school', in T. Köllner ed., *Orthodox Religion and Politics In Contemporary Eastern Europe: on Multiple Secularisms and Entanglements* (2019), pp. 109–122, and 'The changing scope of religious authority and reconfigurations of social status in postsocialist Russia', *Religion, State, and Society* (2018).

Julie McBrien is Associate Professor of Anthropology at the University of Amsterdam and the Director of the Amsterdam Research Center for Gender and Sexuality. Her research interests include religion, secularism, gender, and development. She is the author of *From Belonging to Belief: Modern Secularisms and the Construction of Religion in Kyrgyzstan* (2017).

Vlad Naumescu is Associate Professor of Anthropology at the Central European University (Vienna/Budapest). He has conducted extensive fieldwork in Eastern Europe and South India looking at practices, institutions and politics that shape Orthodox communities. He is the author of *Modes of Religiosity in Eastern Christianity: Religious Processes and Social Change in Ukraine* (2007), co-editor of *Churches In-between: Greek Catholic Churches in Postsocialist Europe* (2008), and a forthcoming monograph on ritual, history and ethics in the Russian Old Belief.

Agnieszka Pasieka is a Visiting Professor of Anthropology at the University of Bayreuth and Research Fellow at the University of Vienna. She specialises in anthropology of religion and anthropology of politics. She is the author of *Hierarchy and Pluralism: Living Religious Difference in Catholic Poland* (2015) and co-editor of the forthcoming

Rethinking Modern Polish Identities: Transnational Encounters. Her new book focuses on the transnational networking of European far-right movements.

Edyta Roszko is Research Professor at the Chr. Michelsen Institute in Bergen, Norway and a Fellow of the Young Academy of Europe. She has published articles on ocean-related issues and the politics of religion and heritisation in *Anthropological Quarterly, Singapore Journal of Tropical Geography, Journal of Contemporary Ethnography, Nations and Nationalism* and others. Her first book, *Fishers, Monks and Cadres: Navigating State, Religion and the South China Sea in Central Vietnam*, was co-published in 2020 by NIAS and the University of Hawai'i Press and is available in open access format at http://hdl.handle.net/10125/76750.

Davide Torsello is Professor of Anthropology and Organizational Behavior at the Central European University, Vienna. He has extensive experience of ethnographic field research in organisations and communities in Japan, Italy and Eastern Europe. Davide has studied political and business corruption and has published over sixty journal articles and book chapters and eleven books, the latest (in press) being *The Cultural Theory of Corruption. Institutions, Cognition and Organizations*. He has consulted for international organisations (UNODC, EU Parliament) and corporates; he is advisor to the nomination committee for the Nobel Prize in Economics.

Tommaso Trevisani is Associate Professor at the Department of African, Asian and Mediterranean Studies, University of Naples L'Orientale, where he teaches Societies and Cultures of Central Asia. He has conducted extensive fieldwork in Uzbekistan and Kazakhstan. His research interests include agrarian and environmental change; class and industrial work; ritual, marriage and society.

Introduction

Juraj Buzalka and Agnieszka Pasieka

It has been more than thirty years since the fall of the Berlin Wall and the collapse of communist regimes in numerous countries. A watershed moment, the developments in 1989 and thereafter were—quite unsurprisingly—studied and analysed by numerous scholars. Much of this research had a very practical orientation, as it aimed at providing tools for "dealing" with socio-political transformation and addressing the issues of apparent change. For socio-cultural anthropologists, however, ethnographic studies conducted in the period of post-socialist transformation meant both an engagement with issues that have long been at the heart of the discipline and an opportunity to shed a new light on those matters. These were, among others, questions about the relation between morality and other spheres of social life; the everyday operation of political and economic institutions; people's agency and their ways of dealing with social changes; grassroots political and civic activism, as well as the manifold continuities and validity of a *longue-durée* approach to the post-socialist transformation, sharply contrasting with the emphasis on dramatic rupture brought by the 1989 transition.

In short, the anthropological investigations of the micro-level transformations provided a perspective on an alternative model of modernity, different from the capitalist one that had dominated the scholarship for decades. It is a perspective that continues to inspire comparative research. To name but a few recent examples, the societal reactions to the COVID-19 pandemic, responses to the refugee crisis and the rise of right-wing populism in Eastern Europe so tragically materialised in Putin's Russia's aggression on Ukraine can be productively analysed in the broader context of post-socialist transformation. Questions of "capitalism without liberalism" (as

 https://doi.org/10.11647/OBP.0282.11

emblematically developed in China) and the dynamics of neoliberal politics after state socialism open space for a productive discussion about the deeper layers of transformations of former state-socialist societies. Yet another example is the socio-religious landscape: religions have re-emerged as powerful public actors in the aftermath of one-party states that themselves often appeared as religious regimes in their own right. The religious-national conflicts in the region have been explained as having their own socialist, as well as post-socialist, trajectories.

This volume offers a social anthropological perspective on the vast region that Professor Chris Hann, prominent figure in the research and theorisation of post-socialism, designates as Eurasia. Director for over two decades at the Max Planck Institute for Social Anthropology (MPISA) in Halle/Saale, Germany, Professor Hann supported and supervised several generations of socio-cultural anthropologists carrying out fieldwork in numerous countries across Eurasia. Building upon Chris Hann's life-long, fieldwork-based familiarity with regions as different as Central and Eastern Europe, Turkey, and the Chinese north-west, this collection of essays represents a joint effort by his former doctoral students to reflect upon his work in light of their own. Since the establishment of the MPISA in the late 1990s, doctoral training has been a fundamental aspect of the advancement of its research agenda. Thanks to the opportunities for PhD students to conduct long-term fieldwork and develop their work in conversation with senior researchers, whether fellows of the institute or prominent visiting scholars, a visible generation of specialists in former state-socialist countries has formed. After graduating, they have found employment in different academic settings in Europe and North America, successfully carrying on the legacy of a particular—ethnographic, comparative and historically informed—perspective on complex transformations within and beyond the post-socialist realms. Without Chris Hann's ambitious plan and tenacious work, MPISA's contribution to the academic world would not have had the same impact on academic discussions.

This book *is not* a collection of conference papers. It aims at engaging with enduring questions in Chris Hann's work, identifying those issues which were at once most prominent in his scholarship, and which have had the biggest impact on his students' work and their scholarly trajectories. This book thus ought to be seen as a multivocal conversation between the mentor, his students, and numerous other scholars who have critically engaged with his work. Each author takes Hann's ideas as the starting point of his or her consideration, and then polemically expands them through their own ethnographic insights. Indeed, the volume's biggest strength is the fact that all of the contributors draw on long-term ethnographic research, providing a novel perspective on the post-socialist transformation in Central and Eastern Europe (CEE) and the former Soviet Union, as well as globally. The volume thus addresses political, economic and religious questions provoked by the thirty-year anniversary of the 1989 revolution, illustrating the inter-disciplinary and inter-generational dialogue generated by the study of post-socialist transformation, productively expanded and inspired by Chris Hann's work.

In the following, we describe in more detail the themes we have chosen for this "conversation" and briefly summarise the structure of the volume. Rather than trying to systematically cover Hann's impressive scholarship—something our senior colleagues have already successfully attempted in another volume (Kaneff and Endres 2021)—our aim has been to engage with those topics we find most appropriate for telling a story about *scholars, scholarship* and *mentoring*. We have singled out a few important ideas Hann proposed along the years, the focus on which allows us to demonstrate not only some *final* "products"—be it articles, book chapters or new concepts—but products in the *making*: a story of interactions, exchanges, and inspirations that led to the final works. For this purpose, we have decided to foreground two of Hann's contributions, his 2011 Erfurt lecture "Eastern Christianity and Western Social Theory" and a relatively recent (2018) article "Moral(ity and) Economy. Work, Workfare, and Fairness in Provincial Hungary," relating them to Hann's broader vision of an anthropology of transformation in Eurasia.

Key Terms, or: The Title of the Volume Explained

At a time when disciplinary canons are being reconsidered and the boundaries between disciplines contested, it is important to ask: what do we understand by "anthropology"? At the MPI for Social and Cultural Anthropology, the answer to this question has been rather straightforward. Hann's conviction of the value of long-term ethnographic fieldwork can be said to be the core *creed* transmitted to generations of his students. This academic ethos grew from the empiricist tradition of British social anthropology and motivated his own long-term ethnographic studies in four countries (in Hungary, Poland, Turkey, and China). Hann kept returning to his various fieldsites over the years and, despite embarking on new projects, remained vividly interested in developments in the areas of which he had deep knowledge. Moreover, the quality of ethnographic material—that is, ethnography that gives insights into lived realities and which leads to new theoretical insights—has always been the key criterion through which he valued his students' work.

Hann's work has always been ethnographically grounded; "Moral(ity and) Economy" is a superb example of this approach. Drawing on field research in a Hungarian village he has known for over forty years, Hann critically engages with recent attempts to "expand" the concept of moral economy. The (over)emphasis on "tensions" and "contradictions" which supposedly characterise moral economies leads, in his view, to a downplaying of the economic dimension and ultimately weakens the very concept of "moral economy." Hann highlights instead long-term, collectively held values—such as the value of work as an object of moral sentiment—a "dimension" he was able to observe and theorise precisely due to his long-term engagement with a specific locality, ethnographic "revisits" and close contacts with several generations of inhabitants. Notably, the works he engages with to corroborate his arguments are likewise products of intense field research (e.g. Lampland 1995).

In arguing against the "lumpish" concept of moral economy, Hann suggests that it is unhelpful in grasping the post-socialist transformation. As mentioned above, he argues that in recent reiterations the concept has not made space for engaging with "embedded moral values" and especially the resilience of "work as value." These points well illustrate an approach Hann has persistently put forward and propagated— tracing "dominant values" through history and connecting them to their "concrete enactments" in social relations observed in the field.

The question of embeddedness—inspired by the seminal work of Karl Polanyi (Polanyi 1978[1944]), which Hann considers to be one of his key inspirations—leads to the second key term, "transformation." Hann's research experience in socialist countries made it possible for him to conduct a series of inspiring studies on complex, socio-political changes that have been taking place since the 1980s. Stressing the social costs of transformations, Hann, like his fellow anthropologists, critically engaged with the teleological narrative on the transition from communism to liberal democracy (for an overview, see Hann, Humphrey and Verdery 2001). The common feature of anthropological studies of socialism and post-socialism has been their stress on the distinctive character of the socialist regime and the legacies of state-socialist and pre-socialist regimes for contemporary socio-political developments (Hann et al. 2001).

Hann et al.'s (2001) focus on economic transformation (with a special emphasis on the transition from socialist to capitalist economy) is of course but one of his engagements with the question of transformation. He has also written a series of highly inspiring works on religion, nationalism and ethnicity, demonstrating once again how an ethnographically grounded perspective and attention to history enables us to examine complex processes of collective identity formation and, indeed, social-political transformation (see Hann 1998; Hann 2000; Hann and Pelkmans 2009). His work on Eastern and Western Christianity (Hann and Goltz 2010) emphasised a long history of interactions, mutual influences and related "hybridisation" of religious traditions beyond nation-state borders. These observations allowed him to make a series of strong arguments against the reified concept of "culture," whether used in ethno-nationalist exclusionary discourses or the supposedly benign discourse of multiculturalism (see Hann 2002)

Moreover, his long-standing interest in the in-betweenness of Greek Catholics in CEE and Eastern Christianity more broadly led to another fundamental contribution to the study of transformation, namely an encouragement to rethink the genealogies of modernity. Hann's Erfurt lecture (2011) is a *tour de force* which exposes the ethnocentrism of social theory that constructs its vision of modernity in "Western" terms. In exemplifying this problem through scholarship on religion and the Protestant bias characterising the anthropology of Christianity, Hann demonstrates the ways in which this mode of theorising ends up portraying Eastern Christianity as non-modern and immutable. Importantly, and reflecting Hann's vision of anthropology mentioned above, his call to challenge this bias simultaneously indicates the need for a more thorough ethnographic engagement. Quite tellingly, the section of the lecture which best exposes a more complex understanding of Western and Eastern Christianity is titled "Enter the ethnographers".

In his Erfurt lecture, Hann refers to yet another scholar who, in addition to Polanyi, has been one of his most important sources of inspiration: Jack Goody. Hann draws on Goody's criticism of Weber's Eurocentric approach and his understanding of Eurasia. For Hann, as for Goody, the adoption of the term "Eurasia" is not only a way to challenge Western exclusivist conceptions of modernity and change, but also a means to highlight connections, interactions, and exchanges between Europe and Asia. In other words, the concept of Eurasia is an answer to an epistemological question: a commitment to understand the complexities of societies inhabiting the "supercontinent" through a focus on interconnections and commonalities (rather than taking as a point of departure demarcations and differences between the two continents). As such, this idea perfectly illustrates what lay at the heart of Hann's key contributions over the years, whether devoted to religion, populism, agrarian economy or ethnic identities. Hann developed his concept of Eurasia to go beyond Eurocentrism, which envisioned "Europe" as unique and distinct, and to provide normative frameworks and frames of comparison.

To sum up, Hann's critical engagement with the reified notions of culture and modernity, attention to history and emphasis on exchanges/ interactions demonstrate his position among the scholars of (post-socialist) transformation as one who vehemently challenged the West/East binary. Fundamentally, this criticism, as well as his broader theory, is built from in-depth ethnographic studies; ethnographic observations—whether his own or those of scholars who inspired him—have always been the most fruitful sources of his theoretical and empirical engagements. It is an approach shared by the authors of this volume, as the short summary below demonstrates.

The book opens with a chapter by Davide Torsello, the first PhD graduate of Chris Hann after the opening of the MPI in Halle. Torsello argues, through examples from southern Italy and East Central Europe, that the complexity brought about by high social uncertainty and marginalisation requires actors to invest in forms of trust which can continuously and efficiently be re-negotiated and rendered impermanent. These forms not only include strategic resorts to trust and distrust, but also the blurring of the boundary between interpersonal and institutional trust.

Carolin Leutloff-Grandits links the question of property to the post-war transformation of Croatia and the ongoing ethno-nationalism under the post-socialist transformation. Inspired by Chris Hann's conceptualisation of property contrasting with the dominant individualist private property preferences of the international actors, she discusses the housing property and explores in which way this housing property is embedded in forms of community and socialising which reach back to socialist and pre-socialist times, creating not only a roof over one's head, but identity and belonging, which are embedded into specific forms of livelihood, and social security, which is also closely linked to the workplace.

The chapter by Julie McBrien and Vlad Naumescu revisits the 'post-socialist religious question' twenty years later, reflecting on its theoretical import and contribution to broader debates on religion, modernity and social transformation. It draws on the comparative work produced by the MPISA research group on 'Religion and Civil Society' focused on the 'religious revivals' in CEE and Central Asia. The authors argue that while some of the trends identified by this group were ephemeral products of the 'transition period,' others proved more durable, like the thorny ethno-national-religious knot and its impact on regional, national and global politics. Moreover, they demonstrate that the Civil Religion Group's attempt to answer the post-socialist religious question proved that the post-socialist context was a laboratory for anthropological thought which still bears on contemporary issues.

Agata Ładykowska's chapter follows Hann's critical reflection on how religious ideas are being invoked to explain changes in societal organisation, at least since Weber (Hann 2012). Hann's preoccupation with the Eastern Christian perspective (e.g. Hann and Goltz 2010; Hann 2011; 2012) allowed for a critique of unidirectional models of modernity that was grounded in an interweaving of secularity, individualism and the spread of capitalism. His work paved the way for an anthropological search for alternative notions of modernity, secularity and identity at play, which has been Ładykowska's main research question.

The chapter by Tommaso Trevisani looks at the transformation of Uzbek society by investigating the changing nature of authoritarianism from a moral economy perspective. The focus of his analysis is on the relationship between informal economy and authoritarianism in

Uzbekistan. The chapter takes inspiration from Hann's (2018) approach to moral economy, in which the study of the transformation of social values across history figures prominently and it explicitly compares the Uzbekistan case study with his Hungarian case study.

Katerina Ivanova, who completed her PhD studies at MPI around the time of Hann´s official retirement, focuses on unemployment and the different values, meanings and morals associated with it in Zwickau, an industrial city in eastern Germany. In her approach, she follows Chris Hann's (2016: 7) recognition of "a moral dimension in the sense of a collective and systemic basis in long-term shared values", which captures both the dynamic nature of morality and economy, and the resilience of some long-term dominant values.

László Fosztó argues that our ability to understand and address xenophobia and anti-Gypsyism will be greatly enhanced if we look beyond legal definitions of human rights, without falling back on cultural explanations, or simply blaming racist attitudes. Addressing themes frequently discussed by Chris Hann, Fosztó shows how ethnic diversity is embedding economic relationships. Ethnicity, in his view, provides local modes for interaction which buffer local communities, reducing the impact of exclusionary political rhetoric and exacerbating xenophobia.

Juraj Buzalka´s chapter follows Chris Hann's long-term interest in peasants and their transformations. It complements Hann's perspective on the introduction of post-socialist liberalism in Hungary by presenting some arguments about socialist and post-socialist politics in Slovakia. Chris Hann has pointed to the consolidation of reactionary right-wing populism under the leadership of national bourgeoisie as a consequence of the introduction of free-market liberalism and the state's reduced provision of social welfare for the Hungarian population. However, the Slovak case shows that one ought to pay equal attention to the values represented in rural progressivism—a kind of autochthonous liberalism—as an important component of social and political emancipation, complementing reactionary post-peasant populism.

Agnieszka Pasieka's contribution engages with Hann's recent work on right-wing populism in Hungary by discussing the activism of a Polish "national socialist" movement. A discussion of young activists' views on the economy, Europe, the place and role of the nation-state is for her a point of departure for considering broader developments as well as the role of anthropology in studying the far right and right-wing populism.

Edyta Roszko's chapter engages with Chris Hann's concept of Eurasia. Emphasising the interconnected singularity of the ocean (rather than the Eurasian supercontinent) for an understanding of non-Eurocentric connectivities, she proposes a new paradigm—Transoceania. Transoceania foregrounds the seafaring peoples who have always been mobile, thereby connecting various continents and ocean basins beyond territorially bounded nation-states and homogeneous national histories.

Chris Hann's School of Anthropology

In this second part of this introduction, we reflect on Chris Hann's influence on the intellectual and professional trajectories of his students, whose work, under his supervision, was shaped by post-Cold War conditions and European integration. We believe that the generations of academics born between the 1970s and 1990s—the cohort of Chris Hann's students predominantly represented in this volume—have benefited greatly from post-socialist changes, as opportunities to study formerly state-socialist societies abounded and worldwide academic interest in post-socialism dramatically increased. An important legacy of Chris Hann's work at the MPISA are the research groups he led for almost twenty years. These included a mix of PhD students and postdocs, organised in regional and thematic clusters. The contributors to this volume were hired as PhD students in the first focus groups, 'Property Relations' (2000–2005) and 'Religion, Identity, Postsocialism' (2003–2010), the latter of which evolved in two consecutive stages with strong continuities between them: 'Religion and Civil Society' and 'Religion and Morality'. Besides shaping their members' academic output, these groups also formed these students' intellectual and professional development. This distinguished their training from other PhD programmes in anthropology, placing it somewhere between the Anglo-American model and the Eastern European ethnographic tradition of collective fieldwork. While long-term ethnographic fieldwork is central to anthropological training and research, undertaking it in a team is less common. Field trips and workshops were an important part of this process, in which teams came together to discuss points of comparison and to mark individual progress at each site. Workshops also fulfilled an important emotional and pedagogical function which, even if it was not articulated explicitly, played a big role especially for the CEE cluster whose work to a certain extent followed Hann's earlier research in the region.

Many of Chris Hann's students came from post-socialist countries and, when they returned home, contributed to improving the cosmopolitan profile of their respective national traditions of anthropology. Others, students of anthropology from Western Europe or the US, contributed to the spread of analyses of the former Soviet bloc, thus de-orientalising the dominant perspective of scholars in the West about tribal, ethnic, or autocratic legacies of the East. This educational trend reflected Hann's long-term interest in the different national traditions and his hope to create a dialogue between these traditions and the Anglo-American anthropology his students learned (Barth et al. 2010). His preference for a plural history and promotion of a more diverse anthropology of transformation (Boskovic and Hann 2014; Hann, Sarkany, and Skalník 2005; Mihailescu, Iliev, and Naumovic 2008), has not always been fully acknowledged by his contemporaries but it has borne fruits in the ongoing generational takeover in East European academia. Various regional clusters were created during this time and the institute brought together scholars working on Siberia, Central Asia, the Caucasus and former socialist states like the GDR, China or Vietnam. These groups included PhD students, some of whom are also represented in this volume. In retrospect, MPISA in Halle was an extraordinary place for PhD students. From the institute's inception, it had a reputation of being one of the largest and most prestigious centres for anthropological research. It was equipped with the best technology available for fieldwork at the time, resources for travelling and conferences, and an excellent anthropological library which could deliver any book or text requested. Moreover, the steady rotation of top scholars in the fields of social and cultural anthropology, sociology or history who visited the institute, often for extended periods, and with whom it was easy to talk in the corridors or the pubs around Reileck, the urban hub near the institute, all made MPISA a haven for doctoral studies. The departmental routines were marked by Hann's rather intimidating work ethic. Hann arrived early in the morning, taking a frugal lunch—usually eating a sandwich he made at home—and not wasting time with small talk or after-work socialising. Still, he was fully attentive to our work, responding promptly to emails—the almost exclusive means of communication between offices—and sending detailed comments on entire chapters or abstracts in no time.

While informal exchanges about work took place at *kaffeeklatschen* in Chris Hann's winter garden next to his spacious office, the forum for organised discussion and feedback on our work was the Tuesday weekly seminar which Chris Hann attentively led and expected everyone to attend. He was evidently regretful when he could not make it to the seminar, and usually asked one of his senior colleagues such as Frances Pine or Lale Yalcin-Heckmann to lead the event, in an effort to stick to the schedule and rhythm it imposed on us. Both PhD students and postdocs were expected to present their work; initially just their pre-fieldwork projects, then after returning from the field they would present more frequently, sharing chapter by chapter to receive constructive criticism from colleagues. Preparing for the seminar was stressful and time-consuming work that took several weeks, but the discussion and colleagues' help were highly beneficial. Many senior researchers read our ethnographies closely, and made detailed comments on our written work. But the main event was the collective discussion that followed the thirty- or forty-minute presentation. Hann would always conclude the session punctually after one hour and a half, so everybody knew that they had to make their point in time. There were also plenary sessions at the institute where students learned to become conversant in intellectual debates and academic performance. The ironic or controversial comments of academic stars—frequent guests of the institute—were especially appreciated and welcomed, and these meetings cultivated a familiarity that was not to be found in formal events or conferences. This mode of socialising between junior and senior researchers, PhD students and the big men and women of anthropology was central to MPISA's culture while still maintaining unspoken hierarchies.

And then there was a *Stammtisch*—a weekly fixed meeting over a beer—where informal, social news was exchanged. Enlarging the circle to include colleagues across the street, from the Institute of Social and Cultural Anthropology at Martin-Luther University, this was a more casual event where one could learn about different opportunities, and find out more about how the German academic system worked (here, as in most MPIs, our life was somewhat sheltered from the everyday practices of German institutions). Post-conference socialising was another highlight, albeit always in the German Protestant style of moderation. It was nevertheless made clear that guests should not provoke the generosity of German taxpayers, as the director usually put it. There was rigorous auditing of costs per person per day, which continues up to the present day when events within the Visegrad Anthropologists' Network are organised outside of the institute. All of these rituals, big and small, enabled PhD candidates to mature into anthropology professionals within an almost monastic culture of well-kept academic estate, to use a metaphor that would probably resonate with Professor Hann.

On Method

Hann was very particular about long-term, uninterrupted ethnographic fieldwork for a duration of at least one year and did not favour multi-sited fieldwork, which was in vogue during the globalising liberalism of the 1990s and 2000s. He advised his students to stay in one community, immersing themselves in people's lives, conducting participant observation and writing systematic fieldnotes. Other methods such as household surveys or archival research were also advised, to ensure a better grasp of the socio-historical context and a familiarity with the particular histories of respective communities. This was especially important for comparing the post-socialist present with the socialist past, which was essential for understanding social transformation. Chris Hann's close engagement in supervising his students' fieldwork also manifested in a series of workshops and group field trips to fieldsites. Among others, he visited Carolin Leutloff-Grandits in Croatia and Davide Torsello in Slovakia, Julie McBrian and Mathijs Pelkmans in Kyrgyzstan, Katerina Ivanona in East Germany, and (with the whole Civil Religion group) Hann also visited Laszlo Fosztó in his Transylvanian fieldsite and Juraj Buzalka in Przemyśl, Poland. When visiting, Hann stayed with his students' host families, walked around with them and met their informants, asking questions and making astute observations on their research sites.

Hann's insights bore different weight in each case since his relationship with the fieldsites of those working in CEE was somewhat different than with those working in Central Asia or other regions where he had never lived or conducted research. His intimate knowledge of

CEE and long-term ethnographic and intellectual engagement with the region and its sociological tradition was bound to shape his students' research. Not only did he generate the theme for each research cluster, but Hann also invited his PhD students and postdoctoral researchers to visit his own fieldsites in Hungary (Tázlár) and Poland (Przemyśl/ Wisłok Wielki). This was an ingenious way of familiarising them with the region and the ethnographic grounding of his ideas about post-socialist transformation, expounded upon in his numerous books and articles which they had already read. Some of his students, like Juraj Buzalka, were invited to follow in his steps and revisit these sites years later to pursue their own ethnographic studies. Buzalka arrived in 2003 in Przemyśl, a border city not far away from his major fieldsite in Wisłok Wielki (Hann 1985) to observe the same Greek Catholic Jordan ceremony Hann had described in the 1980s (Hann 1988). Buzalka and a few other colleagues—especially his fellow PhD candidate working across the border in Lviv, Vlad Naumescu (2007)—were part of a research cluster focused on Greek Catholics that was sparked by Hann's own interest in the subject. Taking up Hann's initial observations on post-socialist deprivatisation of religion and his critique of liberal multiculturalism, Buzalka went on to produce a nuanced portrayal of post-socialist transformation in Poland and the emergence of post-peasant populism in the region (2007).

In a similar vein, also working in a region close to Hann's Polish fieldsite, Pasieka conducted research on the grassroots production of pluralism (2015). The others pursued similar questions in different localities in the region (Mahieu and Naumescu 2008) and the whole cluster met halfway through their fieldwork in March 2004 for a field workshop in Cluj, Transylvania. Similarly, a larger, post-fieldwork workshop took place in Przemyśl in 2005 when all the members of the Religion & Civil Society group travelled by train from Halle through Berlin and Kraków to Przemyśl, in south-east Poland to work together on a comparative CEE-Central Asia volume (Hann at al. 2006). While group field trips in Central Asia, where several members of the group worked, were impossible, Hann did have at least one opportunity to practice his fieldwork pedagogy in the region. An academic exchange brought him and Ildiko Beller-Hann to Bishkek, Kyrgyzstan in summer 2003, just as researchers from the Central Asia Cluster were settling into their fieldsites around the region. On that occasion, he seized the opportunity to travel with Julie McBrien to "her village", in southern Kyrgyzstan. McBrien served as translator to Hann's never-ending stream of questions for every guest-house owner, shrine guardian, market seller, taxi-driver, and waiter they encountered along the way, including for many residents of the small town that would become McBrien's fieldsite. His perseverance during that very short visit in learning as much as he could about a new region from those living in it served as a mini-lesson in the kind of fieldwork he encouraged his students to pursue. At MPISA research was not only geographically coordinated to allow for meaningful comparisons but also temporally synchronised, with all researchers in a given cluster leaving for fieldwork at the same time and returning together after fifteen months. Once back from the field, Hann advised his students not to return there, attend conferences, give classes at the university, or commit to collective publications, but to concentrate solely on writing their dissertations.

This aside, he did not push his students to adopt a particular approach in their work or to pursue his ideas, yet he made a point of testing them on every hypothesis they presented and offering critical, yet generous comments and reading suggestions. He was a very thorough supervisor, closely reading and commenting on all drafts sent to him, demanding timely presentations of empirical findings at the Tuesday seminars and an individual contribution to the final conference that marked the end of a three-year research cycle. The tight schedule meant that everyone finished their PhD thesis (more or less) on time. Moreover, his mentoring extended beyond this point, and he guided most of his students through the process of turning their theses into monographs to be published in Lit Verlag's Halle Series in the Anthropology of Eurasia. He also committed himself to assist the work of one of his students and our dear colleague, Irene Hilgers, whose life ended unexpectedly while visiting her friend in Uzbekistan. This assistance resulted in the publication of a joint research monograph (Hann and Hilgers 2009). Hann established this ambitious series in 2003 to promote original research produced in his department. The number of monographs published in the series since then testifies to the great productivity of the research groups he led for over thirty years, as do the multiple monographs and edited volumes originating from research conducted at the MPISA but published with other prestigious university presses. As this volume testifies, these conversations on social transformation in Eurasia, which began at the MPISA, have continued over the years. Hann continues to cultivate these dialogues and to create new spaces for them to take root.[1] We are grateful for a further opportunity to contribute to this ongoing conversation with this volume.

References

Barth, Fredrik, Andre Gingrich, Robert Parkin, and Sydel Silverman. 2010. *One Discipline, Four Ways*. Chicago: University of Chicago Press.

Boskovic, Aleksandar and Chris Hann. 2014. *The Anthropological Field on the Margins of Europe, 1945–1991*. Berlin: Lit Verlag.

Hann, Chris. 1985. *A Village without Solidarity: Polish Peasants in Years of Crisis*. New Haven, CT: Yale University Press.

Hann, Chris. 1988. Christianity's Internal Frontier: The Case of Uniates in South-East Poland. *Anthropology Today* 4 (3), 9–13.

Hann, Chris. 1998. Postsocialist Nationalism: Rediscovering the Past in Southeastern Poland. *Slavic Review* 57 (4), 840–863.

Hann, Chris. 2000. Problems with the (De)privatization of Religion. *Anthropology Today* 6 (6), 14–20.

Hann, Chris. 2002. All Kulturvölker Now? Social Anthropological Reflections on the German-American Tradition: In: R. Fox and B. King (eds), 2002. *Anthropology beyond Culture*. London: Routledge, pp. 259–276.

Hann, Chris and Civil Religion Group. 2006. *The Postsocialist Religious Question: Faith and Power in Central Asia and East-Central Europe*. Münster: Lit Verlag.

Hann, Chris. 2011. Eastern Christianity and Western Social Theory. *Erfurter Vorträge zur Kulturgeschichte des Orthodoxen Christentums* 10, 5–32.

Hann, Chris. 2012. Personhood, Christianity, Modernity. *Anthropology of This Century* 3, http://aotcpress.com/articles/personhood-christianity-modernity/.

Hann, Chris. 2016. The moral dimension of economy: work, workfare, and fairness in provincial Hungary. *Max Planck Institute for Social Anthropology Working Papers* 174, https://pure.mpg.de/rest/items/item_2353110/component/file_2353109/content.

Hann, Chris. 2018. Moral(ity and) Economy: Work, Workfare, and Fairness in Provincial Hungary. *European Journal of Sociology* 59 (2), 225–254, https://doi.org/10.1017/S000397561700056X.

---

1   An important legacy of his vision and pedagogical work matured in the Visegrad Anthropologists' Network, established in 2017, whose members come from the Halle school of anthropology and affiliates of the institution led by Chris Hann until 2021, https://www.eth.mpg.de/4638135/Visegrad_Network.

Hann, Chris, Caroline Humphrey and Katherine Verdery. 2001. Postsocialism as a Topic of Anthropological Investigation. In: Chris Hann (ed.), 2001. *Postsocialism: Ideals, Ideologies and Practices in Eurasia*. London: Routledge, pp. 1–28.

Hann, Chris, Mihály Sárkány, and Peter Skalník. 2005. *Studying Peoples in the People's Democracies. Socialist Era Anthropology in East-Central Europe*. Berlin: Lit Verlag.

Hann, Chris and Mathijs Pelkmans. 2009. Realigning Religion and Power in Central Asia: Islam, Nation-State and (Post)Socialism. *Europe-Asia Studies* 61 (9), 1517–1541.

Hann, Chris and Hermann Goltz (eds). 2010. *Eastern Christians in Anthropological Perspective*. Berkeley, CA: University of California Press.

Lampland, Martha. 1995. *The Object of Labor. Commodification in Socialist Hungary*. Chicago: Chicago University Press.

Mahieu, Stephanie and Vlad Naumescu. 2008. *Churches In-Between. Greek Catholic Churches in Postsocialist Europe*. Berlin: Lit Verlag.

Mihailescu, Vintila, Ilia Iliev and Slobodan Naumovic. 2008. *Studying Peoples in the People's Democracies II*. Berlin: Lit Verlag.

Polanyi, Karl. 1978[1944]. *The Great Transformation: The Political and Economic Origins of Our Time*. Boston: Beacon.

Works of Former PhD Students

Buzalka, Juraj. 2007. *Nation and Religion. The Politics of Commemoration in South-East Poland*. Münster: Lit Verlag.

Fosztó, L. 2009. *Ritual Revitalisation after Socialism: Community, Personhood, and Conversion among Roma in a Transylvanian Village*. Münster: Lit Verlag.

Hann, Chris and Irene Hilgers. 2009. *Why Do Uzbeks Have to Be Muslims? Exploiting Religiosity in the Ferghana Valley*. Münster: Lit Verlag.

Leutloff-Grandits, Carolin. 2006. *Claiming Ownership in Postwar Croatia. The Dynamics of Property Relations and Ethnic Conflict in the Knin Region*. Münster: Lit Verlag.

Naumescu, Vlad. 2007. *Modes of Religiosity in Eastern Christianity. Religious Processes and Social Change in Ukraine*. Münster: Lit Verlag.

Pasieka, Agnieszka. 2015. *Hierarchy and Pluralism. Living Religious Difference in Catholic Poland*. New York: Palgrave.

Torsello, Davide. 2003. *Trust, Property, and Social Change in a Southern Slovakian Village*. Münster: Lit Verlag.

1. Voiced versus Acted Trust

Managing Social Uncertainty and Marginalisation in Rural Southern Italy and Central Eastern Europe

Davide Torsello

Trust is a form of social interaction and of cognitive evaluation of the risks of such interaction, hence it is a socio-cognitive process subject to multiple variations. At the core of trust is the tension between individual rational choice and collective expectations of social performance generated when the trustor enters into a fiduciary relationship with the trustee. In spite of the rich theoretical models which are imbued with the scientific traditions of each discipline and of the sophisticated elaborations of simulation games, trust has still received comparatively poor empirical elaboration. I shall identify a number of reasons for this shortcoming. First, scholarly observation of the mechanisms of trust building has seldom paid adequate attention to the social conditions in which trust is required (Rothstein and Eek 2009). This problem becomes particularly evident in simulation and laboratory games which create a reality abstracted from the social world in which trust is deeply embedded, dramatically reducing the analytical potential of this notion. As such, trust is one of the most effective analytical tools to understand mechanisms of social exchange, empathy, solidarity and power, but only as long as the social conditions underlying such mechanisms are considered (Hardin 1995). Secondly, the application of trust to conditions of high social uncertainty is often problematic. Sociological tradition, from the works of Niklas Luhmann (1979) and James Coleman (1990) onwards, has been attributed to trusting the power to mitigate widespread social uncertainty. Trust, as one of the

  https://doi.org/10.11647/OBP.0282.01

side-products of modernity, could help to reduce the complexity and the volatility of social roles (Giddens 1990; Seligman 1997). However, as many sceptics have revealed, trust is at the same time about the sum of all these benefits and the absence thereof. If it is commonly assumed that a lack of trust severely undermines the proper functioning of, for example, a democracy, it is similarly recognised that distrust may have a functional role in politics, social and even market relations when high social uncertainty is at stake (Gambetta 1988; 1993; Hardin 1995; Levi 2000; Torsello 2005).

This leads to the third point: the blurring of the functional boundaries between trust and distrust. Even if we accept the assumption that trust is a prerequisite of cooperative behaviour, this does not exclude the fact that distrust may also foster human interactions. To put it in other terms, the (social) conditions generating distrust and hampering cooperation in some cultural contexts may, in others, generate trust and thus enhance cooperation. Robert Putnam (2000) has attempted to resolve this theoretical impasse by distinguishing between "bridging" and "bonding" social capital, as a way to differentiate between exclusive and more general trust (Yamagishi 2002). This approach, however, fails to explain both the high variability of trust in different institutions (Hann 2008) and the inadequacy of the trust-distrust dichotomy (see also Lewicki et al. 1998; Letki 2006). This chapter argues that the complexity brought about by high social uncertainty and marginalisation requires actors to invest in forms of trust which can continuously and efficiently be re-negotiated and rendered impermanent. These forms not only include strategic resorts to trust and distrust, but also the blurring of the boundary (more analytical than factual) between interpersonal and institutional trust. The study of the socio-cognitive processes underlying trust in conditions of generalised uncertainty becomes, therefore, a complex and often unproductive task to the social scientist. I will demonstrate that trust can, in these conditions, be tackled only through an integrated approach based on the distinction between voiced and acted trust. Voiced trust refers to the forms of communication through which social actors express their ideas about trustworthiness. Acted trust, on the other hand, refers to the individual choices and actions which generate and use trust in interpersonal and individual-institutional relationships. I argue that, in order to analyse the difference between these two domains of trust, an analytical distinction between three dimensions of trust must follow: instrumental, emotional and moral trust. I will make use of ethnographic data collected in two case studies: southern Italy and Central Eastern Europe. These are cases characterised by high degrees of social uncertainty. I define social uncertainty as: 1) incomplete information about the trustee, 2) high probability that the trustee will aim to exploit the trustor, 3) rapidly and frequently changing social roles.

The first part of the chapter introduces some of the most relevant theoretical foundations of trust in conditions of high social uncertainty, underlining the domains to which trust can be applied as a socio-cognitive process. The second part deals with the social and cultural conditions in which trust is built and expressed verbally in the case studies. The third part introduces the empirical data obtained in the two case studies through ethnographic research.

Analytical Approaches to Trust

Trust is defined here as "the psychological state comprising the intention to accept vulnerability based upon positive expectation of the intentions or behaviour of another". From this definition it emerges that trust can be about dispositions, decisions, behaviours, social networks and institutions. The richness and multiplicity of these domains is one of the main deterrents to the construction of a single empirical model which accounts for the variations of trust in societal contexts. In order to deal with the complexity of these notions scholars have limited the sphere of analysis, following a number of analytical approaches to the notion. One of these approaches distinguishes between trust in persons and in abstract entities, or institutions. Giddens formulated the difference between facework commitments (trust in persons) and faceless commitments (trust in abstract systems) (Giddens 1990: 87–88). The former, to him, is functional to the latter in the common effort to regain control over the uncertainty of modernity (what he terms "social re-embedding"), which requires continuous faceless commitments. However, since the degree and kind of risk, the major component in the trust relation, is different in the cases of interaction between individuals and interaction between institutions, the two become mostly separate forms of social exchange. In the case of institutional trust, the access to information about the institution, the frequency of the interaction, the distance (geographical and social) from the trustee and the specific purpose of the fiduciary relationship are conditions for the assessment of trustworthiness.

On the other hand, in the case of interpersonal trust a number of socio-cognitive factors are more directly involved, including experience of social interaction with the trustee and momentary assessments based on visual perception, moral and emotional arousal. This approach, although of strong appeal to the application of trust in the study of institutions, treats the two types of trust as completely separate entities (Rousseau et al. 1998). The second approach distinguishes between trust in competence and in intentions. Barber (1983) distinguishes between two sub-categories of trust. The first category is defined as an "expectation of technically competent role performance", the second "expectations that the partners will carry out their fiduciary obligations". Yamagishi (2002) underlines that these two types of trust are not mutually interchangeable, since the degree of assurance needed by the trustor to assess trustworthiness in the two cases is different. The problem that this approach gives rise to lies in the analytical difference between trust and trustworthiness. Whereas trust is the assessment of trustworthiness, trustworthiness concerns the actual behaviour of the trustee who responds in a trustworthy manner or not (Yamagishi 2002: 42). Trust, unlike trustworthiness, is inherently cognitive *and* social, in that it serves the task of processing cognitive judgments towards the decision to trust. Hardin points out there has been insufficient attention paid to trustworthiness since this has too often been inferred from trust (Hardin 1996). According to him, trustworthiness is the moralised expression of trust which might "be fully explicable as a capability or as a product of rational expectation without any moral residue" (Hardin 1996: 28). This position, however, follows the assumption that the decision to trust is driven by the rational choice of the trustor who seeks to minimise the risks of the social interaction (and/or economic transaction) in order to maximise the benefits of the action. This perspective, however, fails to take into due consideration the several possible deviations from the rational choice model (Barbalet 2009). There may be instances when distrust is more rational than trust, and it functions to establish and maintain social relations, or others when emotions affect the predisposition to trust more compellingly than rational calculation does.

The third approach takes a culturalist perspective and points out that particular institutional arrangements and cultural norms can affect the process of trust building.

Yamagishi et al. (1998) treat the relevance of these arrangements, introducing the distinction between the "institutional view of culture" and the "emancipation theory of trust." The former is characterised by strong power differences, hierarchies and a group ideology which supports the existence of "artificial" groups based on cooperation and strong endogenous trust. The latter is the process through which actors build general trust (trust in general social terms), by recognising the limits of relying on endogenous trust only, and by eventually deciding to widen the opportunities they have for trust. The difference between endogenous (within close groups) and exogenous (beyond strict group formations) trust is perhaps an extension of the distinction between positive and negative social capital, strong and weak ties already present in the works of Putnam (1993), Granovetter (1973) and others (Buchan et al. 2002). If these approaches with anthropological and sociological studies of value orientation are linked, the distinction between cultures inclined towards individualistic rather than collectivist values, as well as vertical vs. collateral (or horizontal) ties can be adopted (Kluckhohn and Strodtbeck 1961). With a good degree of generalisation, both southern Italy and Central Eastern Europe have been described as societies characterised by the dominance of strong ties over weak ties and institutional views of culture. This approach, however, also fails to take into account the specificity of the trust mechanism which allows the individual to rely strategically on others even when the cultural constructions and values would prescribe them not to do so.

In a recent article, Chris Hann has engaged with the challenges of dealing with comparison in time and space by using ethnography (Hann 2021). The sophisticated argumentation comes from the analysis of a rich array of ethnographic studies of socialist Eastern Europe. Here, of course, some ethnographies are more comparable than others, demonstrating that economic, geographic and demographic aspects marked the differences. What Hann hints at is a form of socialist morality that seemed to be underpinning the dichotomy between moralism and amoralism, trust and mistrust in rural contexts.

Methodology

I shall present research data based on ethnographic fieldwork undertaken in Central Eastern Europe and southern Italy in 2001 and 2006 respectively. The temporal framework of the empirical research is highly significant to the scope of this chapter since I chose to deal with two historical points at which social uncertainty was at its height. In Central Eastern Europe the ongoing post-socialist transformation had reached its first phase of consolidation, marked by profound socio-economic changes, high degrees of social and work mobility, institutional transformations paving the way towards EU accession, and conflicting new values. In southern Italy, 2006 was the last year of the EU structural funding intervention for "under-developed" regions. At that point the benefits (and drawbacks) of the six-year programme were already visible and the spectre of persisting social, political and economic problems of this region after the end of the intervention had become manifest.

I studied two villages: Kráľová nad Váhom in Slovakia, and Melpignano in southern Italy.[1] The choice of two small "communities" was justified by the need to explore through participant observation the social dynamics of trust building in interpersonal and individual-institutional relations. The population scale of the two villages (1,530 inhabitants in Slovakia and 2,234 in Italy, data from 2007) was roughly equivalent. The Slovak village lies on the Trans-Danubian Plain, the most fertile agricultural region of the country where, until the advent of socialism, agriculture was the dominant economic activity. Socialist collectivisation of land ownership dramatically changed the economic geography of the region and in the 1970s most of the agricultural workforce was transferred to industry, rendering the socialist cooperatives the only productive agricultural institutions. Since the

---

1   I conducted the fieldwork session in Slovakia as part of my PhD research programme at the Max Planck Institute for Social Anthropology, Halle/Saale (Germany). The fieldwork undertaken in southern Italy was part of my post-doctoral research program at the University of Lecce, Italy.

post-socialist transformation, the agricultural cooperative still manages over two thirds of the village land, whereas, since 2000, a gowing number of small enterprises, accompanied by foreign investments in car manufacturing and electronic devices, has attracted much of the village workforce in what has become one of the most prosperous regions in the country.

The southern Italian village is located about twenty kilometres from Lecce, the capital of the province, which lies at the southernmost tip of the Apulian peninsula. Originally an agricultural centre (producing mainly olive oil, tobacco and fruit), it is today an important tourist spot which recently gained national recognition following the institution of *La Notte della Taranta*, presently the largest popular music festival held in southern Italy, with a growing presence of international artists and tens of thousands of tourists who visit every summer.

I followed three methods for the collection of ethnographic data. The first was participant observation, the second was the use of structured and semi-structured interviews with political figures, local entrepreneurs and citizens. The third was a survey questionnaire which I submitted to a sample of 100 households (about one third of the households in the Slovak case and one fourth in the Italian case). The samples were generated randomly and the questionnaire was initially tested with a small number of informants. The questionnaire included three sections: general demographic data, trust and opinions on the performance of public institutions. The outcomes of the survey were discussed with some of the key informants before being analysed.

Voiced Trust

The results of the surveys have been used to investigate the general trends of voiced trust. Two questions tested the perception of trust and how it changed over time. The first question was: "Do you think that since 1989[2] it has become: a) more difficult to trust people; b) less difficult to trust people; c) things have not changed". In the Slovak case, 76% of respondents chose a), 22% chose c), and only 2% b). In the Italian

---

2   In the Italian case the question was: "Do you think that in the last fifteen years it has become...".

case, on average among the three communities 89% chose the answer c), 2% b) and 9% a).

The second question introduced a list of institutions and social actors to which the respondents were asked to attribute a level of trust ranging from 1 (minimum) to 5 (maximum). Table 1 reports the findings of this question. There are some general trends to be observed in these findings. First, both case studies present a clear polarisation between institutions and persons who are closer (in spatial and social terms) to the respondent, and institutions and people who are more distant from the respondent. The reported trust level was much higher in the first cluster including family, close relatives, friends, colleagues, neighbours, villagers, and municipal administration. The second cluster includes distant relatives, the state, the church and the EU. The difference between the average reported trust in the first and second clusters is consistent in both case studies. This suggests that vicinity, which can be measured in terms of frequency of encounters or of interaction with institutions and persons, can enhance trust. The second comparative finding is that there is very little deviation from the results of the first cluster in both cases (Tables 2–3). The number of items with a range difference of between 0 and 0.4 is 5, whereas only in 2 cases is there a range difference of over 0.4 (trust in neighbours and in the municipal administration, this latter scores 0.9 higher in the Italian case). On the other hand, the second cluster presents a more diversified structure of answers with all cases in different ranges. The interpretation of this finding is that increased distance from the trustee generates greater idiosyncrasy in the reported trust level. This is the case to which social conditions apply more significantly. The case of the state is particularly telling of this difference. The higher score in southern Italy suggests that in Slovakia the socialist experience has led citizens to express negative judgments in the operations of the state, whereas southern Italians still believe (as they did at the time of Banfield's research) that state intervention should help to improve their conditions. In spite of this, however, the range level of trust in the state in the latter case remains just above 2.5.

The third finding concerns the municipal administration. In Slovakia it scores just above average (2.7), whereas in southern Italy this proves to be the most trusted institution (3.6), ranking above distant relatives, neighbours and colleagues. In several instances the respondents in

Melpignano underlined that the work of the municipal administration, and above all that of the mayor, has contributed to strengthening public perception of the successful and powerful role of the community in promoting economic development. After showcasing the successful preservation and marketisation of local tradition, the Melpignanesi shared a strong voiced trust in the figure of the mayor. The same cannot be said for Kralova, where respondents were much more ambiguous about reporting trust in the municipal administration, especially in the case of young and middle-aged persons who branded the activities of the former mayor as "prosecutions of socialist-style politics".

Finally, the item "villagers", which had mid-range scores in both cases, was helpful for detecting ambiguity in expressions of trust. In Slovakia some respondents were ready to blame other villagers for a lack of generalised trust since "people became wolves to each other". They mostly imputed the general difficulty in trusting fellow inhabitants to uncertainty generated by the post-socialist transformation. They did so without realising that the category of "villagers" also included (close) relatives and kin members, who were the strongest depositories of personal trust. In Italy, on the other hand, some respondents criticised and even showed frustration with the lack of communication within the village. In 30% of Slovak surveys it emerged that improvements in local economic conditions could come from the citizens themselves, whereas in Italy only 12% indicated this view. On the other hand, the idea that the municipal administration is mainly responsible for development and improved life conditions was shared by 47% of Italians but only 13% of Slovaks.

Acted Trust

The research findings presented so far introduce a situation not too distant from the basic assumptions on trust in conditions of high social uncertainty. Both cases are characterised by high levels of reported trust in items contained in the first cluster (the family, kin, friends). As for those institutions with which respondents have fairly frequent interactions, these score high or mid-range positions. Other institutions are reported as being less trustworthy. Perhaps the only evident difference between the two case studies is the prominence of mid-range trust in the Italian case, whereas the Slovak responses are characterised by stronger oscillations, suggesting that the southern Italian respondents were more cautious in reporting both trust and distrust. What these findings fail to pinpoint, however, is that voiced trust is the expression of people's ideas about persons and institutions, and is a form of communication which need not coincide with acted trust in decision-making processes. This ambivalence can be studied by questioning the difference between interpersonal and institutional trust and by considering the three dimensions of trust. In order to do so, I will focus on three categories: family and kin, villagers and the municipal administration.

Interpersonal Trust: The Kin Group

In spite of its high range of voiced trust, the family did not always prove to be the object of acted trust in Slovakia. For instances of help during the harvest and other agricultural work, money lending, borrowing of tools and machinery, help with repairing houses, babysitting and assistance to elderly people, kin were not the chosen option since trust was directed mainly towards friends, neighbours or work colleagues. The weight of kin obligations, the rigidity of behaviour etiquette and the complex system of reciprocity accompanying kinship relationships have loaded trust among kin with moral connotations. It is believed to be morally good to trust one's relatives since the family is the main depository of interpersonal trust. Often, however, the emotional dimension affects the rationality of trust-related choices. Due to the heavy burden of obligations that kin relations pose to the actors, there is a tendency to limit visits to relatives during festivities and ritual occasions (such as the village festival). Some elderly informants complained that their work-aged children had less and less free time to spend with them, according to some because of hectic work schedules, and according to others because of a widespread disinterest in the elderly.

On the other hand, middle-aged members of large kin networks preferred to reduce interactions with kin, expressing a sense of "fatigue" with these forms of social interaction, which some described as "heavy". When the weight of obligations, which is related to the growing importance of the kin group during uncertain times, becomes too pervasive, family-oriented moral trust is replaced by emotionally driven (and hence instrumental) trust addressed towards friends. These become the only valid social networks outside the sphere of kinship, as they are comparatively free of obligations of reciprocity. This is partly a strategic answer to social uncertainty, and partly the outcome of the resiliency of socialist values, such as sociability, communality, the ability to rapidly adapt to conditions of shortage, and the strong divide between public and private life. In southern Italy, there is a clearer distinction between the reasons for which trust can or cannot be sought from the family. Here financial help is often sought outside the kin sphere, whereas help with babysitting or lending of tools and machinery is preferably entrusted to kin. The need to reciprocate favours is particularly strongly felt only in less frequent trust relationships, such as those between distant relatives. The lower trust in distant relatives for southern Italian respondents than Slovak respondents is an indication of the spatial character of voiced trust in southern Italy. Relying on distant relatives is a more hazardous option than relying on non-kin such as neighbours or friends, since the chances to reciprocate the act of trust are rarer and, as such, less in the control of the trustor. There is a moral component in this kind of distrust which emerges from the often-quoted proverb: *parenti serpenti* (relatives are snakes). On the other hand, relatives who live in the same community are entrusted on an almost daily basis with favours, help, loans, gifts and other forms of service.

The rationale underlying this choice is not merely moral, but also instrumental, since continuous interpersonal interaction actually reduces the social leverage of trust. Moreover, positive emotional approaches to trust among close kin are amplified by values such as commitment to family relationships, the strength and density of networks, and the number of reliable relatives. These aspects are considered as positive values in the communities I investigated. Usually, the larger a person's kin network, the more reliable that person is in the whole community, since the number of possible checks with other relatives increases. Unlike in Slovakia, these values show a degree of continuity with the past and have never actually hampered the consolidation of interpersonal trust among close kin.

Villagers

The category of "villagers" or "community members" is among the most problematic. Unlike verbal expressions of trust in relatives, this category is less likely to indicate identification between trustor and trustee. The general character of this social category calls for more neutral expressions of trust which are not imbued with the sentimental and emotional traits of trust in kin. Nonetheless, in Slovakia I encountered strong emotional (verbal) expressions of distrust towards villagers. To some, the category represented the common problems in their daily social reality and acquired a more notable temporal (rather than spatial) dimension. Distrust in villagers was conveyed as a sign of the times, epitomising the difficulties of the post-socialist transformation.

Acted trust, however, follows different pathways. There are over a dozen social and cultural associations active in the community and the revival of their activity has been one of the most remarkable results of the last twenty years (Torsello 2008). If, under socialism, community-level associations were mainly dependent on the support of local political (the Communist Party section) and economic (the agricultural cooperative) institutions, during the 1990s spontaneous activism became a significant achievement. In the early 1990s the Hungarian majority of the village became involved in this form of activism as a way of shielding themselves against the threat of assimilation (Tóth 2003), but in recent times this has also been morally and emotionally valued as a communal answer vis-à-vis the general loss of community life in rural villages. In the village examined, the rich activity of social and cultural associations, particularly in the last decade, strongly contrasts with the low voiced trust in "villagers" suggesting that this ambivalence is rooted both in the emotional and moral aspects of socialisation and ethnic identity. In the Italian case the ambivalence between voiced and acted trust among community members is also evident. In spite of the wary attitude towards generalised trust, purchasing from street or market sellers coming from the same town, preferring food cultivated in the same town of origin, employing personnel from the same community and avoiding street markets, festivals and cultural events in other towns are all widespread practices. Identification in local social interaction confirms the trend, observed frequently in Italian rural contexts, that *campanilismo* (parochialism) is still alive and can actually become a deterrent to interpersonal trust when relationships with outsiders are in question. As in the case of the difference between close and distant relatives, space influences trustworthiness. Trust in villagers and members of the same community is, again, not only a matter of emotional or moral expression, but also a distinctive feature of the actual possibility to temporally control the trustee through personal or mediated interaction.

In other cases, however, some inhabitants, mostly of the upper-class, often as a matter of social distinction, preferred to shop outside their town, send their children to schools in the province capital, and avoid participating in village festivals and other community events. Many of these decisions were justified by a common dissatisfaction with the community of origin, accompanied, at times, by emotional distrust.. Even in these cases, ambivalence was not absent, as those same members who declared they did not trust local shops could not avoid purchasing from them on a weekly basis when it was inconvenient to travel to the city. On other occasions, participation in large community events such as religious or civil festivals was sought as a way of confirming belonging to a common regional (rather than communal) identity, sharing genuinely good food, enjoying music and dance and staying out late at night. Again, the emotional attitude towards trust could be replaced by instrumental attitudes (moved by pleasure-seeking behaviour and choices too) and this occurred especially in short-term, limited interactions with persons outside the affective sphere.

Institutional Trust

In the case of institutional trust, ambivalence between acted and voiced trust was very widespread. In both cases, the distance of the social actors from the institution was the main criterion in building trust relations. In order to compare the Slovak and the southern Italian cases, I chose to deal with the issue of the municipal administration. This choice was based on three reasons. Firstly, this is the closest political institution to the communities being examined, and as such it is strongly inflected with personal relationships. Secondly, it is the institution about which community members possess the highest degree of information. Thirdly, the moral grounds on which trust is built find their best expression in this institution, since its performances are measured against the collective interests and well-being of the community.

In spite of the different historical features of the administrative contexts. There are two strong similarities between both cases: frequent ambivalence between voiced and acted trust and the transposition of personal and institutional trust. In the latter case, the municipal administration in Slovakia has come to be mainly identified with the figure of the mayor (and less with the council, which until the present day had limited power). This marks a significant change from the former regime, since trust vis-à-vis this institution is today measured against the personal responsibility of the mayor, and not the leading party.

The first democratically elected mayor, Mark, who kept his office for three terms (twelve years) represents a very common figure in the post-socialist period: he was the son of a rich peasant family, he had important social networks with ex-party leaders, regional and district officials who remained mostly in office during the 1990s. Mark had not been an active communist and he ran as an independent candidate. This helped him to gain trust and be re-elected twice, without having to formally give up the social capital he had previously accumulated. Mark was very active in supporting the infrastructural improvement of the social clubs and the church cemetery, and introduced the gas pipeline in the community, gaining most of his support among the elderly village members (who today represent over 65% of the electorate). In 2001 he lost trust and his third election due to allegations of corruption in the gas connection business, whose bid was won by his cousin's company. The new mayor, presently in his second term of office, comes from a family of school teachers, has no personal ties with local politicians and has been described positively as a trustworthy, honest, hard-working person who has reached his position without any help or network inherited from the past. In spite of this openly voiced trust, in some cases the villagers have demonstrated that they distrusted him, as when they decided to turn to the ex-mayor for help with issues related to land purchase, building licences, development funds and social benefits. The preference to resort to informal ties suggests that local institutions are still approached through personal networks, and this is a form of continuity with past practices. Moreover, the ambivalence between voiced and acted trust is here the expression of a need to cope with increased social uncertainty and happens mainly at an instrumental, rather than a moral or emotional, level. As most of the anthropological literature on clientelism has pointed out, a corrupt but effective patron can, in conditions dominated by high social uncertainty, be valued more than an honest one (Gellner and Waterbury 1977; Eisenstadt and Roniger 1981; Chubb 1982).

In the southern Italian case the finding of comparatively high voiced trust in "the municipal administration" is based on a positive assessment of this institution's performance. This derives mainly from the mayor's ability to successfully lobby the region and the province to establish the music festival and eventually to obtain annual (though constantly declining) funding for it. He has been elected twice and in March 2010 left his office to run in the regional elections, where he was appointed secretary. Not all trusted him, however. As in the Slovak case, some had been disappointed after losing employment or entrepreneurial opportunities related to the festival. Others blamed the mayor for his inability to maintain the same amount of external funding for the festival, or for concentrating his efforts on this event and neglecting wider problems such as poor infrastructure and social services. His decision to leave office was even criticised by the local press and the opposition parties as "an act of betrayal" to the town. Even though his recent election to the regional administration may still prove beneficial enough to the whole community, the step up in his political career has caused the resignation of the entire municipal council, which lost support and, more recently, credibility. Even when the mayor and the municipal council were the object of criticism and distrust, however, a common positive evaluation of the cultural events sponsored by the administration was registered. Among the town dwellers interviewed, all those who had voiced distrust in the mayor were nonetheless positive about the outcome of the music festival. Similarly, none of those who expressed low trust in the local municipality chose not to attend the festival and the other religious and civil events. One explanation for this involvement was that the event represented the "success of the community as a whole and strengthened identity among its inhabitants".

Conclusions

What contribution can the comparative analysis of the case studies give to the general theory of trust? First, the widespread ambivalence between ideas and practices renders problematic the deduction that in the two case studies, both of which are dominated by high uncertainty, endogenous trust prevails over generalised trust. Actors may find it strategically appropriate to alternate moral and emotional voiced trust with instrumental acted distrust, or vice versa. Although the family and kin group score highest in levels of reported trust, there are instances in which social practices avoid resorting to kinship ties. Similarly, voiced distrust in local political institutions does not necessarily lead citizens to avoid seeking interaction with key personalities such as the mayor or provincial officials. Hence, voiced and acted distrust are not necessarily causally related as much of the literature wrongly assumes.

Secondly, the hypothesis that the dominance of interpersonal trust in conditions of high social uncertainty hampers institutional trust is not confirmed in the case studies. True, institutional trust is, in conditions of uncertainty, supported by interpersonal trust because actors rely heavily on personal networks and informal practices. However, this type of reliance permits them to convert interpersonal trust into institutional trust, and not, as much of the literature argues, to replace it. Institutional trust is transposed into interpersonal trust because in certain social conditions (ranging from collective to individual-oriented values, rapid and frequent changes in social roles and increasing inequality), spatial and temporal checks of trustworthiness are more successfully established and implemented. To the actors, the ambivalence between voiced and acted trust is the best strategy to perform these checks.

Thirdly, the idea that short-term trust may be ascribed to the domain of rational choice, whereas empathy and emotional sharing promote long-term oriented trust based on common identity structures, also seems weak. On the one hand, emotionally driven expressions of trust may easily leave space for instrumental trust actions. This happens when a high perceived incidence of being deceived and a high level of informality in institutional relations influence the process of individual decision-making. On the other hand, identity-based, long-term commitment may still play an important role in boosting cooperation, but this is deemed to exert mainly a short-term influence on the processes of trust building (both in the interpersonal and institutional domain). As both cases suggest in different ways, trust and distrust are alternative solutions to the constant need to re-configure cognitive ideas of the changing social reality. This shows that the dominant long-term strategy is based on ambivalence between ideas and actions rather than simply on in-group trust and commitment formation as commonly argued.

These research results are in line with other empirical research pointing out the difficulty of fruitfully applying the two dichotomies of trust-distrust, interpersonal vs. institutional trust in conditions of prolonged and generalised social uncertainty. The comparison between Central Eastern Europe and southern Italy emphasises how different social conditions and value orientations, affected by different historical paths of institutional development, can produce rather similar outcomes in the field of ideas and practices of trust. The Slovak case is characterised by a general concern for the benefits and losses of trust. Because of the profound social and institutional transformation of the last two decades, actors' values and cognitive constructions of trust are still extremely vulnerable and oscillate between lower and higher scores, from strong endogenous trust in the family and in identification-based interest groups, to wariness in interpersonal relationships. The southern Italian case presents a condition in which trust-building choices reflect a constantly instrumental drive. Here, the dominance of mid-range trust scores actually portrays the need to strike a delicate balance between endogenous trust and exogenous distrust. Enduring difficulties in economic development and the pervasiveness of personal and informal ties in institutional arrangements, rather than rapid transformation, lead actors to resort to the ambivalence discussed above. In both cases, however, ambivalence between voiced and acted trust, as well as the transposition of interpersonal and institutional trust are optimal solutions that reduce and give meaning to social uncertainty.

References

Apolito, Paolo. 1990. *Tarantismo, identità locale, postmodernità*. Milano: Feltrinelli.

Bagnasco, Arnaldo. 2006. Ritorno a Montegrano. In: E. Banfield. 2006. *Le basi morali di una società arretrata*. Bologna: Il Mulino, pp. 7–37.

Barbalet, Jack. 2009. A characterization of trust, and its consequences. *Theory and Society* 38, 367–382, https://doi.org/10.1007/slll86-009-9087-3.

Banfield, Edward R. 1958. *The Moral Basis of a Backward Society*. New York: Free Press.

Barber, Bernard. 1983. *The Logic and Limits of Trust*. New Brunswick: Rutgers University Press.

Benassi, David and Enrico Mingione. 2001. Life strategies and social integration in contemporary Italy. *Focaal* 38, 41–54.

Buchan, Nancy, Rachel Croson and Robyn Dawes. 2002. Swift neighbors and persistent strangers: A cross-cultural investigation of trust and reciprocity in social exchange. *American Journal of Sociology* 108 (1), 168–206, https://doi.org/10.1086/344546.

Campbell, John. 1964. *Honour, Family and Patronage*. New York and Oxford: Oxford University Press.

Carrino, Annastella. 1995. *Parentela, mestiere, potere. Gruppi sociali in un borgo meridionale di antico regime*. Bari: Edipuglia.

Coleman, James. 1990. *Foundations of Social Theory*. Cambridge: Harvard University Press.

Chubb, Judith. 1982. *Patronage, Power and Poverty in Southern Italy*. Cambridge: Cambridge University Press.

Delamont, Sara. 1995. *Appetites and Identities. An Introduction to the Social Anthropology of Western Europe*. London and New York: Routledge.

De Martino, Ernesto. 2005. *The Land of Remorse. A Study of Southern Italian Tarantism*. Translated by D.L. Zinn. London: Free Books.

Douglas, Mary. 1992. *Risk and Blame. Essays in Cultural Theory*. London: Routledge.

Eisenstadt, Samuel and Luis Roniger. 1981. The study of patron-client relations and recent developments in sociological theory. In: S. Eisenstadt and R. Lemarchand (eds), 1981. *Political Clientelism, Patronage and Development*. Beverly Hills: Sage, pp. 271–295.

Fukuyama, Francis. 1995. *Trust. The Social Virtues and the Creation of Prosperity*. New York: Free Press.

Gambetta, Diego (ed.). 1988. *Trust: Making and Breaking Cooperative Relations*. Oxford: Basil Blackwell.

Gambetta, Diego. 1993. *The Sicilian Mafia. The Business of Private Protection*. Cambridge, MA: Harvard University Press.

Damasio, Antonio. 1994. *Descartes' Error: Emotion, Reason and the Human Brain*. New York: G. Putnam.

Gellner, Ernest and John Waterbury (eds). 1977. *Patron and Clients in Mediterranean Societies*. London: Duckworth.

Graziano, Luigi (ed.). 1974. *Clientelismo e mutamento politico*. Milano: Angeli.

Falcone, Franca. 2005. *La disoccupazione: teorie, terapie ed esperienze dei giovani del sud*. Roma: Edizioni Scientifiche Italiane.

Féhervary, Magda. 1988. *Parasztgazdaság a XX Század Első Felében* (Peasant economy in the first half of the twentieth century). Budapest: MTA Néprajzi Kutatócsoport.

Fél, Edit and Tamás Hofer. 1969. *Proper Peasants. Traditional Life in a Hungarian Village*. Chicago: Aldine.

Giddens, Anthony. 1990. *The Consequences of Modernity*. Stanford: Stanford University Press.

Giordano, Benito. 2001. 'Institutional thickness'. Political sub-culture and the resurgence of the new regionalism in Italy: a case study of the Northern League in the Province of Varese. *Transactions of the Institute of British Geographers* 26 (1), 25–41, https://doi.org/10.1111/1475-5661.00004.

Granovetter, Mark. 1973. The strength of weak ties. *American Journal of Sociology* 78, 1360–1380.

Gunst, Peter. 1989. Agrarian systems of Central Eastern Europe. In: A. Chirot (ed.). 1989. *The Origins of Backwardness in Eastern Europe*. Berkeley: University of California Press, pp. 53–91.

Hann, Chris, M. 1998. Religion, trade and trust in South-East Poland. *Religion, State and Society* 26 (3/4), 235–249, https://doi.org/10.1080/09637499808431828.

Hann, Chris M. (ed.) 2002. *Postsocialism. Ideas, Ideologies and Practices in Eurasia*. London and New York: Routledge.

Hardin, Russel. 1995. *One for All: The Logic of Group Conflict*. Princeton: Princeton University Press.

Hardin, Russel. 1996. Trustworthiness. *Ethics* 1, 26–42.

Herzfeld, Michael. 1980. Honor and shame. Problems in the comparative analysis of moral systems. *Man* 15, 339–351.

Herzfeld, Michael. 1984. The horns of the Mediterraneanist dilemma. *American Ethnologist* 11, 439–454.

Kornai, János, Bo Rothstein, and Susanne Rose-Ackerman. 2004. *Creating Social Trust in Post-socialist Transition*. New York: Palgrave Macmillan. Kluckhohn, Florence R. and Fred Strodtbeck. 1961. *Variations in Value Orientations*. Evanston: Row, Peterson and Co.

Letki, Natalia. 2006. Investigating the roots of civic morality: trust, social capital and institutional performance. *Political Behavior* 28, 305–325, https://doi.org/10.1007/s11109-006-9013-6.

Levi, Margaret. 2000. When good defenses make good neighbors. In: C. Menard (ed.). 2000. *Institutions, Contracts and Organizations: Perspectives from New Institutional Economics*. Colchester: Edward Elgar, pp. 137–157.

Lewicki, Roy, Daniel McAllister and Robert Bies. 1998. Trust and distrust: new relationships and realities. *The Academy of Management Review* 23 (3), 438–458.

Luhmann, Niklas. 1979. *Trust and Power: Two Works by Niklas Luhmann*. Chichester: John Wiley and Sons.

Malinowski, Bronislaw. 1919. Kula: The circulating exchange of valuables in the Archipelagoes of Eastern New Guinea. *Man* 20, 97–105.

Mead, Margaret. 2001. *Russian Culture: The Study of Contemporary Western Cultures*. Oxford: Berghahn.

Meloni, Benedetto (ed.). 1997. *Famiglia meridionale senza familismo. Strategie economiche, reti di relazione e parentela*. Catanzaro: Meridiana.

Miller, William, Åse Grødeland and Tatyana Y. Koschechkina. 2001. *A Culture of Corruption? Coping with Government in Post-communist Europe*. Budapest: CEU Press.

Mingione, Enzo. 1993. Italy: The resurgence of regionalism. *International Affairs* 69 (2), 305–318.

Misztal, Barbara. 1998. *Trust in Modern Societies. The Search for the Bases of Social Order*. Cambridge, MA: Polity Press.

Misztal, Barbara. 2001. *Informality: Social Theory and Contemporary Practice*. London: Routledge.

Pardo, Italo. 1996. *Managing Existence in Naples. Morality, Action, and Structure*. Cambridge: Cambridge University Press.

Pine, Frances. 2002. Retreat to the Household? Gendered Domain in Postsocialist Poland. In: C.M. Hann (ed.). 2002. *Postsocialism. Ideals, Ideologies and Practices in Eurasia*. London, Routledge, pp. 95–113.

Pizza, Gianni. 2004. Tarantism and the politics of tradition in contemporary Salento. In: F. Pine and D. Kaneff (eds). 2004. *Memory, Politics and Religion: The Past Meets the Present in Europe*. Münster: Lit Verlag, pp. 199–223.

Putnam, Robert. 2000. *Bowling Alone. The Collapse and Revival of American Community*. New York: Simon and Schuster.

Róna-Tas, Akos. 1998. Path-dependence and capital theory: Sociology of the post-communist economic transformation. *East European Politics and Societies* 12 (1), 107–131.

Rose-Ackerman, Susanne. 2001. Trust and Honesty in Post-Socialist Societies. *Kyklos*, 54, 415–444, https://doi.org/10.1111/1467-6435.00161.

Rothstein, Bo and David Eek. 2009. Political corruption and social trust. An experimental approach. *Rationality and Society* 21 (1), 81–112, https://doi.org/10.1177%2F1043463108099349.

Rousseau, Denise, Sim Sitkin, Burt, Ronald and Colin Camerer. 1998. Not so different after all: a cross-discipline view of trust. *Academy of Management Review* 23 (3), 393–404.

Sahlins, Marshall. 1972. *Stone Age Economics*. Chicago: Aldine.

Schneider, Jane. 1971. On vigilance and virgins: honor, shame and access to resources in Mediterranean societies. *Ethnology* 9 (1), 1–24.

Schneider, Jane (ed.). 1998. *Italy's "Southern Question". Orientalism in One Country*. Oxford: Berg.

Seligman, Adam B. 1997. *The Problem of Trust*. Princeton: Princeton University Press.

Simmel, Georg and K.H. Wolff (ed.). 1964. *The Sociology of Georg Simmel*. New York: Free Press.

Sztompka, Piotr. 1999. *Trust: A Sociological Theory*. Cambridge: Cambridge University Press.

Švecová, Sona. 1991. A szlovák és a cseh parasztcsalád (The Slovak and Czech peasant family). *Ethnographia* 102, 89–119.

Tarrow, Sidney. 1967. *Peasant Communism in Southern Italy*. New Haven: Yale University Press.

Tarrow, Sidney. 1996. Make social science work across space and time: a critical reflection on Robert Putnam's *Making Democracy Work*. *American Political Science Review* 90 (2), 389–397.

Torsello, Davide. 2003. *Trust, Property and Social Change in a Southern Slovakian Village*. Münster: Lit Verlag. Torsello, Davide. 2005. Managing instability. Trust, ambiguity and social relations in postsocialist Slovakia. In: P. Skalnik (ed.). 2005. *Anthropology of Europe: Teaching and Research*. Prague: SET-OUT, pp. 153–176.

Torsello, Davide. 2008. Trust, kinship and civil society in a Slovakian village. *Sociologia—Slovak Review of Sociology* 40 (6), 514–529.

Tóth, Károly. 2003. A village on the ethnic periphery, The case of Dlhá nad Váhom, southern Slovakia. In: D. Torsello and M. Pappova (eds). 2003. *Social Networks in Movement. Time, Interaction and Interethnic Spaces in Central Eastern Europe*. Dunajska Streda: Lilium Aurum, pp. 117–140.

Tullio-Altan, Carlo. 2000. *La nostra Italia. Clientelismo, trasformismo e liberismo dall'Unità al 2000*. Milano: Egea.

Uslaner, Eric. 2002. *The Moral Foundations of Trust*. Cambridge: Cambridge University Press.

Viesti, Gianfranco. 2009. *Mezzogiorno a tradimento, Il nord, il sud e la politica che non c'è*. Roma: Laterza.

Viesti, Gianfranco. 2010. *Più lavoro, più talenti: giovani, donne, Sud. Le risposte alla crisi*. Roma: Donzelli.

Yagi, Kazuo and Satoshi Mizobata (eds). 2008. *Melting Boundaries. Institutional Transformation in the Wider Europe*. Kyoto: Kyoto University Press.

Yamagishi, Toshio, Karen Cook and Motoki Watabe. 1998. Uncertainty, trust and commitment formation in the United States and Japan. *American Journal of Sociology* 104 (1), 165–194.

Yamagishi, Toshio. 2002. *The Structure of Trust. An Evolutionary Game of Mind and Society*. Hokkaido Behavioral Science Report 13, Hokkaido University. White, Carolin. 1980. *Patrons and Partisans*. Cambridge: Cambridge University Press.

Zinn, Dorothy. 2001. *La raccomandazione. Clientelismo vecchio e nuovo in Italia*. Roma: Donzelli.

Appendix

Tables

Table 1: Reported trust levels.

	Slovakia	Southern Italy
Family	4.6	4.9
Close relatives	3.9	4.1
Distant relatives	3.1	2,6
Friends	3.5	3.9
Colleagues	3	2.6
Neighbours	3.2	2.7
Villagers	2.4	2.6
Municipal administration	2.7	3.6
State	1.6	2.8
Church	2.9	3
European Union	1.9	2.5

Source: author survey.

Table 2: Differences between the two cases, Cluster 1.

	0–0.4	0.5–0.9	1.0–1.4
Family	0.3		
Close relatives	0.2		
Friends	0.4		
Colleagues	0.4		
Neighbours		0.5	
Villagers	0.2		
Municipal administration		0.9	

Source: Author survey.

Table 3: Differences between two cases. Cluster 2.

	0–0.4	0.5–0.9	1.0–1.4
Distant relatives			
State			1.2
Church	0.1		
European Union		0.6	

Source: author survey.

2. Property Relations and Ethnic Conflict in Post-war Croatia

Reflections on Conceptual Approaches and Research Findings

Carolin Leutloff-Grandits

Introduction

When conducting my fieldwork in a former war region of Croatia in the year 2000–2001, I was part of the "Property Relations" Focus Group at the Max Planck Institute for Social Anthropology, established under the guidance of Chris Hann. I wanted to look at the reconciliation and reestablishment of a local community after ethnic war in post-socialist Croatia from a property relations perspective, especially considering housing property. Within the region of Knin that I selected for fieldwork, almost all inhabitants had experienced (forced) migration during the war and the years after. They were either returnees to the place they had left due to the war, or they were new settlers who had come to the region on the promise that they would find a new home there—a home which they had either lost in war, or which they had not been able to finance during the precarious post-war times. In fact, in the Knin region, the local situation and the relations between people were very much based on housing relations, as houses had been destroyed during the war, and those still intact had been redistributed on the basis of mainly ethno-national criteria. As such, the violent war along ethno-national lines, which had occurred in Croatia from 1991–1995, was prolonged by other means.

© 2022 Carolin Leutloff-Grandits, CC BY-NC 4.0   https://doi.org/10.11647/OBP.0282.02

With the proclamation of Croatia as an independent nation-state in 1991, the Serb inhabitants of Croatia, who made up a little over 12% of all citizens, suddenly became a national minority. This was soon followed by the military occupation of certain territories of Croatia, in which the Serb inhabitants built a majority, via the Serbian army, and the declaration of the never internationally recognised "Republic of Serbian Krajina" in 1992, of which Knin was the capital. In the aftermath, Serbian militia forcefully expelled the native Croatian inhabitants. For years to come, the situation remained relatively stable, until 1995, when the Croatian state managed to reintegrate the territory through two military actions—the smaller action *Bljesak* (Flash), which took place in May 1995, and the larger action *Oluja* (Storm), which took place in August 1995. During the latter, about 180,000 Serbs fled the region for the Serbian-held territories of Bosnia and Serbia, fearing Croatian revenge. These military actions were followed by the massive destruction of Serb-owned houses, as soldiers of the Croatian army used grenades to blow up the roofs of ten thousand Serb houses.

This was soon also followed by the return of (at least a part of) the native Croatian population, and also partly the settlement of Croats from Bosnia. Even years after the end of the war, the return of Serbs was obstructed through manifold ethno-national discrimination—especially in the housing sector, but also regarding pension payments—and meagre economic possibilities. As a result, Serbs accounted for only 4.54% of citizens in the 2001 census, and 4.36% in 2011. This means that only about one third of pre-war Serb inhabitants had returned to Croatia after the war (and the UNHCR found that only about 50% of those registered as having returned live permanently in Croatia), and that the number of Serbs in Croatia has been shrinking again in the new millenium. Those who returned were mainly elderly who eventually passed away some years after their return, while most young families stayed abroad. Knin thus remained a place of continuous ethnic engineering even after the war. The city had and has an important place in Croatian national historiography as well as a strategic and symbolic dimension for the territorial integrity of the Croatian state and therewith for the question of state borders and legitimate ownership. Thus, the return to one's house and region held symbolic—as well as social and economic—dimensions. Knin served as a home, and as a marker of ethno-nationality.

Within this chapter, I will link the question of property to the post-war transformation and the ongoing ethno-nationalism, to the post-socialist, neoliberal transformation, and to Croatia's accession into the EU. For this, I focus on housing property and its many dimensions. More concretely, I will outline what people mean when they speak about their housing property, what kind of relations they have in mind and what kind of social, economic—but also emotional and symbolic—values they attach to it. In doing so, I will also take a historically informed perspective and explore how housing property is embedded in forms of community and socialising which reach back to socialist and pre-socialist times, creating not only a roof over one's head, but an identity and belonging which are embedded in specific forms of livelihood and social security, and closely linked to the workplace. Such relations have been overlooked by international actors, who have followed and continue to follow a narrow, neoliberal conceptualisation of property as private ownership when analysing the situation on the ground. I will then broaden the perspective by analysing the erection of war memorials that convey a particular reading of history and serve as legitimation for certain citizens'—often nationalistic—claims to be rightful inhabitants and legitimate home-owners of the region. This has created twists and unforeseen side-effects shaping not just the past and present, but also the future. In order to underline this, I will juxtapose the economic and symbolic dimensions of housing relations and link them not just to the ethno-nationalist and neoliberal policies prevalent partly until today, but also to the concepts of civility and social security.

I begin with a description of the concept of housing relations and provide a general overview of the transformation of housing conditions in post-socialist, post-war Croatia. I then turn to the perspective of Knin's inhabitants and their housing relations in post-socialist, post-war Croatia and the policies of the Croatian state and international actors, after which the housing conflict was considered resolved. In the last section, I focus on the symbolic dimensions of property relations that revived ethno-nationalism and the experience of being stuck on the periphery of the nation-state in the wake of EU accession.

The Concept of Housing Relations and Their Transformation in Post-socialist, Post-war Croatia

Property relations, as Chis Hann (1996; 2015) always highlighted, have manifold dimensions. Besides the juridical dimensions of property rights, which are often the concern of political actors on an international and national level and which may themselves be divided into ownership and use rights, there are also various social, economic and, not least, symbolic and material dimensions. The fact that property relations are social relations that are symbolically and emotionally imbued has been discussed at length—in addition to Chris Hann—by various scholars in the post-socialist context, such as Kideckel (1993), von Hirschhausen (1997), and Verdery (1996; 1998; 2003) in Romania, Creed (1998) and Kaneff (2004) in Bulgaria, Torsello (2003) in Slovakia, and Humphrey (1998) in Russia, amongst others. While these studies mainly focus on landed property, such as fields, meadows and forest, housing property has been largely neglected, although it also underwent a reconfiguration of social relations during the post-socialist transformation.

Houses may be owned by the state or may be held in private ownership. Ownership and usage rights may be passed down to the next generation, based on inheritance laws, which may include all children, or only one, or a few, depending on criteria such as male inheritance rules, primogeniture or similar. Ownership and use rights of houses may also be linked to a workplace or membership in a residential community. Housing property—including apartment houses—can look different from region to region, or between rural and urban areas, and may also express social organisation and notions of modernity and tradition. Housing property can also be inhabited differently—be it by nuclear or complex families, or by large or small households, or even various households. Embedded in family and community relations as well as social and economic relations, houses, and property more generally, may be concrete expressions of "living standards, work patterns, group relations, social inequalities, and collected notions of belonging to a community", as Chris Hann (2003: 1) has outlined. Houses give not only shelter by providing a roof over one's head, but they also receive economic, social, cultural and symbolic meanings through interactive processes between people, such as (re-)distribution, selling, exchange, and daily use. This is why the functions and meanings of houses do not only differ from house to house, but also from person to person (see also Roth 1983: 64–65).

Forms of power over housing may also reach beyond the individual and family sphere and may include the real-estate market and the state. Housing projects in many countries are often financed by the state or local government, influenced by state ideologies, and designed by state planners. To whom housing rights are given when housing is planned and built or even confiscated by the state is also a political question and is based on values of social equality, deservingness, and social relations. In order to analyse housing relations, one can, according to Franz and Keebet von Benda-Beckmann (1999: 20), differentiate four interrelated layers of social organisation: the cultural ideological notions, the legal regulations and institutional frameworks, the social property relationships and the practices. A house may, as Frances Pine (1996) has outlined, symbolise belonging to a certain kin group, but it may also symbolise belonging to an ethno-national group or other communities. Access to housing as well as ownership and property rights are regulated by state laws and administrative procedures as well as cultural practices. At the same time, housing is also integrated in social, economic and ecological relations. Housing may be regarded as a social entitlement and may be linked to other social entitlements, like state benefits or a work space or more generally the possibility to make one's living in the reach of the living space, but it may also be detached from such entitlements and norms of social security (Hann 2000; 2006). Housing can also be a simple market commodity that can be bought, sold, invested in, and resold. In socialist Yugoslavia, including socialist Croatia, houses, at least in rural areas, were largely built by families with the help of neighbours. Houses, as well as land, were largely held in private ownership and were often passed down according to male inheritance rights—at least in the countryside. The house and the land were important markers of kinship and belonging to a place. In the Knin region, and more generally in rural regions of the Balkans, houses were often clustered in a so-called *bratstvo*, a brotherhood, a settlement which often reached back centuries and whose organising principle was patrilineal inheritance, which was more or less equally divided among brothers, while women were largely excluded from heritage. In socialism, private housing property was built on privately held land, often with the help of relatives and neighbours, and on the basis of the salaries earned in socially owned firms and factories, as well as on the basis of the agricultural products the inhabitants produced on their own land attached to the houses, which they either used for themselves or sold to the agricultural collective. In urban areas, where the Yugoslav state or, more precisely, firms in collective ownership (*društveno vlasništvo*) built apartment houses, these apartments were bound to the workplace and were distributed to workers according to a special key. Although formally they remained in collective ownership, these use rights could still be passed on to children. As such, ownership and use rights of housing property were also closely related to and embedded in other relations like workplace, agricultural, kinship, and community relations.

During the 1990s, the Croatian state privatised the collectively held housing property and tenants who held use rights were given the right to buy their dwelling for a subsidised price. The post-socialist transformation took place alongside an ethno-nationalist war in Croatia, and the ongoing privatisation of formerly socially owned housing property also had an ethno-national dimension. Within the areas occupied by Serbs, privatisation was postponed, and at the end of the war, when the regions were reintegrated into the Croatian state, Serbs who had fled Croatia and who wanted to return had difficulties in claiming their rights to their former homes, which were instead given to Croats and then privatised. Moreover, during the war along ethno-national lines, people who were regarded as belonging to the "wrong" ethno-national group were expelled from their houses and apartments, and their housing space was either destroyed or redistributed according to ethno-national criteria—not just within the direct warzone, but also in those regions not directly affected by the war. This was exacerbated by the crumbling economy, which was also affected by the war and the post-socialist transformation and which again made it difficult for many inhabitants to invest in housing, or even to pay their rents. In fact, housing became a scarce commodity even for those who were not directly affected by the war. In this situation, access and distribution of housing followed mainly ethno-nationalist criteria—a situation which continued even after the end of the war in 1995, when the Croatian state passed laws which legalised the occupation of houses which Serbs had abandoned during the war in order to create housing space for Croatian families in need. At the same time, houses destroyed during the war were rebuilt at different speeds, by different actors. The Croatian state financed the rebuilding of houses owned by Croats, while houses owned by Serbs were rebuilt by international aid organisations—often slightly later owing to divergent criteria and budget considerations. Investments in the economy, however, continued to be side-lined by the Croatian state as well as international actors. Instead, they believed that the privatisation of firms would bring enough momentum to the crumbling economy—even if this soon proved to be an illusion. As has also been described by Stef Jansen (2006) with regard to post-war Bosnia-Herzegovina, in the war-torn areas, housing was often cut off from its social base, as inhabitants no longer had any means by which to make a living.

The fact that conflicts and discrimination along ethno-national lines—which also affected access to and rebuilding of houses— continued well after the official end of the war, the Dayton Peace Agreement in 1995, was also a result of investment in war-related memorials and ritualised, collective performances. Such investment helped to sanctify the collective memory underlying ethno-national group identities and to support the differentiation and identification of individuals according to ethno-national markers. As such, these memorials also legitimised the occupation of houses, or more generally the distribution of property along ethno-national criteria. Memorials and rituals allow participants to transcend borders in both time and space, reaching back to former and forward to future generations—as if the story presented, the identity given, has been and always will be true. But abandoned houses can also be turned into or perceived as a monument. As long discussed in theories on material culture, houses and monuments are not dead objects, but carriers of social relations (Lévi-Strauss 1969) which link the past with the future and which have not only a spatial, but also a temporal dimension (see Dalakoglou 2009; Hurd, Donnan and Leutloff-Grandits 2017). Such bordered time-spaces are anchored in the material, as memorials envision a past time and make a claim for the future and buildings carry traces of the past and may invoke alternative (and transnational) histories and collectives.

Housing Relations as Social Relations in Post-war, Post-socialist Knin

When I arrived in the Knin region, finding a family who could host me was not easy, although the village I chose had a relatively large percentage of Serb returnees, a small number of local Croatian families who had returned and more than forty Croatian settler families who had settled in Serb-owned houses. As such, it was more alive than most other villages in the former war region of Croatia. In the process of finding a host and choosing a house to stay in, the relational character of housing property was immediately evident. It became clear to me that the choice of the house and family I stayed with would also affect my relations with the inhabitants and the local community. In the search for a host, it was clear to me that I did not want to stay with Croats who had occupied the houses of Serbs, as this would mean that I would be paying rent for a room which my landlords were using "for free", and possibly at the expense of the true owners, who were prevented from returning to their home. I found it ethically problematic, even though I knew that these Croatian settlers had the express permission of the Croatian state, and most of them had nowhere else to go, having lost their own housing during the war or simply not having enough money to rent a house or flat in the more prosperous regions of Croatia. Most of the Serb returnees were however in their old age and lived in precarious conditions, and were unable to host me, owing either to the state of their health, or to the state of their houses, which were minimally equipped. Thanks to the help of the local mayor and a local employee at the UNHCR, I finally managed to find a willing elderly couple in a large but rather empty house, where I could inhabit a room on the first floor. Staying there initially meant I had a room and a bed but no door, as the couple had returned to a plundered and devastated house—like all houses that had been abandoned during the war. The couple, thanks to the intervention of their Croatian son-in-law, had managed to repossess their house, which was occupied by a Croatian family. With the passing of time and not least thanks to my rent, the couple slowly but surely managed to buy more furniture, not just for their own living room, but also for my room.

Sharing everyday life with this couple, I could grasp why my hosts—as well as many of the other elderly members of the community—had returned. They felt very attached to their house and their land, for which they had saved and in which they had invested all their life, and they started to work hard on their vineyards again, in order to produce their own wine. Most received a small pension from the Croatian state that enabled them to live, if only at a very basic level. Many of them had also felt useless (and even burdensome) in the limited housing that they had shared with their children or other relatives after fleeing to Serbia, often to Belgrade. In their own property and using their own land resources around their houses in Croatia, on the other hand, they regained agency and could even be useful to their children, since by returning, they were also rescuing the property for their children (Leutloff-Grandits 2005).

It was however also noticeable that their house had lost value and meaning, not only because it was plundered, but also because many neighbours had not returned, and community life was only returning slowly, as the younger generation especially was missing. As such, houses were disconnected from the social relations for which they once stood. When I did my fieldwork in the years 2000/01, my landlady would tell me the stories of all those families whose houses were either destroyed, locked or occupied, and who had not returned yet. The houses served as a memorial for all those who had not returned, but their stories could only be gleaned from those who had experienced life before the war. In fact, the house of my landlady's first neighbour had been blown up, and the neighbouring house opposite hers was occupied by a Croatian couple from Bosnia with three children, whose youngsters had harassed them during the first years after their arrival.

Sharing the house with the elderly couple and sharing food and much more also meant that we grew together and established family-like relations. The daughter of my hosts lived at a considerable distance in Croatia's capital Zagreb and visited only a few times within the year. Because she was only a little older than myself and was also a scientist, I somehow took her place and became a kind of adopted daughter to my hosts. This meant that I was very well cared for, in both an emotional and mental sense, as I shared daily intimacies and sorrows with my landlady and was able to take her advice. Living with the elderly couple and trying to understand this community meant grasping their perspective and also relating to their pre-war time existence, while at the same time trying to talk to all people, including the newcomers who had settled in the region after the war, in order to obtain a cross-section of perspectives. However, in the post-war scenario in which violence and suffering had been—and were partly still—based on ethno-national markers, socialising with Croats occupying the houses of Serbs felt like a betrayal of the Serb owners, as living in this local community also meant becoming enmeshed with its history, in which there was no "neutral" stance.

Those younger Serbs who had returned were mostly unmarried men, who had followed their elderly parents in order to support them, and who knew that they would ultimately inherit the property. Their days were mostly boring, as there was hardly any work besides some basic agriculture. Many spent their days in front of the local shop, often a bit drunk, either buying beer if there was money available, or bringing their own beverage—wine, *bewanda*, a mix of wine and water, or *raki* (schnapps), all made from self-grown grapes. Due to the missing income of the younger generation, who could hardly find permanent work, roles within the household were somewhat disrupted, as younger and middle-aged people also depended largely on the pensions of their elderly parents. Most had no means or possibilities to establish a family and remained unmarried, with years passing by. For them, returning to their homestead often meant entering a dead end, as most did not manage to develop their lives or establish their own family. The purposes of houses, often built in this region to house the family of the grown-up children and to be passed on from parents to the future generation, could thus not be fulfilled. Most of the younger, unmarried women or whole families with underage children—apart from a few isolated cases—visited only in summer for a limited time. They happily socialised with those who had returned, had barbecues and jointly recalled stories from their childhood or youth, when this region was full of social life, but they saw no future in it, even if their houses were neither occupied nor destroyed, as there were no jobs in the region and houses could not be eaten. While they clearly did not socialise with the Croats who had recently settled in the region, there were however some local Croats who joined these gatherings, as they had grown up as part of the community until the war had divided them.

In fact, as also explored by Jasna Čapo Žmegač (2007; 2010) in her study on Croats from Vojvodina who had exchanged houses with Serbs from Croatia in order to settle there at the end of the ethno-national war, divisions within the local community run not necessarily along lines between Croats and Serbs, but rather between locals and settlers. Local people—returned Serbs and returned Croats alike—emphasised that they did not differ much in their habits and ways of securing or earning their livelihood. For Serb and Croat returnees, civility, understood in the terms of Chris Hann (2002) as grown forms of sociability linking the private and the public and as the underlying moral values on which a community is based, was an important basis of conviviality in the region, and was also reflected in property relations. Local inhabitants—Serbs and Croats alike—stressed that they respected private property, and regarded Croatian settlers who had occupied Serb property as suspicious and potentially uncivil. They argued among others that many unemployed Croatian settlers received social benefits from the Croatian state, which classified them as without property although they were legally occupying the housing property of others, while Serbs and Croats who lived in their own houses did not qualify for such social entitlements, even though their social situation was by no means better (Leutloff-Grandits 2002; 2006).

The Housing Conflict, the Croatian State and the International Neoliberalist Policy

At the time of my fieldwork, in 2000–2001, international aid organisations, many of which were active in the Knin region—such as OSCE, UNHCR, and German organisations like Arbeiter Samariter Bund—were very busy with the reconstruction of destroyed Serb houses. At the same time, they pressured the Croatian state to find solutions for returning occupied houses to their lawful (Serb) owners. However, there were various problems involved. First of all, many of the owners were still in Serbia and not in Croatia. Secondly, not all Serb homeowners had their ownership documents, which they needed as a proof in order to apply for the rebuilding or repossession of a property. In fact, during socialism, the practice of registering property in the cadastre was largely abandoned in order to circumvent state-imposed restrictions on the construction of private property. As the land on which the property was built was often registered under the name of already deceased relatives, who themselves had various children, the provisions for reclaiming ownership rights could become very complicated. It meant contacting all possible heirs of the land who might be spread throughout the world, as this was a necessary step for homeowners to prove their property rights (Leutloff-Grandits 2003). Still, when the international community pressured the Croatian state to enable Serbs to gain repossession of their occupied houses, the Croatian settler families who had occupied the houses of Serbs also felt that pressure. Many of them had moved to the region with several children and lived in precarious conditions, having suffered from the difficult economic situation and often being jobless. Being war refugees themselves and/or without alternative housing, they had nowhere else to go. Croatian settlers then tended to vote for right-wing Croatian nationalist parties like the *Hrvatska Stranka Prava* (HSP), as they believed that they would fight hardest to secure their rights (Leutloff-Grandits 2008).

In order to solve the housing conflict and still enable Croats to stay in the region, the Croatian government tried to offer alternative housing for Croat families. To this end, the Croatian state financed the construction of new housing settlements in the region for Croatian families. Furthermore, a state agency for property transfers was founded and tasked with buying up the houses of Serb owners who had fled and redistributing them to Croat settlers who were forced to move out of the houses they had occupied. The agency mainly relied on houses which they bought from Serbs who did not plan to return. The Croatian state thus created an artificial market for houses which would likely have been unsaleable without state finances, as no one in the region had the money to buy housing property. Nor would they have dared to buy such a house in this region, as its economic prospects were meagre and foreseeing a future there was thus difficult. Nevertheless, the Croatian state, as well as international organisations, regarded the agency's efforts as a win-win situation, as it would ease the ethno-national conflict around housing.: Serbs received money from the selling of their houses—albeit at a relatively low price—and Croatian settlers received a permanent housing solution in the former war regions in Croatia. In some cases, the settlers did not even need to move out of the house they were occupying, as the absent owners could sell their houses, even when settlers inhabited them, for a relatively cheap price.

Simultaneously, however, this practice also cemented the ethno-national engineering of the war and immediate post-war period. In fact, with this procedure, Serbs, who had no realistic possibility to return for good—as there were no working positions in the region for them—were encouraged to sell their houses. With the money they could buy property in Serbia (this was in fact possible even though the prices offered were very low by Croatian standards, as by Serbian standards they were decent), and thus permanently settle down there. It was also clear that the elderly returnees would die eventually, and that without younger people, without children, there was no future for Serbs in the region (see also Mesić and Bagić 2010; Djurić 2010). Croatian settlers, on the other hand, who up to this point had been insecure about their stay in the region—also because of the difficult economic conditions they encountered—gained a reason to stay as they received permanent housing property in the region (Leutloff-Grandits 2016).

In 2006, about 90% of privately owned houses were officially repossessed by their lawful owners and the Croatian state declared the housing question, which had been regarded as a priority for solving the ethno-national conflict, as solved and international actors complied with this view. Subsequently, the political—and international—attention to the region and to monitoring and supporting post-war reconciliation in the former war areas decreased. The solving of the housing question had however not necessarily contributed to a lasting return of Serbs. In the village in which I did fieldwork, of the forty houses which had been occupied by Croatian families from Bosnia in 2001, by 2008, all of them had been returned to their Serb owners. But this was only a reason to return for a very small number of Serb house owners, and many others simply sold their house to the agency. This had enabled seventeen Croatian settler families to remain in the village, as they had received housing property that Serbs had sold to the state agency for property transfer. The other Croatian setter families had moved out of the village, either to the neighbouring town of Knin or to a newly built settlement in another village municipality, where about 300 Croatian settler families had received housing.

Following a neoliberal logic, the focus of international organisations on the return of private property however also largely ignored formerly socially owned property, which had existed in the form of flats and which had been the main form of housing in urban areas during socialism. Outside the former war areas, such socially owned flats had been privatised in the early 1990s, and the tenants had been given the possibility to buy them at a highly subsidised price—which most of them did. In the aftermath of the war in the Knin region, these flats had also been occupied by Croats, who replaced fleeing Serbs. But Serbs had also been living in such flats outside the former warzone, where economic possibilities were much more promising than in the region of Knin, and again, Serbs were prevented from repossessing the flats they had abandoned during the war. Only many years after the war did the international community revise its politics, pressuring the Croatian state to pay financial compensation to the former tenants of such flats—without however granting them the possibility of reclaiming possession rights. This policy again meant that the possible return of Serbs to urban centres had been postponed for years, effectively preventing the Serbs from returning to Croatia. More generally, international organisations largely disregarded the fact that a successful return—and more generally the possibility to build up a livelihood in the region—was not only based on the return of private property rights, but on an embedded notion of housing property, taking into account property forms which had been central during socialism, such as socially owned housing, as well as linking the value of housing property—and the sustainable return to one's house—to the possibility of making a living, and more generally to an economically and socially vital community. Following a narrow neoliberal ideology, international organisations believed that the restitution of private property rights would be a starting point for economic development, without realising that in the post-war, post-socialist Knin area, the entire former socialist economy had collapsed, and neither the repossession of private housing nor the privatisation of firms and other forms of property, including formerly socially owned flats, was sufficient to revitalise the community and substitute the lost workplaces (Leutloff-Grandits 2016; Jansen 2006).

In fact, alongside the repossession of private housing property by Serbs, there was a continual privatisation of firms by so called *tajkuni* (tycoons), powerful businessmen who bought former socialist firms, which had suffered during the war and the disintegration of the former Yugoslav market, often only to then dismantle them, and to destroy economic opportunities for the region's inhabitants. This led to high numbers of unemployed individuals dependent on the meagre social support of the state, and a general feeling that there was no future in this region. This feeling was present across ethno-national boundaries. While this prevented younger Serbs from returning, it also affected Croatian families who had returned or settled in the region. In 2008, the former rail and steel factory TVIK, then renamed as DIV, which had been the main employer during socialism, was finally privatised. Happily, it was renovated and restarted operations. But unlike 1990, when more than 1000 people had worked there, only around 200 people were employed.

The Re-entry of Ethno-nationalism through Spiritual Property Relations

In 2000–2001, in the face of the difficult economic conditions, it was not the local state, but the Catholic Church that tried to improve the precarious living conditions in this region by opening a soup kitchen in order to feed "the hungry Croats" in Knin. As in other post-socialist countries (Hann 1998; Hann et al. 2006; Pina-Cabral and Pine 2008), religious institutions, and in this case the Catholic Church, provided an anchor of hope and a sense of security and social relation as Croats felt cared for by the Catholic Church and connected to the community of Croatian believers (while most Serbs followed the Orthodox faith and thus felt excluded). Next to opening a soup kitchen as a basic form of social security, Catholic Church representatives stressed that settlers would contribute to the future of the Croatian state and nation when they endured in this area—despite the difficult conditions they met here. Remaining in this region thus acquired a higher meaning sanctified by the Catholic Church, as it gave settlers spiritual support for enduring the hardships in life (Leutloff-Grandits 2009). In fact, as Keebet and Franz von Benda-Beckmann (1994) have stressed, the spiritual dimensions are an important layer when considering social security.

The Catholic Church invested simultaneously in the construction of a new church building in Knin and it was rumoured that a large part of the donations was used for the latter. In order to house the many Croats who had settled in Knin after the war, the new church building was planned to be a few times bigger than the existing church, which had been built at the end of the nineteenth century. The large church building however also served as a national marker, symbolising the legitimate presence of Croats in the region, who in fact held a majority over Serbs since the end of the war in 1995, while this region had had a strong

Serbian-Orthodox majority for decades and even centuries (Leutloff-Grandits 2009). The spiritual claim to the region was furthermore stressed with a new, huge cross on Dinara Mountain above Knin, which war veteran associations placed there and which was visible for all those travelling from Zagreb via Knin to the seaside. In Knin, and all over Croatia from the 1990s onwards, religion played an important role for claiming ethno-national belonging (Schäuble 2014) and the right to a certain place as well as property (see also Pina-Cabral and Pine 2008). It created, as Chris Hann (1998) highlighted in his case study of symbolic struggles between Greek Orthodox and Catholics in Przemyśl in south-eastern Poland as well as in other post-socialist contexts (Hann 2006: 9) "a sense of belonging to a nation". In the years to come, other symbolic monuments were added all over Croatia, which dwelled on the war of the 1990s and outlined the history of suffering along ethno-national lines, thus perpetuating the two incommensurable stories (Pavlaković 2014; Schäuble 2014).

In Knin, most important in this regard was the erection of the memorial "*Oluja '95*", commemorating the successful military operation *Oluja* by the Croatian army, which led—from the Croatian point of view—to the glorious liberation of the Serb-occupied territory of Croatia in the so-called Homeland War (*Domovinski Rat*). *Oluja* was equated with the rebirth of the territorial integrity of the Croatian state within its legitimate borders and the rebirth of the Croatian nation. The *Oluja* memorial consists of two main elements: an approximately nine-metre-high, abstract victory sign, symbolising the victory over Serb insurgents in 1995, and a black, monumental stone chapel about seventeen metres long and eight and a half metres high. The chapel houses an altar and a cross as well as information plates about the military action of the Croatian army, naming the fallen soldiers. In this reading of history, the Serbs appear only as "the evil Other" that the Croatian army managed to defeat. There was no mention of the fact that for Serbs, this military action forced them to flee from their homes, and caused the deaths of civilians who remained and the looting and destruction of their houses as well as an enduring suffering in the post-war period. The erection of the monument in Knin was again initiated by Croatian veteran organisations and then taken up by the local government of Knin and supported by the Croatian state. After an approximately three-year-long planning and construction phase, the monument was inaugurated on 5

August 2011, the anniversary of "Homeland Gratitude", celebrating the day the Croatian army reached Knin in order to 'liberate' the Serb-held regions of Croatia. The festive anniversary of *Oluja* attracted masses to Knin and, in the speeches of state officials, the Croatian version of the war was revitalised, dividing Croats and Serbs into defenders and aggressors respectively. Local newspapers reported that the monument cost eight million Kuna, or more than one million Euros, and was financed in part by veterans' associations as well as the national and local state authorities. The high costs were especially considerable as Knin was one of those towns with the highest number of socially dependent citizens in Croatia as well as the highest number of young people due to the Croatian families which had settled in the Knin region after the war, many of them unemployed and without a perspective. This means that the municipality urgently needed the money in question for economic or social projects, especially as the municipal budget was small due to limited tax income and high expenses. Obviously, however, those who decided on the use of the money privileged the erection of a memorial commemorating the Croatian version of the war, and focusing on spiritual dimensions of ethno-national belonging rather than material and social improvement which could have served the community beyond national affiliations.

It is thus no wonder that Serbs who had returned did not participate in the celebrations on this day (Leutloff-Grandits 2004), and instead built their own memorials commemorating their experiences of victimhood during the war. One of them, consisting of a cross and a memorial plate in Cyrillic letters that names the local Serbian civilians who had died in connection with *Oluja*, was erected only two months later, in October 2011, in front of the Orthodox church building in the village of Golubić near Knin. The village had about 1400 (mainly Serb) inhabitants before the war, of which about one third had returned by 2011, while a few hundred Croats from Bosnia had received new houses that were constructed by the Croatian state in the village after the war. In collaboration with local villagers, the Belgrade-based, Serb refugee association *Suza* (Tear), which deals with the search and identification of Serbs who went missing during the 1991–1995 war in Croatia, had planned and constructed the monument. However, Croatian hardliners soon demolished this monument, arguing that it was placed there illegally, as they regarded the involvement of associations based outside

Croatia as action by a foreign state representing the wrong version of history. Serb representatives again argued that the demolition of this monument showed that European values—and here especially the minority rights of Serbs and the right to remembrance—were not respected in Croatia. More generally, with the competing memorial culture, a struggle over the reading of history along ethno-national lines continued, and was used for the legitimation of settlement rights and belonging in the former warzones of Croatia. Other monuments, like partisan monuments erected by the (local) state during socialism and commemorating certain socialist ethics, like that of brotherhood and unity of the different national groups in former Yugoslavia, had been destroyed during the war along ethno-national lines of the 1990s and remained in ruins.

EU Accession and the Experience of Layered Time and Stagnation at the Margins of the Nation State

The international presence in Knin, which had been strong after the end of the war in 1995, fully ceased with the accession of Croatia to the EU in 2013. At the same time, various local NGOs, which had been heavily dependent on international funding, had closed down—thus supporting Chris Hann's (2002) finding that so-called civil organisations may not reflect the civil state of the community, but rather may be imported from outside. During my visit in 2010, Knin appeared to me a very provincial, sleepy place despite attempts to promote it as a tourist destination, advertising the natural beauty of the Dinara region with its limestone and springs and historical excavations of Croatia's mediaeval past. This was not in the least the case because a new highway to the popular Croatian tourist destinations on the coast circumvented Knin, thus marginalising it in a geographical sense, as most traffic now surpassed it. While in many Serb households, elderly, single people dominated, there were also fewer new-born children among Bosnian Croatian settler families than before.

In fact, in 2007/08 the Šibenik-Knin county had the largest decline in birth rate compared to other counties in the country. There was furthermore a growing number of three-generation households among Croatian settler families, which was an indicator of the diminishing possibilities of Bosnian Croats in the Knin region. As opposed to the period directly after the war, when young families moved to the region in order to occupy property and establish their own household, now young couples, who often got married soon after school, could not get a house as easily. As renting a flat was rather expensive, many lived with their parents (-in-law). While young men worked in some rather low-paid jobs in Knin or the surroundings, young women mainly stayed at home to take care of the kids. This situation gave only little hope for savings, investments or the establishment of one's own household in the near future, and was, most of all, accompanied by feelings of disappointment and disillusionment. When settlers from Bosnia came to the region in 1995/96, they had imagined starting a new, good life; in 2000/01, they now feared losing their new-found rights. In the following years, the lives of Croatian settlers had been consolidated by the receipt of their own housing properties, but they also had a feeling of being marginalised, stuck and forgotten. This was the time the Catholic Church became an important pillar of strength and sense of community among Croats who had settled in the region. And although the Catholic Church remained important for Croatian settlers, many young people found their own town very boring and wanted to move out of the region as soon as possible, as they saw no future there. This was the case for Croats, and even more so for Serbs, who experienced ongoing discrimination in places in which Croats were the majority, as in Knin after the war (in 2011, Serbs comprised about 25% of the population of the Knin municipality, while Croats made up 75%, and with that, the pre-war ethnic distribution had been reversed). The negotiations for EU membership did not bring about much change for the better, at least locally, as the EU regarded the problems of Serbs in Croatia as largely solved. The fact that the Serbian SDSS (*Samostalna demokratska srpska stranka*, the Independent Democratic Serb Party) participated in the national *Sabor* (parliament) by supporting the reigning HDZ (*Hrvaska demokraska zajednica*, the Croatian Democratic Union) from 2007 onwards served as another sign to the EU that Serbs had been reintegrated into political life and society in Croatia, and thus contributed to the commencement of negotiations for EU accession. This however did not stop clientelism and corruption, which went to the very top of the state, nor indeed the general marginalisation of the region, which affected all local inhabitants, but especially Serbs, and which affected their self perception and their views to the future.

In 2000/01 Serb returnees had stressed that the war had set them back twenty years, but they still hoped that more young people would return soon and that the villages would be revitalised, even if they knew that it would take a long time to regain what they used to have, "maybe twenty years," as they said. They somehow still believed in the linear progress of modernity, as Stef Jansen (2014) had stressed in regard to post-war Bosnia-Herzegovina, and thought—or at least hoped—that the war had been an outlier, a crisis of modernity and civility, which could be overcome. By 2014, this hope had disappeared, as the long-awaited progress had failed to materialise. While the larger return movement of younger families had not taken place, an EU-supported elderly service became one of the main employees for local (Serbian) women in the region, helping those fragile elderly individuals left alone in their houses. Furthermore, an increasing number of Serb-owned houses was becoming empty again, as their elderly owners had died. Other Serbs who had returned soon left again on realising that the repossession of houses alone could not feed them. Their houses remained empty, locked, abandoned, and even fell into decay after the war. Some remote villages have never attracted returnees due to their remote location or a continued lack of electricity and running water. Again other houses remained destroyed, as the owners had never returned and thus had not cared or been able to reconstruct them. In fact, in this region, destroyed and abandoned houses were like ghosts of a time past, or, to use Foucault's (1986) term, so called "heterotopias". Forgotten and left to decay, the ruins and empty houses and villages, as well as the demolished monuments of the socialist past, became partly overgrown with trees and brushwood. Still, they remain 'living' memorials of the immediate socialist past, in which the inhabitants of this region lived a 'normal', lively and hopeful life, Serbs alongside Croats, but which is officially ignored and forgotten, as the glorious victory in the so-called homeland war and the victorious liberation of Knin are important tropes of Croatia's past, directly alluding to an imagined medieval Croatian kingdom dating back to the tenth century, which again had its seat in Knin.

Simultaneously, the abandoned houses are also memorials of a missing future. They are symbols of decline and of a massive depopulation in the Dalmatian hinterland after the demise of socialist Yugoslavia and with the war, and which is—after the heights of the state-organised settlement project of Croats in these regions in the direct aftermath of the war and the then partial return of Serbs which had been encouraged by international organisations—again continuing. The ongoing depopulation and economic marginalisation are the opposite of what Croatia—and in fact also the EU—claimed to achieve: a prospective, forward-looking future for its citizens. Being more or less isolated in the Knin region, without powerful social contacts in the region or even beyond, in Croatia, Serb returnees often have difficulties building up or even imagining a future for their children in Croatia, and instead rely on their networks abroad—either in Serbia, or other EU countries—to create a sense of social security and a future for their children. Croatian settlers, on the other hand, have established themselves as a permanent community in Knin thanks to the housing solution, but they also leave the region as soon as better options occur—migrating instead to more prosperous EU countries, as enabled by Croatia's accession to the EU.

In 2020, property conflicts had long been solved in the region, and generally, interethnic antagonisms in local, everyday life hardly occur. Instead, people often highlighted that they were on good terms with each other, and that there was an everyday conviviality in their local communities. Local Serbs were however also aware of the ongoing discrimination of Serbs and the marginalisation of largely Serb-inhabited regions in Croatia. However, for this they held state politics, and not their Croat neighbours, responsible. Furthermore, violent incidents against ethnic minorities still happen, and are often initiated by people coming into local communities from outside. What unites people locally is the fact that they feel powerless. They are convinced that the state is not caring enough, but that it is corrupt and clientelist. While neoliberalism, consumerism and privatisation have indeed ultimately entered the region, centralisation, clientelism, and nationalism have remained dominant concepts in politics, hindering the development of local communities, and impinging on agency and trust. Still, local people also have a certain power, and in their fight for *opstanak* (staying) in the region, for their economic and social survival, they are increasingly united.

On 5 August 2020, for the first time since the end of war in 1995, a Serbian member of parliament took part in the official celebrations of the Croatian day of liberation by *Oluja* in Knin, while a Croatian official participated in the commemoration of Serbian victims of the same military action, celebrated a few days later in the village near Knin, next to the memorial for civil victims of the war established by Serbs. This mutual acknowledgement received a lot of attention both nationally and internationally. It was seen as a sign of interethnic tolerance and reconciliation, a victory for civil rights and interethnic respect. Some local Serbs, however, were rather indifferent to it. For them, another apology for war crimes or another symbolic gesture of mutual recognition was still only lip service, and not a move towards a better future for the local community, as these state officials returned to Zagreb the next day, while economic and social investments in the region are yet to materialise.

Conclusions

In the war along ethno-national lines, housing politics became a means of supporting ethno-national engineering, which in turn lasted long after the end of the war itself. The neoliberal politics put forward by the international community, which focused on the return of private property while ignoring the realities of housing in socialism, was only partly successful in undoing the war-related ethno-national reality. The fact that Serbs had regained the private property rights over their houses may have solved the housing conflict, but this did not necessarily enhance the return of Serbs, as houses were useless without an economic basis on which their inhabitants could live. In post-war, post-socialist, neoliberal Croatia, the entanglement of housing and labour—which had been a major principle in socialism—became dissolved, as neither the state nor the international community pushed forward economic investments in the region. In this situation, it was mainly the Catholic Church which cared for the inhabitants who found themselves in precarious economic situations by distributing food and giving spiritual support. Here, however, not necessarily civil values, but rather ethno-national values were at stake. In fact, after the end of war, the Catholic Church and other, so-called civic, but highly nationalist organisations like the veteran associations, invested in a symbolic landscape, claiming Croats' ethno-national ownership rights to the region, while the development of local prosperity and conviviality faded into the background. As such, the investment in memory culture contributes to what has been going on in the last years: the silent but ongoing diminishing of the Serbian population in the Knin region. The houses of those who have not returned and those who have died, but who have no living offspring in the region, establish (unofficial) monuments of a time-space that is past, although or because they are neglected and left aside. The fact that in this climate, local Croats also leave, leads—maybe unexpectedly—to local forms of inter-ethnic solidarity, or to new forms of conviviality, as locals today jointly face what local Serbs term the "economic *Oluja*". This time, it is not nationalism which makes the younger generation leave the region, but economic motives. These young people mainly seek greener pastures in more prosperous EU countries. The Croatian government—as well as the EU—seems rather indifferent to this state of affairs.

References

Barić, Nikica. 2008. The Rise and Fall of the Republic of Serb Krajina (1990–1995). In: Sabrina P. Ramet, Konrad Clewing and Reneo Lukic (eds). 2008. *Croatia Since Independence: War, Politics, Society, Foreign Relations.*Munich: Oldenbourg, pp. 89–105.

Benda-Beckmann, Franz and Keebet von. 1994. Coping with insecurity. In: Franz and Keebet von Benda-Beckmann (eds). 1994. *Coping with Insecurity. An "Underall" Perspective on Social Security in the Third World*. Indonesia: Pustaka Pelajar & Focaal Edition, pp. 7–31.

Benda-Beckmann, Franz and Keebet von. 1999. A functional analysis of property rights, with special reference to Indonesia. In: Toon van Meijl and Franz von Benda-Beckmann. 1999. *Property Rights and Economic Development. Land and Natural Resources in Southeast Asia and Oceania*. London and New Yord: Kegan Paul International, pp. 15–57.

Čapo Žmegač, Jasna. 2007. *Strangers Either Way. The Lives of Croatian Refugees in Their New Home*. Oxford: Berghahn Books.

Čapo Žmegač, Jasna. 2010. Različiti pristupi povratnim migracijama: primjer Hrvatske. *Studia ethnologica Croatica*, 22, 11–38, https://hrcak.srce.hr/62238.

Creed, Grald. 1998. *Domesticating Revolution: From Socialist Reform to Ambivalent Transition in a Bulgarian Village*. Pennsylvania: Penn State Press.

Croatian Bureau of Statistics. Population By Ethnicity—Detailed Classification, https://dzs.gov.hr/en.

Dalakoglou, Dimitris. 2009. Building and Ordering Transnationalism: the 'Greek House' in Albania as a Material Process. In: Daniel Miller (ed.). 2009. *Anthropology and the Individual.* Oxford: Berg, pp. 51–68.

Djuric, I. 2010. The post-war repatriation of Serb minority internally displaced persons and refugees in Croatia—Between discrimination and political settlement. *Europe-Asia Studies* 62 (10), 1639–1660, https://doi.org/10.1080/09668136.2010.522423.

Foucault, Michel. 1986. Of Other Spaces. *Diacritics,* 16 (1), 22–27.

Hann, Chris. 1998. Introduction. In: Chris Hann (ed.). 1998. *Property Relations. Renewing the Anthropological Tradition.* Cambridge: Cambridge University Press, pp. 1–47.

Hann, Chris. 1998. Postsocialist Nationalism: Rediscovering the Past in Southeast Poland. *Slavic Review* 57 (4), 840–863.

Hann, Chris. 2000. The tragedy of the privates? Postsocialist property relations in anthropological perspective. *Max Planck Institute for Social Anthropology Working Paper,* 2, https://www.eth.mpg.de/cms/en/publications/working_papers/wp0002.

Hann, Chris. 2002. Farewell to the socialist 'other'. In: Chris Hann (ed.). 2002. *Postsocialism. Ideals, Ideologies and Practices in Eurasia.* London and New York: Routledge, pp. 1–11.

Hann, Chris. 2003. Introduction. Decollectivisation and the moral economy. In: Chris Hann et al. (eds). 2003. *The Postsocialist Agrarian Question. Property Relations and the Rural Condition.*Münster: Lit, pp. 1–46.

Hann, Chris. 2006. Introduction: faith, power, and civility after socialism. In: Chris Hann et al. (eds). 2006. *The Postsocialist Religious Question: Faith and Power in Central Asia and East-Central Europe.* Münster: L, pp. 1–26.

Hann, Chris. 2006.'Not the Horse We Wanted!': Postsocialism, Neoliberalism, and Eurasia. Münster: Lit.

Hann, Chris. 2015. Property: Anthropological Aspects. In: James D. Wright (ed.). 2015. *International Encyclopedia of the Social & Behavioral Sciences,* 2:19, Oxford: Elsevier, pp. 153–159.

Hirschhausen, Béatrice. 1997. *Les nouvelles campagnes roumaines. Paradoxes d'un retour paysan.* Paris: Mappemonde.

Humphrey, Caroline. 1998. *Marx Went away—But Karl Stayed behind.* Ann Arbor, MI: University of Michigan Press.

Hurd, Madeleine, Hastings Donnan and Carolin Leutloff-Grandits. 2017. Introduction: Crossing Borders, Changing Times. In: Hastings Donnan, Madeleine Hurd, Carolin Leutloff-Grandits (eds). 2017. *Migranting Borders and Moving Times. Temporality and the Crossing of Borders in Europe.* Manchester: Manchester University Press, pp. 1–24.

Jansen, Stef. 2006. The privatization of home and hope: Return, reforms and the foreign intervention in Bosnia-Herzegovina. *Dialectical Anthropology*, 30, 177–199, https://doi.org/10.1007/s10624-007-9005-x.

Jansen, Stef. 2014. On Not Moving Well Enough. Temporal Reasoning in Sarajevo Yearnings for "Normal Lives". *Current Anthropology* 55, 74–84.

Kaneff, Deema. 2004. *Who Owns the Past? The Politics of Time in a 'Model' Bulgarian Village*. Oxford: Berghahn.

Kideckel, David, A. 1993. *The Solitude of Collectivism: Romanian Villagers to the Revolution and Beyond.* Ithaca: Cornell University Press.

Leutloff-Grandits, Carolin. 2002. Claiming Ownership in Post-War Croatia: The Emotional Dynamics of Possession and Repossession in Knin. *Focaal. European Journal of Anthropology. Special Issue on 'Politics and Emotions in Post-Cold War Contexts'*, ed. by Maruska Svasek, pp. 73–92.

Leutloff-Grandits, Carolin. 2003. Houses Without Owners? Historical Insights into Missing Ownership Documents of Houses in Rural Croatia in the 1990s. In: Hannes Grandits and Patrick Heady (eds). 2003. *Distinct Inheritances. Property, Family and Community in a Changing Europe.* Münster: Lit Verlag, pp. 371–388.

Leutloff-Grandits, Carolin. 2004. Religious Celebrations and the (Re)Creation of Communities in Postwar Knin, Croatia. In: Frances Pine, Deema Kaneff and Haldis Haukanes (eds). 2004. *Memory, Politics and Religion. The Past Meets the Present in Europe.* Münster: Lit Verlag, pp. 229–254.

Leutloff-Grandits, Carolin. 2005. Return as a Strategy of Social Security? Generational and Family based Approaches to Return of Serbian War-Refugees to Croatia. In: Haldis Haukanes and Frances Pine (eds). 2005. *Generations, Kinship and Care. Gendered Provisions of Social Security in Central Eastern Europe.* University of Bergen: Centre for Women's and Gender Research, pp. 207–230.

Leutloff-Grandits, Carolin. 2006. Claiming Ownership in Post-War Croatia. The Dynamics of Property Relations and Ethnic Conflict in the Knin Region. *Halle Studies in the Anthropology of Eurasia* 9, Münster: Lit Verlag.

Leutloff-Grandits, Carolin. 2008. Contested Citizenship between National and Social Rights in Post War Knin, Croatia. *Sociologija* 4, 371–390, DOI:10.2298/SOC0804371L.

Leutloff-Grandits, Carolin. 2008. Croatia's Serbs Ten Years after the End of the War. In: Sabrina Ramet, Konrad Clewing and Reneo Lukic (eds). 2008. *Croatia since Independence.* Munich: Oldenbourg, pp. 141–169.

Leutloff-Grandits, Carolin. 2009. 'Fight against Hunger'. Ambiguities of a Charity Campaign in Post-War Croatia. In: Carolin Leutloff-Grandits, Anja Peleikis and Tatjana Thelen (eds). 2009. *Social Security in Religious Networks.* New York: Berghahn, pp. 43–61.

Leutloff-Grandits, Carolin. 2016. Post-Dayton Ethnic Engineering in Croatia through the Lenses of Property Issues and Social Transformations. *Journal for Genocide Research* 18 (4), 485–502, https://doi.org/10.1080/14623528.2016.1230299.

Lévi-Strauss, Claude. 1949. *The Elementary Structures of Kinship*. Boston: Beacon Press.

Mesic, Milan and Dragan Bagic. 2010. Serb returnees in Croatia—The question of return sustainability. *International Migration* 48 (2), 133–160.

Miller, Daniel. 2010. *Stuff*. Cambridge: Polity Press.

O'Loughlin, J. 2010. Inter-ethnic friendships in post-war Bosnia-Herzegovina: Sociodemographic and place influences. *Ethnicities* 10 (1), 26–53, https://doi.org/10.1177/1468796809354153.

Pavlaković, Vjeran. 2014. Fulfilling the thousand-year-old dream: Strategies of symbolic nation-building in Croatia. In: P. Kolstø (ed.) 2014. *Strategies of Symbolic Nation-building in South Eastern Europe*. Farnham: Ashgate, pp. 19–50.

Pina-Cabral de, João and Frances Pine. 2008. On the margins: an introduction. In: Frances Pine and João de Pina-Cabral (eds). 2008. *On the Margins of Religion*. Oxford: Berghahn, pp. 1–12.

Pine, Frances. 1996. Naming the House and Naming the Land: Kinship and Social Groups in Highland Poland. *The Journal of the Royal Anthropological Institute* 2 (3), 443–459, https://doi.org/10.2307/3034897.

Roth, Klaus. 1983. Zum Umgang des Menschen mit seiner Wohnumwelt.I In: Konrad Köstlin (ed.) 1983. *Umgang mit Sachen. Zur Kulturgeschichte des Dinggebrauchs*. Regensburg: Hermann Bausinger, pp. 62–67.

Schäuble, Michaela. 2014. *Narrating Victimhood: Gender, Religion and the Making of Place in post-war Croatia*. New York: Berghahn.

Torsello, Davide. 2003. *Trust, Property and Social Change in a Southern Slovakian Village*. Münster: Lit Verlag.

Verdery, Katherine. 1996. *What Was Socialism, and What Comes Next?* Princeton: Princeton University Press.

Verdery, Katherine. 2003. *The Vanishing Hectare: Property and Value in Postsocialist Transylvania*. Ithaca: Cornell University Press.

3. The 'Post' in Perspective

Revisiting the Post-socialist Religious Question in Central Asia and Central and Eastern Europe

Julie McBrien and Vlad Naumescu

This chapter revisits the 'post-socialist religious question' twenty years later, reflecting on its theoretical import and contribution to broader debates on religion, modernity and social transformation. It draws on the comparative work produced by the MPI research group on 'Religion and Civil Society' focused on the 'religious revivals' in CEE and Central Asia. Observing the fast re-emergence of religion in the public space, its rapid pluralisation and its entanglement with secular politics, this ambitious project managed to simultaneously interrogate the aftermath of secular-atheist experiments in the region and the 'post-secular' deprivatisation of religion and its global reordering. In this chapter we argue that while some of the trends identified by the Civil Religion Group were ephemeral products of the 'transition period' others proved more durable, like the thorny ethno-national-religious knot and its impact on national, regional, and global politics. Moreover, methodological impulses important to the group, like the inclination to start from an analysis of religion's internal logics in the interrogation of social and political phenomena, contributed significantly to broader anthropological discussions and developed new directions of research. Ultimately, we argue that the Civil Religion Group's attempt to answer the 'post-socialist religious question' proved that the post-socialist context was a true laboratory for anthropological theorisation.

      https://doi.org/10.11647/OBP.0282.03

Introduction

If, fifteen years ago, Chris Hann conceded that the title of the book—
The Postsocialist Religious Question—was a conceit for its simplification
of the variegated questions raised about the new relationship between
religion and power across the former socialist world, then our attempt
to reflect on those findings in light of more recent literature and
transformations in the field is even more limited. Yet we will do so, for
the trends Hann identified in his analysis of the research performed by
his fourteen co-authors, the Max Planck Focus Group "Religion and
Civil Society", are worth reexamining; many characterisations remain
salient and have been taken further, in new research directions, while
those that have not are still worth exploring for the transformations they
reveal. As the book's abstract points out, until the volume's publication
in 2006, investigations of religion and secularisation had primarily, if
not exclusively, been focused on capitalist versions of modernity; the
socialist experiment with atheism had been left out of these analyses.
While the research presented in the book had been undertaken after the
collapse of the Soviet Union, not more than a decade had passed since
its fall and the majority of the region's adult inhabitants had matured
during socialism. Moreover, the ideas, institutions, and infrastructure
that were still influential in everyday life had been formed under
socialism; its legacies profoundly impacted the shape religion took in the
newly independent states, whether as an element in ethno-nationalist
narratives, in institutional politics or in personal religious experiences.
The socialist experiment with atheism and its impact on contemporary
religious and secular landscapes became one of the unifying themes
of the work in the team and hence of the volume. The formal focus of
the Civil Religion Group, as it came to be called in the creation of the
volume, was "religion and civil society" and though most of us did
not engage specifically with either the term or the phenomena of civil
society, we were nearly all concerned with the politics of religion in one
form or another. Few of us, however, addressed religion in its own right,
an omission partially inherited from the anthropology of socialism,
where religion mostly featured as a condition of Soviet modernity
(Rogers 2005), but also from the theoretical models we employed.
The anthropology of Christianity with its call to foreground religion's

cultural logic in the analysis of social change was still incipient; Hann would go on to critique this emerging field based on this group's work and his own research (Hann 2007; Robbins 2007).

Hann's attempt to work with the notion of 'civil society' was at least partly rooted in a desire to critically engage with political scientists and development professionals working in the region at the time. 'Civil society' was the buzz-term for post-socialist societies among them. In asking us to utilise the term, Hann endeavoured to establish a common field of interest and dialogue across disciplinary boundaries, while also demonstrating to those in other fields the value of sustained ethnographic research. There were, however, problems with the terminology. To get around both the restriction and difficulties of a term like 'civil society', which he himself criticised in earlier work (Hann 1996), Hann proposed the concept of *civility*. Many of us were wary of the ethnocentrism we read in the term, but Hann spent much time making a case for why *civility* productively engaged the phenomena pointed to under the related terms 'civil society' and 'civil religion'. Moreover, he argued, if taken as a basic mode of peaceful co-existence, *civility* was much less loaded with the troublesome normativity found in connected notions like *civil, civilised* and *civilisation*, most notably in the form of Norbert Elias's *civilité* (1982).

For Hann, the term *civility* was important not only to provide a common research theme, but because it also gave a framework for interrogating questions of plurality and diversity, which must have been for him one of the hallmarks of the new religious terrain across the post-socialist world. His interest in 'civility' at the time also resonated with other intellectuals searching for a common ground in societies where secular, multicultural models seemed to fail, such as Charles Taylor's reinterpretation of Rawlsian 'overlapping consensus' (1999) or Jürgen Habermas's (2006) proposal for an ethics of citizenship based on mutual recognition and institutional translation. Hann's intervention, motivated by similar questions about the return of religion and the challenges of religious pluralism, assumed a different starting point—socialist modernity. In this sense, it was an early comparison of two 'posts', but rather than the 'post' of post-colonialism (Chari and Verdery 2009) it was an interrogation of post-socialism and post-secularism (though a critique of modernity was common to all three posts).

Our research group was intended to follow Hann's interest in *civility* by investigating the premise which prompted his initial interest, namely that a new alignment of religion and power in the post-socialist period produced a wider scope for the practice and presence of religion, including a more diverse religious field. Understanding this new positioning of religion and power was central to the post-socialist religious question and, for Hann at least, civility was a potential answer to the challenges these new arrangements posed. The 2006 collective volume therefore started by cataloguing the various legal, political and institutional situations of religion in Central and Eastern Europe (CEE) and Central Asia, the regions under consideration in the volume, by devoting a substantial section of a chapter each time a new country was introduced. From there, the contributions diverged, pursuing the questions that were relevant to the researcher and their interlocutors, producing finally the diverse field of inquiry Hann hinted at in his opening sentences. Despite the variety found in the volume, there were, in retrospect, several throughlines in our collective work. First, beyond engaging with Hann's questions about civility, thinking about religion and power necessitated the consideration of secularism, both past and future. This meant engaging with the incipient literature on post-secularism and the question of how socialist secularism compared to its counterparts in Europe and the US, but also places like Turkey or Egypt. Instead of asking how socialism repressed religion, an important political question of the Cold War, we began to ask how socialist modernity transformed religion and how this compared to other secular modernising projects.

Second, while the focus on religion and power laid these processes bare, it may have also blinded us to the internal logics of the religious traditions we faced. The majority of us were not primarily concerned with inherent religious dynamics *an sich*, and here, we argue, our investigations may have fallen short. Yet, when we did examine religious phenomena more fundamentally, our initial insights became productive directions for research on religion in the discipline more broadly, like the renewed attention to religious institutions and collective dynamics (Handman and Opas 2019), the focus on conversion and the agency of religious actors (Pelkmans 2009), and the contemporary interest in morality and ethics. Indeed, if the post-socialist religious question was, for our group, mostly about politics and institutional dynamics, the following group led by Hann in the Religion, Identity, and Postsocialism cluster (2010), focused on 'Religion and Morality', looking at individual transformation and modes of self-cultivation. Our combined efforts made a significant contribution to what was to become the anthropology of ethics and morality (Heintz 2009; Rasanayagam 2011; Zigon 2007; 2010; 2012). Third, the push towards the politics of religion inherent in Hann's interests in religion and civility led us to examine belonging and community more broadly, while the focus on secularism demanded that we ask questions about power, governance, and belonging at the nation-state level, past and present. What quickly became apparent as a result was that religion and ethno-national identity were extraordinarily tightly woven together across the post-socialist landscapes. Despite the diversity of locations in which we worked, the religions we investigated, and the questions we asked, none of us could escape the ethno-national-religious knot. It was, perhaps, the most ubiquitously shared finding across all of our work and it stands as one of the most enduring qualities of the post-socialist landscape identified by the Civil Religion Group. Its persistence indicates the lasting impacts of socialist transformations on contemporary social, religious and political landscapes and provides critical insight into pressing political developments across the region, making us rethink, once again, the relevance of post-socialism as an analytical trope.

In this chapter, we discuss the post-socialist religious question, and the collective labour it represents, following the three themes just discussed as a guide: 1. Secularism reconsidered; 2. Religious transformations and collective dynamics; 3. Ethno-national religious belonging and political movements. We set our discussion of the volume against a review of the literature on religion in CEE and Central Asia, brought together for the first time since the volume's publication, to evaluate the state of the field and the role that the post-socialist religious question played in shaping it. We argue that the empirical findings highlighted in this volume have proven to be some of the most salient and durable qualities of religion across the post-socialist landscape. Beyond this, we argue that our fieldwork provided the ground upon which the Civil Religion Group was able to contest dominant paradigms in the anthropology and sociology of religion and secularism, and post-socialist studies, both in this 2006 volume and beyond, retrospectively showing our collective fieldwork to have been a laboratory for anthropological theorising.

Secularism and Religion between the 'Posts'

The Civil Religion Group started by questioning the obvious: 'religious revivals' were sweeping across the former socialist region with both 'new' and 'old' actors making claims on public space. Their visible publicness aside, we wanted to uncover the structural changes that led to such 'revivals', the new religious forms emerging in this process and their interaction with the post-socialist state and other social actors. The term "post-secular" was not yet established (Habermas 2008) but sociologists of religion had already signalled the resurgence of religion globally (Berger 1999) and its "deprivatization" as Jose Casanova (1994) put it. Could one talk about a similar process in the post-socialist region, as Hann (2000) suggested? What difference had Soviet/socialist atheism made to the post-socialist vs. the post-secular conditions?

By nature, terms that start with 'post-' gain their meaning with reference to an implied previous condition; 'posts' compel comparisons between what came before and what came after. Our research was no different. But unlike the literature on secularism and post-secularity that had developed in sociology, our reference points were not Western modernity, Protestantism, and liberal notions of secularism. Rather, focused on post-socialist transformations, our research engaged with the Soviet and socialist variants of secularism, how they reshaped religion, and their aftermath. This position allowed us to start from different premises than the sociological literature of the time and the emerging post-secular debate, circling around normative models of both modernity and secularism (Berger 1999; Casanova 1994; Davie 1994; Hervieu-Léger 2006). Our ethnographies thus approached the religious revivals in light of the socialist experiment to create a society without God. Through in-depth ethnographic studies, we documented the shifting place of religion in post-socialist European and Asian societies, a large part of which was observing the decay, transformation and, in some cases, continuity of socialist-era notions, practices, and institutions in the early post-socialist years. Most of us, for example, uncovered ways in which religion, however muted and altered, persisted during the socialist period, and became entangled with other logics at work in post-socialist political programs, one effect of which was the further entanglement of religion and nation. These findings contributed to a broader rethinking of the relationship between religion, modernity and secularism, and continue to provide rich material for further comparisons with other secular (modernising) projects across the world and their aftermath (Bielo 2015; Ngo and Quijada 2015; Bubandt and van Beek 2012; Cannell 2010; Warner, Van Antwerpen and Calhoun 2010). Building on work Hann, Goltz, and their contributing authors would produce on Eastern Christianities (2010), and the work on Islam carried out by the Civil Religion Group, among others, McBrien (2017) asked questions about the nature of the category of religion within (post)Soviet secularism. If Western secular articulations of religion grew from Protestant notions of individuality and interiority, might not the Soviet formation, rooted as it was in Orthodoxy, and later influenced by Islam, have crafted a notion of religion more bound up with collective practice and belonging? McBrien's work, like that of Martin's (1969; 2017) and Hann's (2011), questioned the prominence of Protestantism and Western European political histories in theory formation.

This line of research was likewise pursued by other anthropologists of post-socialism who, asking similar questions, at times in conversation with us, dug deeper into the nature of Soviet secularism (Luehrmann 2011; Rogers 2009; Wanner 2012). Through archival research, they were able to provide the empirical substantiation of the secular-religious configurations we observed mostly through reflection on the ethnographic present. Sonja Luehrmann (2015) for example pointed out that the "exclusive humanism" of Western secularism described by Charles Taylor (2007) resonated with Soviet secularism and its attempt to forge a social transcendence by stressing faith in people over gods and reclaiming human agency as an engine of social transformation. The Soviet state in practice, however, she argued, used secularisation to manage ethno-religious differences and build new communities, an important corrective to the idea that secularism and liberal individualism are inherently linked (Luehrmann 2011: 6–7). Even if Hann had not sent us out to the field (explicitly) to interrogate the post-secular condition, he wanted us to address the resurgence of religion and challenges of religious pluralism in the post-socialist context. In an article anticipating our project, and a comparison of the 'posts', "Problems with the (de)privatisation of religion", he drew a comparison between the shifting place of religion in Poland and Turkey based on the Polish-Ukrainian conflict over Przemsyl Cathedral in eastern Poland (Hann 2000). He used this analysis to criticise the Western liberal model of governance that was at the time being projected on to post-socialist Europe, a model which promoted civil society and the public sphere, and which assumed that the separation of church and state would lead to the desired "marketplace of religion".

Hann argued instead for the conceptual melding of civil religion and civil society into something he described as 'civility'. Civility, he then argued, could serve as a potential solution to religious monopolies and post-secular conflicts he (and we) witnessed in the field. This move simultaneously broadened Robert Bellah's concept of "civil religion" beyond the US context, where Christian symbols and myths continue to provide the basis of a civil religion despite the formal separation of church and state, and challenged the generalisation of the Western concept of 'civil society' (see also Hann and Dunn 1996). Hann's push for an empirical study of forms of 'civility' in concrete localities proved more fruitful for our work than the influential models in the sociology of religion at the time. It provided an excellent entrypoint for investigating the constituency and quality of relationships among citizens and between citizens and the state. It also allowed us to explore the underlying moral norms and expectations that constituted the grounds for social interaction and coexistence, even if we each gave it different names at the time, or only addressed it in subsequent work: "Orthodox imaginary" (Naumescu), "agrarian tolerance" (Buzalka), "rural civility" (Foszto), "cosmopolitanism" (Richardson), "charity" (Mahieu), "tolerance" as conformity to civic (rather than religious) norms (Heintz), "temperance and tolerance" (Kehl-Bodrogi 2010), "solidarity" (McBrien 2010), "morality" (Rasanyagam 2010; 2011; Stephan 2010), or "neighbourliness" (Pelkmans).

Even if 'civility' didn't become an analytical concept in our research, it provided a starting point for exploring similar dynamics in the field and showing how religion could offer resources for building communities in times of radical change. Ritual revitalisation, practices of sharing and redistribution, or the rebuilding of churches, mosques, and shrines, all mobilised individuals and collectives, substituted failing state institutions and provided forms of solidarity and sociality on the ground. These acts of reconstruction competed at times with the values and institutions inherited from the socialist state, occasionally relying on neo-liberal logics or institutions (McBrien 2017; Pelkmans 2006) but more often than that they appropriated socialist-era tools. There was a lot of "recycling" of people, spaces, institutions and skills in the post-socialist context (Luehrmann 2005) and socialist values like 'working with people' (*rabota s liudmi*) and doing 'society work' (*obshchestvennaia rabota*), or 'culturedness' (*kul'turnost'*) were still largely shared in the post-socialist space (Rasanayagam 2014; Rogers 2009).

In this competition between state-sponsored 'traditions' and 'society work' the latter seemed to resonate more with communities, not least due to the resilience of socialist patronage networks, which were more able to mobilise local resources than the weak post-socialist state. Apparent puzzles, such as how the alliance of local socialist officials turned post-socialist entrepreneurs, and religious leaders, played a key role in the religious revivals, were suddenly not surprising anymore. Local dynamics, like those we described, remained largely unnoticed by post-socialist scholarship focused primarily on broader economic and political transformations even when tackling the resurgence of religion. By searching for explanations of religious change in the social-economic transformations that defined post-socialism, this literature overlooked religion as a potential drive for social change. The focus on 'civility' through long-term ethnographic fieldwork helped us to see it. In the intervening years, this early omission in the literature has been corrected. It has become impossible to ignore religion's sway in society and the role it has in social phenomena formerly seen as firmly in the realm of the (secular) state is inescapable. Various social actors, rather than institutions, find new ways to insert religion in public spaces while acknowledging—even when challenging or renegotiating—the tenets of secularism. Geertz (2005) pointed out the emergence of religious persuasion as an instrument of public identity ("the religious mindedness" of people) already in the 1960s, but we see lately more concerted efforts to reclaim spheres of life that were for a long time the domain of the secular (socialist) state—for example, gender and reproductive politics (Luehrmann 2018a; Mishtal 2015), life-cycle rituals (Cleuziou 2019; Cleuziou and McBrien 2021; McBrien 2020; Roche and Hohmann 2011), education (Köllner 2016; Ladykowska and Tocheva

2013), economy (Botoeva 2018; Fomina 2020; Köllner 2020), and public space (Tateo 2020).

Religion's new role in public life has not been universally well received, especially as it has grown in strength and prominence. However, while in the past the state was the main regulator of religion's public presence, non-state, secular actors now bring religious-secular conflicts into the sphere of 'civility'. The 2012 'punk prayer' of Russian feminist band Pussy Riot in a Moscow cathedral challenged the sacredness of church and state and their 'symphonic' relationship, managing to disturb both religious and secular sensibilities (Bernstein 2013; Shevzov 2014). Others have taken to court their claims for public institutions to remain free of religious symbols, challenging the post-socialist alliance of church and state by appropriating the repertoire of their opponents, whether 'blasphemy' in the case of Russian courts or 'human rights' in the case of Romanian schools (Horvath 2009). Such developments do not belong to post-socialism anymore. They echo global trends and reconfigurations of the secular and the religious worldwide, whether in the Middle East, North America or Western Europe (Heo 2013; Kaell 2016; Oliphant 2012).

Religious Transformations and Collective Dynamics

Scholars of post-socialist religiosity did not have many resources to start from when trying to account for its transformation; anthropologies of religion under socialism were scarce and local scholarship was 'biased' by atheist ideology (Luehrmann 2015). However, a visible (and ethnographically accessible) site to grasp individual and collective transformation was the religious conversion, both to historical traditions and new religious movements, proliferating after the collapse of socialist regimes. For many, religion became an opportunity for radical change; conversion provided a clear moment of rupture in their lives which resonated with the broader post-socialist transformations they were experiencing. In this sense, conversion could have become the impetus for anthropologists of post-socialism to take individual agency seriously, taking inspiration from the post-colonial literature on conversion and modernity as JDY Peel (2009) suggested in the postface of another volume emanating from our group's work. Some in our group have tried, even if implicitly, through the lens of morality, acknowledging people's conscious orientation towards different ideas of the good, proper or virtuous, and pointing to distinct paths to moral formation and conceptions of personhood that accounted for religious subjectivities beyond utilitarian approaches (Foszto 2009; Hilgers 2009; Pelkmans 2009; Rasanayagam 2011). A focus on morality also seemed to better reflect everyday realities on the ground: the times in which old social contracts were discredited and new ones were not yet in place, when the language of change was itself moralising and the new politics were articulated in an ethics of reform (Nazpary 2002; Steinberg and Wanner 2008; Zigon 2007).

But conversion also challenged ingrained forms of civility and kin relations and the ethno-religious knot in post-socialist countries, with missionaries trying to decouple individual belief from collective belonging (McBrien and Pelkmans 2008). This meant that even when focusing on individual belief and practice, we could not ignore the politics of religion as shaped by post-socialist state-building processes. The forms of 'civility' that sustained communities also played into the politics of differentiation fuelled by ethno-nationalist mobilisations across the post-socialist space. Hann (2003) had already indicated this with the example of sacred music which, he argued, could unite and yet also separate people along confessional, ethnic, and national boundaries (see also Engelhardt 2014 and Luehrmann 2018). Our work further substantiated these findings, showing how dominant religions exerted their exclusive hold in the face of religious 'others' (Buzalka; Hilgers; Foszto; Pelkmans; Naumescu), while also suffering from competing interpretations of the same faith and of their religious past (Hilgers; Kehl-Bodrogi; Mahieu; McBrien; Rasanayagam; Stephan).

The post-socialist conflicts over property split communities and mobilised both old and newly recruited believers (Leutloff-Grandits 2006; Naumescu 2010). Most of us paid particular attention to the state-citizen nexus and the possibilities for religious faith and practice in the new institutional arrangements. The simultaneous assertion of post-socialist states as secular and as having a religious base for their national projects, a legacy of the socialist era, was the backdrop against which many of the individual and collective religious projects we investigated played out. Here, the view 'from below,' which attended to lived religion as well as local institutional dynamics, made a difference; the relationship between religious 'revivals' and secular politics was not straightforward in the post-socialist context. Religion had been highly politicised during socialism and its publicly tolerated forms had been moulded by the state into what has been described in the literature as compliant official institutions and secularised cultural performances, part of national heritage or folklore. Many of us started out by interrogating this model of socialist-era religion, arguing against bifurcated notions like 'official/ unofficial' religion, or 'secularised' religion, showing rather the spaces where, and ways in which, religion persisted in the late Soviet period and the complex ways in which secularising policies *transformed* its practice and understandings of it (Hilgers 2009; Jessa; Kehl-Bodrogi 2008; McBrien 2010; 2012; Rasanayagam 2006; 2011; Stephan).

In the post-socialist period these localised practices and institutions became the grounds for the religious 'revivals' which were however also shaped by the transnational connections that religious groups maintained, revived or formed after 1989. Kehl-Bodrogi, Naumescu, and McBrien, for example, found examples of the former. Kehl-Bodrogi's work argued that in both the Soviet and post-Soviet era, most Khorezmians expressed their Muslim identity through the observance of life-cycle rituals (2010). McBrien (2017) traced the ways that the initial interest in Islam in small towns of southern Kyrgyzstan was facilitated by networks of Islamic scholars trained during the Soviet period. Naumescu (2007) pointed to the religious practices and institutions maintaining a vibrant local tradition in Soviet Ukraine that defied both Soviet atheism and the post-socialist politics of differentiation pursued by Ukrainian churches after independence. Pelkmans's (2007) and Hilgers's (2009) work, in contrast, illustrate the latter, showing how the transnational connections of Evangelical Christians and the massive inroad of Western missionaries in the region produced unexpected synergies with socialist cultural legacies, while also triggering serious tensions. The interaction between local traditions and global actors shaped the religious landscape as much as the nation-building processes and the resacralisation of politics that post-socialist states pursued (Smolkin 2018; Verdery 1999). This implied that religious fragmentation was not just a condition of the rapid pluralisation of post-Soviet society. It was also a result of competing visions of 'religion' (as well as of 'culture', 'tradition' and 'nation') and its place in society. The whole process was in turn affected by salient beliefs and practices, people's mistrust of institutions and church-state relations (another legacy of the socialist period) and the pervasiveness of historical traditions (Islam, Orthodoxy) in society and culture. In many cases, Islam and Orthodox Christianity functioned as an 'ambient faith' (Engelke 2012) in national contexts, articulating a mode of belonging to the nation relatively independent from changing political regimes. In Ukraine, for example, a diffuse Orthodoxy remained salient during the Soviet times as much as in the post-Soviet period, defying the boundaries between private and public and the initial separation—and later alliance—between church and state (Naumescu 2007; Wanner 2014). Like the various modes of 'civility' our group depicted, an ambient faith falls in between well-defined social categories and institutional frames, defying politics of differentiation yet being potentially recruited by them to create difference. Inserting itself in secular space without challenging it directly, and being susceptible to politicisation without being explicitly political, ambient Orthodoxy remains even today an important mobilising factor in Ukraine to legitimise nationalist causes or sustain a war against an enemy that shares the same faith (Wanner 2020).

An ambient faith raises the broader question about the sharp division between (an assumed secular) politics and religion that continues to inform contemporary studies of religion and post-secularity. Their entanglement was visible in the 1990s 'revivals' as it is in the religious mobilisations of today. The establishment of a national Orthodox Church in Ukraine in 2019 and the ensuing schism between Moscow and Constantinople Patriarchates mobilised people and churches in Ukraine and Russia, and across the Orthodox world. Drawing parallels between the patterns of mobilisation around this conflict and those from the 1990s, Kormina and Naumescu (2020) observe how Orthodox Churches' struggles for sovereignty ('autocephaly') have long been entangled with state sovereignty. This relationship is reflected in disputes over 'canonical territory' which follow the post-Soviet reorganisation of state borders, and in a theopolitics of 'communion', and of belonging (or not) to the sacred community of faith and nation. As theological-political formations, 'communion' and 'canonical territory' offer a space for divinely sanctioned action that reaches beyond the religious sphere, constituting an effective means of collective mobilisation. Without an awareness of Orthodoxy's inherent dynamics, one can easily overlook the galvanising potential of religion subordinating it to secular politics. In Central Asia, education, business, and development have been domains in which the lines between the religious and the secular have not always been clearly demarcated and in which religion, politics, national and international actors overlap in mutually constituting fields, belying easy distinctions between them and contesting notions that see religion merely as the instrument of politics (or business). From the 'Turkish' secondary schools of the 1990s and the contemporary mountain university built by the Aga Khan Development Network, to Islamically inspired development projects and Muslim entrepreneurialism across the region, Islamic actors and institutions occupy an interstitial social space in which they work out their religiously-inspired economic, educational, and humanitarian projects (Balci 2003; Botoeva 2020; Clement 2007; Mostowlansky 2017). 'Religion' in their work can neither be seen as the essential cause, as if they were only missionaries in disguise, nor merely a device for educational, economic or political endeavours; the two act mutually and both are constitutive of their efforts. The religious formations which shape the social and economic work warrant research in their own right, such as recent inquiries into Islamic economy in Kyrgyzstan and Kazakhstan (Botoeva 2018) and Muslim humanitarianism in the borderlands of Central and South Asia (Mostowlansky 2020).

Recent anthropological work on religious-secular contestations in the post-socialist space sheds additional light on the entanglements of religion and politics beyond the common tropes of 'instrumentalisation of religion,' or the 'Orthodox symphonia' between church and state (Köllner 2020). Such ethnographies delineate several levels of relatedness between religious and political actors and a space of institutional-organisational dynamics between lived religion and the state (Halemba 2015; Doolotkeldieva 2020; Tocheva 2018). These arrangements complicate the image of 'civility' Hann proposed, pointing to the historical and institutional dynamics that allowed for 'civility' to emerge in its various forms in the first place. They resonate with recent calls in the anthropology of Christianity for a shift of focus from individual faith and ethical pursuits towards religious institutions and (infra)structures of sociality (Handman and Opas 2019), something that should concern anthropologists of religion more broadly. It certainly applies to our regions, where Muslims and Orthodox Christians live their faith primarily through collective practice and community, the focus on which would not only produce fuller empirical renderings of religion in the region but would also continue to provide a corrective to the 'Protestant bias' of the anthropology of Christianity (see also Boylston 2013; Hann 2007; Meyer 2017).

Nationalism, State and New Political Mobilisations

When we started our research on religion and civility, we were confronted with a literature on secularism and religion that had failed to consider socialist secularism and bypassed consideration of Eastern Christianity, which is prevalent in the region. We were also faced with a body of work on religion under socialism, which had yet to move beyond the Cold War-era frames in the way research on economy (Dunn 2004; Hann 1998; Humphrey 1998; Verdery 2003) or ethnicity and nationalism (Bringa 1995; Grant 1995) had. Western European and American researchers examining religion during the late socialist and early post-socialist era, tended towards repression/revival models to describe and interpret it (Liu 2017; Pelkmans 2006).

This mode of thinking generally posited that religion, repressed by atheism, reappeared after the demise of socialism, largely unscathed and unchanged. The model had interesting congruences with other Cold War-era frameworks, namely those developed about national identity. In this case, there were two reigning models, one which argued that ethno-national identity was repressed by the USSR, only to revive at its demise, unchanged. The other, that nations had been rather arbitrarily invented in the early Soviet period and that in the absence of a strong Soviet state, they would fall apart or devolve into ethnic conflict. The Ferghana Valley of Central Asia was often taken as an example for the potential occurrence of the latter while the Caucasus was held up as evidence of the former (Pelkmans 2006). Following the collapse of socialism, anthropologists and historians picked up the investigation of nations and nationalism first, demonstrating the ways that already existing modes of ethnic or national belonging had been profoundly altered by Soviet-era policies and programmes. In other cases, in which early socialist-era interventions played a role in creating nations, researchers demonstrated not only the nuanced ways in which these modes of belonging were constructed but their durability after the union's collapse (Hirsch 2000; 2005; Slezkine 2000). Most of us were already aware of this research when we set out to investigate religion, and it is perhaps because of the nuanced, complicated picture this research painted about how power operated during the socialist era that we began to ask questions about the accuracy and utility of repression/revival models for understanding the post-socialist religious landscapes. The stories we heard from many of our interlocutors who reached adulthood during the socialist era added to these doubts, as they detailed for us the ways in which they attempted to live good Christian or Muslim lives during socialism. Importantly, these were not only stories of hidden, underground religion—though there were those, too as the case of Greek Catholics in CEE has shown (Mahieu and Naumescu 2008).

These were stories of how religious norms and values, for example, mingled and melded with socialist ones (Heintz; Tocheva 2011); of religious leaders who were also proud socialist workers (McBrien 2017); or of a generational specialisation in which religious/secular commitments were mapped onto different ages allowing for the reproduction of both (Naumescu 2016; Ładykowska, this volume). What we saw in the early 2000s, then, were not simply revivals of pre-Soviet religion; they were religious ideas, practices, and institutions profoundly shaped by and formed in response to the socialist experience (see also Rogers 2009; Tasar 2017; Wanner 2007). There were often marked differences between what we found in CEE and what we saw in Central Asia, despite the shared socialist experience. The regions had vastly different pre-socialist modes of economic and political organisation, and how they became socialist states or Soviet republics varied significantly, too. Importantly, we also researched different religions. While some worked on minority religions like Evangelicalism or Baha'I (Hilgers; Pelkmans), the two main religions under study were Eastern Christianity and Islam. Despite these differences, there was a striking similarity across socialist space when it came to the intertwining of religious, ethnic, and national belonging.

Our research revealed that an inadvertent by-product of the attempt to eradicate, or at least tightly control, religion under socialism was the strengthening of its ties to ethno-national identity. While certain elements of religious life had been effectively eliminated by early anti-religious campaigns and later religious restrictions, other elements of religious practice had been tacitly (or explicitly) allowed to remain and were in some cases appropriated by the state. In both Central Asia and CEE these were often life-cycle events and rituals connected to the home. For religious practitioners, these remained important religious customs and were inextricably linked to a sense of religious belonging (Kligman 1988). At the same time, in public secular life, these same elements were often celebrated as components of culture that were integrated into reinvented folk traditions to be performed on the national stage (Cash 2012). The religious quality was either left unmarked as such, denied, or tolerated as an 'in-the-meantime' step towards religious eradication. The net effect for many across the socialist region was that religion became an essential component of ethno-national identity, such that in the early post-socialist period when we conducted our research it was nearly unthinkable for our interlocutors to imagine a non-Orthodox Russian or Ukrainian, or a non-Muslim Uzbek or Kyrgyz, for example. In Ukraine, an Orthodox imaginary was inclusive only of those belonging to the same historical tradition (Kyivan Rus), supporting an ambient faith blended with national identity and excluding those of "foreign import" (Naumescu). Intriguingly, the same logics meant that in Ukraine, Kyrgyzstan, and all across the socialist world, many a foreign missionary, regardless of their faith, struggled with this ethno-national religious knot and worked as hard to convert people to new boundaries between religion and culture as they did to the specific religion they were proselytising (McBrien and Pelkmans 2008; Wanner 2007). When socialism ended, religion not only remained a vital aspect of national identity, it was in many ways strengthened. As the new nation-states asserted their independence, an important element was the (re)construction of their national narrative and a national sense of belonging. Religion played a key role in these nation-building endeavours in all the former socialist countries. As we explored the question of religious pluralism and forms of civility or tolerance, we quickly saw that while there was room for religiously-based alliances among citizens and between citizens and the state, it had its limits.

Articulations of a given religion that were alternative to that endorsed by the state were criticised, discursively demonised, or violently repressed (Hilgers; Jessa; Kehl-Bodrogi; McBrien; Rasanayagam; Stephan). Even in post-Soviet countries like Ukraine or Kyrgyzstan where the state has apparently allowed for a marketplace of religions to emerge, there were clear boundaries as to what constituted acceptable religion. Minority religions that crossed ethnic-national bounds or missionaries trying to break the ethno-religious bond were not tolerated (Hilgers; Pelkmans). Co-religionists belonging to different nation-states started to draw religious boundaries when the newly established borders or political conflicts set them against one another. So while in the thirty years since socialism ended, the varying trajectories of the independent nation-states have resulted in significant divergences between the countries, this ethno-national-religious knot remains strong. It has proven to be one of the most durable effects of the socialist period. The contemporary rise of conservative populist politics across the former socialist world has seen the persistent articulation of religion in nationalist rhetoric and a potential for politicised religiosities. This includes, for example, the post-peasant populism that Buzalka (2008) described for CEE, a political discourse that draws on elements of peasant culture (values, symbols, practices) to mobilise mostly rural populations. Since religion is an integral part of this political culture (anti-modern, anti-Western/liberal, etc.), mainstream churches tend to sustain it as another opportunity to reaffirm their close ties with the nation and state. Yet the nationalist-populist movements of CEE seem to gravitate nowadays towards the global conservative trend where Christianity features as a moral and civilisational dimension rather than national-identitarian alone, a possible legacy of the Christian, anti-communist rhetoric that characterised Cold War politics (Kirby 2014). Poland and Hungary are presented as examples of this shift (Brubaker 2017; Mishtal 2015) while in Ukraine, Russia or Romania the Orthodox Churches remain closely entangled in state politics and national identity in ways that go beyond a simple instrumentalisation of religion (Köllner 2020; Laruelle 2020; Wanner 2020). In Central Asia, religion is mobilised for political manoeuvres, but then often in service of internal repression or control. Governments have continued to utilise their self-appointed authority to assess 'correct' interpretations of Islam in order to shape, censor and sometimes violently repress alternatives by co-religionists. In addition, some states, notably Tajikistan and Uzbekistan, have used this same power to (violently) repress political opponents, whether or not religion was actually an issue in their disagreement.

Central Asia remains a predominantly Muslim region, but the diversity of ways in which Islam is interpreted and lived out has grown significantly in the twenty years since the research of the Civil Religion Group was carried out. Increased contact with other parts of the Muslim world, the proliferation of movements like the Tablighi Jamaat and the investment of foreign Muslim donors in the region, combined with an established network of local Islamic schools and greater access to Islamic materials at home, has led to a variegated religious sphere (Botoeva 2018; Doolotkeldieva 2020; Nasritdinov 2012; Nasritdinov and Esenamanova 2017; Pelkmans 2017; Stephan-Emmrich 2018; Toktogulova 2014). Labour remittances and the growth of a middle class in places like Kyrgyzstan and Kazakhstan has also led to the development of a religious middle class, with its incumbent consumption patterns and tastes (Bissenova 2017; Botoeva 2020; Stephan-Emmrich and Mirzoev 2016). Easy, affordable access to the Internet has facilitated the growth of popular Islamic teachers who weigh in on national trends and affairs (Bigozhin 2019). Politicians now readily proclaim their piety and their religiously-informed political positions. Yet, what has not altered, is the link between religion and ethno-national identity, even if varying interpretations of Islam and different understandings of national belonging have led to a diversity of ways this link is made and understood (Artman 2019; Toktogulova 2020).

Central Asia has seen its own form of populism, notably in the nationalist movements of Kyrgyzstan where religion has been a less visible force than in Europe. Nonetheless, as in Buzalka's notion of post-peasant populism, religion is intimately intertwined with populist notions of political community in Kyrgyzstan, especially when nationalist movements take 'anti-Western' stances in defence of 'local' norms. While the ethno-national religious knot works itself out differently in Europe and Asia, the persistence (and similarity) of these phenomena across time and space reaffirms the value of comparisons between 'posts', one that accounts for the continuing effects of global Cold War politics in the religious and political mobilisations of today.

Conclusion

Answering the 'post-socialist religious question' Hann raised for the Civil Religion Group revealed that the 'religious revivals' were not just outcomes of the post-socialist transformations, making us reconsider the role and impact of socialist modernity on these processes and religious forms. The work of our group proved the lasting presence of Soviet secularism and of religiously-grounded forms of 'civility' that shaped the post-socialist society and religious landscape in important ways. There were obvious continuities behind these 'revivals', especially in the realignment of religion, state and post-socialist nation-building in CEE and Central Asia (see Hann and Pelkmans 2009 for a comprehensive comparison). Yet, by becoming public, religion challenged the power of post-socialist states to define appropriate religious forms and their place in society as well as established connections between ethnicity-nation-religion at the local level. Religion became, at the same time, an agent of social mobilisation and a primary means for individual transformation across the post-socialist space. Conversion, for example, was a key site for negotiating the personal and the political and from which for us to reconsider individual agency within the broader structural processes that defined this period. This was an opportunity for our group to take religious commitments seriously rather than as a sign of self-interest exacerbated by the new market economy, identity politics or ideological commitments.

However, these investigations did not prompt a more systematic reflection on religion in its own right. While our group focused on religion's entanglement with socio-economic transformations and secular politics we did not examine, in depth, how contemporary adaptations of religious forms in the 'post' context were shaped by the theological and historical traditions of the different faiths. Hann raised this question in his Erfurt Lecture, "Eastern Christianity and Western Social Theory" (2011), reflecting on the Protestantism of anthropology and of social theories of modernity. Besides opening the possibility to rethink the genealogies of 'modernity', including religious modernities, in a global frame, this question invites us to reconsider the relationship between religion and politics beyond the modern-secular understanding of the political as devoid of religion.

Hann's search for 'civility' is also validated by the ongoing polarisation of societies stirred by populist politics and growing inequalities, as his latest contributions attest (2020; also Buzalka, Pasieka this volume). The illiberal discourses in the region continue to be partially structured by socialist narratives, namely an anti-Western posturing that resembles the Second- and First-World relations of the Cold War era, perceived marginalisation within the broader political structures, conspiratorial visions of multiculturalism and liberal agendas imposed by the EU, etc. These developments reflect global trends and the continued relevance of Cold War legacies, making us ask whether, despite the thirty years that have passed since the collapse of the Soviet Union, the concept of post-socialism does not still make sense. Discussions of the utility of the term 'post-socialist' remain commonplace today and some researchers are leaving the framework behind (e.g. Müller 2019; Ibanez-Tirado 2015) while others extend and embrace it as a global condition (Chari and Verdery 2009; Gille 2010; Rogers 2010). Important among the latter for our continued reflection on the religious question between 'posts' are considerations about how Cold War configurations of knowledge and power have shaped and continue to shape social theory and politics (not least through the salience of modernisation theory and secularism in the different 'posts'), how imperial legacies have shaped socialist nationalities policies and post-socialist politics of recognition as well as neocolonial claims, and the emergence of contemporary populist, nationalist movements across the region that join a global conservative surge.

References

Artman, Vincent M. 2018. Nation, Religion, and Theology: What Do We Mean When We Say "Being Kyrgyz Means Being Muslim?". *Central Asian Affairs* 5 (3), 191–212, https://doi.org/10.1163/22142290-00503001.

Balci, Bayram. 2003. Fethullah Gülen's Missionary Schools in Central Asia and their Role in the Spreading of Turkism and Islam. *Religion, State & Society* 31 (2), 151–177, https://doi.org/10.1080/0963749032000074006 .

Bielo, James S. 2015. Secular studies come of age. *Thesis Eleven* 129 (1), 119–130, https://doi.org/10.1177/0725513615592986.

Berger, Peter L. 1999. *The Desecularization of the World: Resurgent Religion and World Politics*. Washington, D.C. Grand Rapids, Michigan.

Bernstein, Anya. 2013. An Inadvertent Sacrifice: Body Politics and Sovereign Power in the Pussy Riot Affair. *Critical Inquiry* 40 (1), 220–241, https://doi.org/10.1086/673233.

Bigozhin, Ulan. 2019. "Where is Our Honor?" Sports, Masculinity, and Authority in Kazakhstani Islamic Media. *Central Asian Affairs* 6 (2–3), 189–205, https://doi.org/10.1163/22142290-00602006.

Bissenova, Alima. 2017. The Fortress and the Frontier: Mobility, Culture, and Class in Almaty and Astana. *Europe-Asia Studies* 69 (4), 642–667, https://doi.org/10.1080/09668136.2017.1325445.

Botoeva, Aisalkyn. 2018. Islam and the spirits of capitalism: Competing articulations of the Islamic economy. *Politics & Society* 46 (2), 235–226, https://doi.org/10.1177/0032329218776014.

Botoeva, Aisalkyn. 2020. Measuring the Unmeasurable? Production & Certification of Halal Goods and Services. *Sociology of Islam* 8 (3–4), 364–386, https://doi.org/10.1163/22131418-08030008.

Boylston, Tom. 2013. Orienting the East: Notes on Anthropology of Orthodox Christianities. https://www.new-directions.sps.ed.ac.uk/orienting-the-east/.

Bubandt, Nils O. and Martijn Van Beek (eds). 2012. *Varieties of Secularism in Asia: Anthropological Explorations of Religion, Politics and the Spiritual*. London: Routledge.

Buzalka, Juraj. 2007. *Nation and Religion: The Politics of Commemorations in South-East Poland*. Berlin: Lit Verlag.

Buzalka, Juraj. 2008. Europeanisation and post-peasant populism in Eastern Europe. *Europe-Asia Studies* 60 (5), 757–771, https://doi.org/10.1080/09668130802085141.

Bringa, Tone. 1995. *Being Muslim the Bosnian Way: Identity and Community in a Central Bosnian Village*. Princeton: Princeton University Press.

Brubaker, Rogers. 2017. Between nationalism and civilizationism: The European populist moment in comparative perspective. *Ethnic and Racial Studies* 40 (8), 1191–1226, https://doi.org/10.1080/01419870.2017.1294700.

Cannell, Fenella. 2010. The Anthropology of Secularism. *Annual Review of Anthropology* 39, 85–100, https://doi.org/10.1146/annurev.anthro.012809.105039.

Casanova, José. 1994. *Public Religions in the Modern World*. Chicago: University of Chicago Press.

Cash, Jennifer R. 2012. *Villages on Stage: Folklore and Nationalism in the Republic of Moldova*. Berlin: Lit Verlag.

Chari, Sharad and Katherine Verdery. 2009. Thinking between the Posts: Postcolonialism, Postsocialism, and Ethnography after the Cold War. *Comparative Studies in Society and History* 51, 6–34, https://doi.org/10.1017/S0010417509000024.

Cleuziou, Juliette. 2019. Traditionalization, or the making of a reputation: Women, weddings and expenditure in Tajikistan. *Central Asian Survey 38* (3), 346–362, https://doi.org/10.1080/02634937.2019.1617247.

Cleuziou, Juliette and Julie McBrien. 2021. Marriage quandaries in Central Asia. *Oriente Moderno 100* (2), 121–146, https://doi.org/10.1163/22138617-12340246.

Clement, Victoria. 2007. Turkmenistan's new challenges: Can stability co-exist with reform? A study of Gülen schools in Central Asia, 1997–2007. In: Ihsan Yilmaz et al. (eds). 2007. *International Conference Proceedings. Muslim World in Transition: Contribution of the Gülen Movement*. London: Leeds Metropolitan University Press, pp. 572–583.

Davie, Grace. 1994. *Religion in Britain since 1994: Believing without Belonging*. Hoboken: Wiley-Blackwell.

Doolotkeldieva, Asel. 2020. Madrasa-based Religious Learning: Between Secular State and Competing Fellowships in Kyrgyzstan. *Central Asian Affairs* 7 (3), 211–235, https://doi.org/0.30965/22142290-bja10010.

Dunn, Elizabeth. 2004. *Privatizing Poland: Baby Food, Big Business, and the Remaking of Labor*. Ithaca: Cornell University Press.

Elias, Norbert. 1982. *Power & Civility*. New York: Pantheon Books.

Engelhardt, Jeffers. 2014. *Singing the Right Way: Orthodox Christians and Secular Enchantment in Estonia*. Oxford: Oxford University Press.

Engelke, Matthew. 2012. Angels in Swindon: Public religion and ambient faith in England. *American Ethnologist* 39 (1), 155–170, https://doi.org/10.1111/j.1548-1425.2011.01355.x.

Fomina, Victoria. 2020. How to Earn a Million in the Glory of God?: Ethics and Spirituality among Orthodox Entrepreneurs in Contemporary Russia. *Anthropological Quarterly* 93 (2), 27–55, https://doi.org/10.1353/anq.2020.0025.

Fosztó, Laszlo. 2009. *Ritual Revitalisation after Socialism: Community, Personhood, and Conversion among Roma in a Transylvanian Village*. Münster: Lit Verlag.

Grant, Bruce. 1995. *In the House of Soviet Culture*. Princeton: Princeton University Press.

Geertz, Clifford. 2005. Shifting Aims, Moving Targets: On the Anthropology of Religion. *JRAI* (N.S.) 11, 1–15.

Gille, Zsuzsa. 2010. Is there a Global Postsocialist Condition? *Global Society* 24 (1), 9–30, https://doi.org/10.1080/13600820903431953.

Habermas, Jürgen. 2006. Religion in the Public Sphere. *European Journal of Philosophy* 14 (1), 1–25, https://doi.org/10.1111/j.1468-0378.2006.00241.x.

Habermas, Jürgen. 2008. Notes on Post-Secular Society. *New Perspectives Quarterly* 25 (4), 17–29, https://doi.org/10.1111/j.1540-5842.2008.01017.x.

Halemba, Agnieszka. 2015. *Negotiating Marian Apparitions, Leipzig Studies on the History and Culture of East-Central Europe*. Budapest: CEU Press.

Handman, Courtney and Minna Opas. 2019. Institutions, Infrastructures, and Religious Sociality: The Difference Denominations Make in Global Christianity. *Anthropological Quarterly* 92 (4), 1001–1014, https://doi.org/10.1353/anq.2019.0058.

Hann, Chris 1996. Introduction: Political society and civil anthropology. In C. Hann and E. Dunn (eds). 1996. *Civil Society: Challenging Western Models*. London: Routledge, pp. 1–24.

Hann, Chris (ed.). 1998. *Property Relations: Renewing the Anthropological Tradition*. Cambridge: Cambridge University Press.

Hann, Chris. 2000. Problems with the (de)privatization of religion. *Anthropology Today* 6 (6), 14–20, https://doi.org/10.1111/1467-8322.00033.

Hann, Chris. 2003. Creeds, cultures and the 'witchery of music'. *The Journal of the Royal Anthropological Institute* 9 (2), 223–240, https://doi.org/10.1111/1467-9655.00147.

Hann, Chris. 2007. The Anthropology of Christianity *per se*. *European Journal of Sociology* 48 (3), 383–410, https://doi.org/10.1017/S0003975607000410.

Hann, Chris (ed.). 2010. *Religion, Identity, Postsocialism*. Halle/Saale: Max Planck Institute for Social Anthropology.

Hann, Chris. 2011. Eastern Christianity and Western social theory. *Erfurter Vorträge zur Kulturgeschichte des Orthodoxen Christentums* 10, http://hdl.handle.net/11858/00-001M-0000-000F-3EC8-8.

Hann, Chris. 2014. The Heart of the Matter: Christianity, Materiality, and Modernity. *Current Anthropology* 55 (S10), S182-S192, https://doi.org/10.1086/678184.

Hann, Chris. 2020. In Search of Civil Society: From Peasant Populism to Postpeasant Illiberalism in Provincial Hungary. *Social Science Information* 59 (3), 459–483, https://doi.org/10.1177/0539018420950189.

Hann, Chris and Elisabeth Dunn (eds). 1996. *Civil Society: Challenging Western Models*. London: Routledge.

Hann, Chris and Hermann Goltz. 2010. Introduction: The Other Christianity? In: C. Hann and H. Goltz (eds). 2010. *Eastern Christians in Anthropological Perspective*. Berkeley: University of California Press, pp. 1–29.

Hann, Chris and Mathijs Pelkmans. 2009. Realigning Religion and Power in Central Asia: Islam, Nation-State and (Post)Socialism. *Europe-Asia Studies* 61 (9), 1517–1541, https://doi.org/10.1080/09668130903209111.

Heintz, Monica. 2009. *The Anthropology of Moralities*. Oxford: Berghahn Books.

Heo, Angie. 2013. The bodily threat of miracles: Security, sacramentality, and the Egyptian politics of public order. *American Ethnologist* 40 (1), 149–164, https://doi.org/10.1111/amet.12011.

Hervieu-Léger, Danièle. 2006. In search of certainties: The paradoxes of religiosity in societies of high modernity. *Hedgehog Review* 8 (102), 59–68.

Hilgers, Irene. 2009. *Why do Uzbeks Have to Be Muslims?: Exploring Religiosity in the Ferghana Valley*. Münster: Lit Verlag.

Hirsch, Francine. 2000. Toward an empire of nations: Border-making and the formation of Soviet national identities. *The Russian Review 59* (2), 201–226, https://doi.org/10.1111/0036-0341.00117.

Hirsch, Francine. 2005. *Empire of Nations: Ethnographic Knowledge and the Making of the Soviet Union*. Ithaca: Cornell University Press.

Humphrey, Caroline. 1998. *Marx Went Away—But Karl Stayed behind*. Ann Arbor: University of Michigan Press.

Ibañez-Tirado, Diana. 2015. 'How Can I Be Post-Soviet if I Was Never Soviet?' Rethinking Categories of Time and Social Change—A Perspective from Kulob, Southern Tajikistan. *Central Asian Survey* 34 (2), 190–203, https://doi.org/10.1080/02634937.2014.983705.

Kaell, Hillary. 2016. Seeing the Invisible: Ambient Catholicism on the Side of the Road. *Journal of the American Academy of Religion* 85 (1), 136–167, https://doi.org/10.1093/jaarel/lfw041.

Kehl-Bodrogi, Krisztina. 2008. *"Religion is not so strong here". Muslim Religious Life in Khorezm after Socialism*. Berlin: Lit Verlag.

Kehl-Bodrogi, Krisztina. 2010. Local Islam in postsocialist Khorezm (Uzbekistan). In: Chris Hann (ed.) 2010. *Religion, identity, postsocialism*. Halle/Saale: Max Planck Institute for Social Anthropology, pp. 30–33.

Kirby, Dianne. 2014. Christian anti-communism. *Twentieth Century Communism 7* (7), 126–152, https://doi.org/10.3898/175864314813903962.

Kligman, Gail. 1988. *The Wedding of the Dead: Ritual, Poetics, and Popular Culture in Transylvania*. Berkeley: University of California Press.

Kormina, Jeanne and Vlad Naumescu. 2020. A new 'Great Schism'? Theopolitics of communion and canonical territory in the Orthodox Church. *Anthropology Today* 36 (1), 7–11, https://doi.org/10.1111/1467-8322.12551.

Köllner, T. 2016. Patriotism, Orthodox religion and education: empirical findings from contemporary Russia. *Religion, State & Society* 44 (4), 366–386, https://doi.org/10.1080/09637494.2016.1246852.

Köllner, Tobias. 2020. *Religion and Politics in Contemporary Russia: Beyond the Binary of Power and Authority.* London: Routledge.

Ladykowska, Agata and Detelina Tocheva. 2013. Women Teachers of Religion in Russia. *Archives de sciences sociales des religions* 162, 55–74, https://doi.org/0.4000/assr.25051.

Laruelle, Marlene. 2020. Ideological Complementarity or Competi tion? The Kremlin, the Church, and the Monarchist Idea in T'day's Russia. *Slavic Review* 79 (2), 345–364, https://doi.org/10.1017/slr.2020.87.

Leutloff-Grandits, Carolin. 2006. *Claiming Ownership in Postwar Croatia: The Dynamics of Property Relations and Ethnic Conflict in the Knin Region.* Berlin/ Münster: Lit Verlag.

Liu, Morgan. 2017. Central Asia Islam Outside a Soviet Box. *News of the Association for Slavic, East European and Eurasian Studies* 57 (3), 3–5.

Luehrmann, Sonja. 2005. Recycling Cultural Construction: Desecularisation in Postsoviet Mari El. *Religion, State & Society* 33 (1), 35–56, https://doi.org/10.1080/0963749042000330857.

Luehrmann, Sonja. 2011. *Secularism Soviet Style: Teaching Atheism and Religion in a Volga Republic.* Bloomington: Indiana University Press.

Luehrmann, Sonja 2015. *Religion in Secular Archives: Soviet Atheism and Historical Knowledge.* Oxford; New York: Oxford University Press.

Luehrmann Sonja (ed.) 2018. *Praying with the Senses. Contemporary Orthodox Christian Spirituality in Practice.* Bloomington: Indiana University Press.

Luehrmann, Sonja. 2018a. Beyond Life Itself: The Embedded Fetuses of Russian Orthodox Anti-Abortion Activism. In: S. Han, T. K. Betsinger and A. B. Scott (eds). 2018. *The Anthropology of the Fetus: Biology, Culture, and Society.* New York: Berghahn.

Mahieu, Stephanie and Vlad Naumescu. 2008. *Churches In-Between. Greek Catholic Churches in Postsocialist Europe.* Berlin: Lit Verlag.

Martin, David. 1969. Notes for a general theory of secularisation. *European Journal of Sociology/Archives Européennes de Sociologie* 10 (2), 192–201, https://doi.org/10.1017/S0003975600001818.

Martin, David. 2017. *On Secularization: Towards a Revised General Theory.* London: Routledge.

McBrien, Julie. 2010. Muslim life in a Kyrgyz-Uzbek town. In: Chris Hann (ed.) 2010. *Religion, Identity, Postsocialism.* Halle/Saale: Max Planck Institute for Social Anthropology, pp. 37–40.

McBrien, Julie. 2012. Watching *Clone*: Brazilian soap operas and muslimness in Kyrgyzstan. *Material Religion* 8 (3), 374–396, https://doi.org/10.2752/175183412X13415044208952.

McBrien, Julie. 2017. *From Belonging to Belief: Modern Secularisms and the Construction of Religion in Kyrgyzstan*. Pittsburgh: University of Pittsburgh Press.

McBrien, Julie. 2020. Regulating, Recognizing, and Religionizing *Nike* in Kyrgyzstan. *Journal of Women of the Middle East and the Islamic World* 20, 55–75, https://doi.org/10.1163/15692086-12341386.

McBrien, Julie and Pelkmans, Mathijs. 2008. Turning Marx on his Head: Missionaries, Extremists and Archaic Secularists in Post-Soviet Kyrgyzstan. *Critique of Anthropology 28* (1), 87–103, https://doi.org/10.1177/0308275X07086559.

Meyer, Birgit. 2017. Catholicism and the Study of Religion. In: K. Norget, V. Napolitano and M. Mayblin (eds). 2017. *The Anthropology of Catholicism: A Reader*. Oakland, CA: University of California Press, pp. 305–315.

Mishtal, Joanna. 2015. *The Politics of Morality: The Church, the State, and Reproductive Rights in Postsocialist Poland*. Athens, OH: Ohio University Press.

Mostowlansky, Till. 2017. *Azan on the Moon: Entangling Modernity along Tajikistan's Pamir Highway*. Pittsburgh: University of Pittsburgh Press.

Mostowlansky, Till. 2020. Humanitarian affect: Islam, aid and emotional impulse in northern Pakistan. *History and Anthropology 31* (2), 236–256, https://doi.org/1080/02757206.2019.1689971.

Müller, Martin. 2019. Goodbye, postsocialism! *Europe-Asia Studies* 71 (4), 533–550, https://doi.org/10.1080/09668136.2019.1578337.

Nasritdinov, Emil. 2012. Spiritual Nomadism and Central Asian Tablighi Travelers. *Ab Imperio 2012* (2), 145–167, https://doi.org/10.1353/imp.2012.0062.

Nasritdinov, Emil and Nurgul Esenamanova. 2017. The war of billboards: Hijab, secularism, and public space in Bishkek. *Central Asian Affairs* 4 (2), 217–242, https://doi.org/10.1163/22142290-00402006.

Naumescu, Vlad. 2007. *Modes of Religiosity in Eastern Christianity: Religious Processes and Social Change in Ukraine*. Berlin: Lit Verlag.

Naumescu, Vlad. 2010. Encompassing Religious Pluralism: The Orthodox Imaginary of Ukraine. In: D'Anieri (ed.) 2010. *Orange Revolution and Aftermath: Mobilization, Apathy, and the State in Ukraine*. Washington, DC: Woodrow Wilson Center Press with Johns Hopkins University Press, pp. 274–299.

Naumescu, Vlad. 2016. The End Times and the Near Future: The Ethical Engagements of Russian Old Believers in Romania. *JRAI* (N.S.) 22 (2), 314–331, https://doi.org/10.1111/1467-9655.12379.

Naumescu, Vlad. 2020. 'A World to be Transfigured': Shaping a Cold War vision of Orthodoxy from the South. In: Todd Weir and Hugh McLeod (eds). 2020.

Defending the Faith. Global Histories of Apologetics and Politics in the Twentieth Century. London: British Academy, pp. 231–248.

Nazpary, Joma 2002. *Post-soviet Chaos: Violence and Dispossession in Kazakhstan*. London: Pluto Press.

Ngo, Tam T. T. and Justine B. Quijada. 2015. *Atheist Secularism and Its Discontents: A Comparative Study of Religion and Communism in Eurasia*. Basingstoke; New York: Palgrave Macmillan.

Oliphant, Elayne. 2012. The crucifix as a symbol of secular Europe. The surprising semiotics of the European Court of Human Rights. *Anthropology Today* 28 (2), 10–12, https://doi.org/10.1111/j.1467-8322.2012.00860.x.

Peel, John David Yeadon. 2009. Postsocialism, postcolonialism, pentecostalism. In: Mathijs Pelkmans (ed.) 2009. *Conversion after Socialism: Disruptions, Modernisms and Technologies of Faith in the Former Soviet Union*. Oxford: Berghahn Books, pp. 183–200.

Pelkmans, Mathijs. 2006. *Defending the Border: Identity, Religion, and Modernity in the Republic of Georgia*. Ithaca: Cornell University Press.

Pelkmans, Mathijs. 2007. 'Culture' as a Tool and an Obstacle: Missionary Encounters in Post-Soviet Kyrgyzstan. *JRAI* (N.S.) 13, 881–899.

Pelkmans, Mathijs (ed.) 2009. *Conversion after Socialism: Disruptions, Modernisms and Technologies of Faith in the Former Soviet Union*. Oxford: Berghahn Books.

Pelkmans, Mathijs. 2017. *Fragile Conviction: Changing Ideological Landscapes in Urban Kyrgyzstan*. Ithaca: Cornell University Press.

Rasanayagam, Johan. 2006. Introduction. *Central Asian Survey* 25 (3), 219–234, https://doi.org/10.1080/02634930601022500.

Rasanayagam, Johan. 2011. *Islam in Post-Soviet Uzbekistan: The Morality of Experience*. Cambridge: Cambridge University Press.

Rasanayagam, Johan. 2014. The politics of culture and the space for Islam: Soviet and post-soviet imaginaries in Uzbekistan. *Central Asian Survey* 33 (1), 1–14, https://doi.org/10.1080/02634937.2014.882619.

Robbins, Joel. 2007. Continuity Thinking and the Problem of Christian Culture. *Current Anthropology* 48 (1), 5–38, https://doi.org/10.1086/508690.

Roche, Sophie and Sophie Hohmann. 2011. Wedding rituals and the struggle over national identities. *Central Asian Survey* 30 (1), 113–128, https://doi.org/10.1080/02634937.2011.554065.

Rogers, Douglas. 2005. Introductory Essay: The Anthropology of Religion after Socialism. *Religion, State & Society* 33, 5–18, https://doi.org/10.1080/0963 9042000330848.

Rogers, Douglas. 2009. *The Old Faith and the Russian Land: A Historical Ethnography of Ethics in the Urals*. Ithaca: Cornell University Press.

Rogers, Douglas. 2010. Postsocialisms Unbound: Connections, Critiques, Comparisons. *Slavic Review* 69 (1), 1–15, https://doi.org/10.1017/S0037677900016673.

Shevzov, Vera. 2014. Women on the Fault Lines of Faith: Pussy Riot and the Insider/Outsider Challenge to Post-Soviet Orthodoxy. *Religion and Gender* 4 (2), 121–144, https://doi.org/10.1163/18785417-00402004.

Slezkine, Yuri. 2000. The USSR as a Communal Apartment, or How a Socialist State Promoted Ethnic Particularism. In: Sheila Fitzpatrick (ed.) 2000. *Stalinism: New Directions*. London: Routledge, pp. 313–347.

Smolkin, Victoria. 2018. *A Sacred Space Is Never Empty: A History of Soviet Atheism*. Princeton: Princeton University Press.

Steinberg, Mark D. and Catherine Wanner. 2008. *Religion, Morality, and Community in Post-Soviet Societies*. Washington, D.C. Bloomington: Woodrow Wilson Center Press; Indiana University Press.

Stephan, Manja. 2010. Moral Education, Islam and bein Muslim in Tajikistan. In Chris Hann (ed.) 2010. *Religion, Identity, Postsocialism*. Halle/Saale: Max Planck Institute for Social Anthropology, pp. 49–52.

Stephan-Emmrich, Manja. 2018. Playing Cosmopolitan: Muslim Self-fashioning, Migration, and (Be-) Longing in the Tajik Dubai Business Sector. In: Marlène Laurelle (ed.) 2018. *Being Muslim in Central Asia*. Leiden: Brill, pp. 187–207.

Stephan-Emmrich, M. and Abdullah Mirzoev. 2016. The Manufacturing of Islamic Lifestyles in Tajikistan through the Prism of Dushanbe's Bazaars. *Central Asian Survey* 35 (2), 157–177, https://doi.org/10.1080/02634937.2016.1152008.

Tateo, Giuseppe. 2020. *"Under the Sign of the Cross": The People's Salvation Cathedral and the Church-building Industry in Postsocialist Romania*. New York: Berghahn Books.

Tasar, Eren. 2017. *Soviet and Muslim: The Institutionalization of Islam in Central Asia*. Oxford: Oxford University Press.

Taylor, Charles. 1999. Modes of Secularism. In: R. Bhargava (ed.) 1999. *Secularism and Its Critics*. New Delhi and Oxford: Oxford University Press, pp. 31–53.

Taylor, Charles. 2007. *A Secular Age*. Cambridge, MA: Harvard University Press.

Tocheva, Detelina. 2011. Crafting ethics: the dilemma of almsgiving in Russian Orthodox churches. *Anthropological Quarterly* 84 (4), 1011–1034, https://doi.org/10.1353/anq.2011.0060.

Tocheva, Detelina. 2018. *Intimate Divisions. Street-Level Orthodoxy in Post-Soviet Russia*. Berlin: Lit Verlag.

Toktogulova, Mukaram. 2014. *The Localisation of the Transnational Tablighi Jama'at in Kyrgyzstan: Structures, Concepts, Practices and Metaphors*. Bonn: Competence Network Crossroads Asia.

Toktogulova, Mukaram. 2020. Islam in the Context of Nation-Building in Kyrgyzstan: Reproduced Practices and Contested Discourses. *The Muslim World 110* (1), 51–63, https://doi.org/10.1111/muwo.12318.

Verdery, Katherine. 1999. *The Political Lives of Dead Bodies: Reburial and Postsocialist Change*. New York: Columbia University Press.

Verdery, Katherine. 2003. *The Vanishing Hectare: Property and Value in Postsocialist Transylvania*. Ithaca: Cornell University Press.

Wanner, Catherine. 2007. *Communities of the Converted: Ukrainians and Global Evangelism*. Ithaca; Bristol: Cornell University Press.

Wanner, Catherine (ed.) 2012. *State Secularism and Lived Religion in Soviet Russia and Ukraine*. Washington, D.C.; Oxford: Woodrow Wilson Press and Oxford University Press.

Wanner, Catherine. 2014. Fraternal Nations and Challenges to Sovereignty in Ukraine: The Politics of Linguistic and Religious Ties. *American Ethnologist* 41 (3), 427–439, https://doi.org/10.1111/amet.12097.

Wanner, Catherine. 2020. An Affective Atmosphere of Religiosity: Animated Places, Public Spaces, and the Politics of Attachment in Ukraine and Beyond. *Comparative Studies in Society and History* 62 (1), 68–105, https://doi.org/10.1017/S0010417519000410.

Warner, Michael, Jonathan Van Antwerpen and Craig J. Calhoun (eds). 2010. *Varieties of Secularism in a Secular Age*. Boston: Harvard University Press.

Zigon, Jarett. 2007. Moral breakdown and the ethical demand: A theoretical framework for an anthropology of moralities. *Anthropological Theory 7* (2), 131–150, https://doi.org/10.1177/1463499607077295.

Zigon, Jarrett. 2010. *HIV is God's Blessing: Rehabilitating Morality in Neoliberal Russia*. Berkeley: University of California Press.

Zigon, Jarrett. 2012. *Multiple Moralities and Religions in Post-Soviet Russia*. New York: Berghahn Books.

4. "We Are Not Believers, We're Workers"

The Synchrony of Work, Gender, and Religion in a Priestless Orthodox Community[1]

Agata Ładykowska

"We are not believers, we are workers", said forty-five-year-old Tatiana on hearing what had brought me to her region. I had arrived in Prichud'e, a region on the western shore of the Peipus Lake that lies between Estonia and Russia, to study the interplay between economy and religion in a chain of settlements where both Orthodox believers and Old Believers have resided for centuries. "Orthodoxy? I have nothing to do with it. And besides, we do not live here; we only come to visit my mother. You know, nowadays, all the young people have left. There are only a handful of old ladies—*babushkas*—who live here. This village is dying." Initially, I was obviously disappointed to hear an answer which suggested that no religious or economic activity was to be found in my chosen fieldsite. However, this encounter proved revealing, as very soon I began to realise that utterances of this type—which I was to hear quite often—were at odds with everyday practice.

Tatiana and her husband did indeed live in Tartu, an urban centre located nearby, and had jobs in the service sector: this was a fact. But each of their visits to the village would last at least four days a week. Moreover, these visits were also enormously busy, filled with providing

---

1   The research on which this article is based was conducted within a project financed by the National Science Centre, DEC-2016/21/B/HS3/03136.

https://doi.org/10.11647/OBP.0282.04

a helping hand to their mothers. The latter needed to be driven by car to visit the church or the cemetery, or a family gathering or neighbours who did not live close enough to be reached on foot. They also asked for assistance in shopping or doing all kinds of renovations in their old houses, and most of all in tending to the gardens on their plots of land. There was an urgent need to mow the lawn, which required regular attention, but most importantly the vegetable plots, which were planted with onions, cucumbers, carrots, potatoes and plenty of other vegetables, begged for the hard and frequent physical work of gardening. While being involved in all of these activities, Tatiana and Sergey demonstrated full familiarity with the local ways of acting: as they had grown up in the countryside, they knew how to cultivate the soil. They were also perfectly in tune with all the church practices. After a while I learnt that Sergey's mother played an important role in the priestless Old-Believer ritual community, and was therefore called by her son "*batiushka*" (lit. 'father'; the term denotes a priest in the Orthodox Church). In light of the couple's initial denial of contact with religion, this information provided firm confirmation not only of the fact that both strands of Orthodoxy can be found here, informing each other in multiple ways, but also that religion mobilises different generations in different ways. It soon became clear that they are not the only middle-generation couple who are closely connected to the village, as on a daily basis many younger faces were also to be seen. Moreover, these people's connection with the village comprised both active engagement in their parents' religious practices, as well as involvement in processes which supported the economic dimensions of their own existence.

The vegetables grown on their mothers' plots were sold by them for a profit, and the empty rooms in their mothers' houses were rented out to tourists and to the fishermen who regularly come to the shores of Lake Peipus to enjoy fishing. I learned that it is particularly in winter, when fishermen regularly come here from Latvia, that local home budgets are supplemented by revenues from tourism. I thus soon understood that, despite my initial apprehensions, both fields of my inquiry, religion and economy, would yield abundant ethnographic information in this site. Only with time, upon hearing the life stories of the older generation, did I begin to see the trajectories of the interconnection between the two which remained invisible to the middle generation. While these trajectories were locally specific, as they were experienced by a specific group in a specific period of time, they proved to be illustrative of more widespread debates concerning the logic of the relationship between economic prosperity and religion, and helped shed light on how this entanglement may be resolved within Orthodoxy.

***

Taking its inspiration from the Weberian agenda (Weber 2001[1905]), this paper aims to illustrate the interrelation between economic decision-making and religious identity within the ethnic Russian Eastern Christian communities inhabiting the western bank of the Chudskoe/Peipus Lake, paying particular attention to the historical dimension from which these interactions emerge. It builds on a combination of archival research, interviews and participant observation in everyday rural life. The study investigates patterns of labour and exchange, gender and age in communities termed here 'priestless Orthodox', and thereby explores the particularities of the alignment of economy and religion in Eastern Christianity. In this way, the study contributes to the project of the anthropology of Christianity by providing a comparative perspective on matters of materiality, individual and collective conceptualisations of personhood and the pertinence of belief.

The anthropology of Christianity is dominated by studies of particular forms of Protestantism, notably Pentecostalism, which results in a series of distortions: 1) an imbalance in representation of other branches of Christianity; and consequently, 2) limited theoretical opportunities for comparative research. A similar state of affairs exists beyond this subfield of anthropology and concerns social theory more widely: existing analytical frameworks within the social sciences are distorted by a 'Protestant bias' (Hann 2007) and as such they do not provide an adequate paradigm for the analysis of the patterns of the Orthodox world. As a consequence, in the scant literature engaging with Orthodoxy this significant branch of Christianity is largely misrepresented. In proposing a historical-ethnographic view on the economic life of Eastern Christians, this article aims to fill the gap in existing scholarship resulting from Protestant overrepresentation and a concomitant lack of interest in Eastern Christianity, and in particular a negligence of its historical dimension. A combination of in-depth anthropological analysis with a historical approach offers an original perspective for ethnographic exploration of Eastern Christians' well-documented adherence to 'Immutable Tradition'. At the same time, it renders religion a contributing, not a 'genetic' factor in long-term patterns of political and economic development. Avoiding simplistic explanations emphasising the absence in the Orthodox tradition of a Protestant ethic based in interiorised asceticism—which identify this as the cause of Orthodoxy's failure to develop the combination of political, legal and economic conditions that enabled the breakthrough to an increasingly secular modernity in the West—this article looks at the distinctive ways in which Orthodoxy has shaped, but not necessarily determined, indigenous conceptions of the relationship between self and wealth.

The article thus places religion within the context of wider institutional changes and power relationships, and their consequences for self-understanding. In this way, by investigating the different, alternative notions of modernity, secularity and identity at play, the study challenges unidirectional models of modernity grounded in an interweaving of secularity, individualism and the spread of capitalism. Inspired by the approach of the historical anthropology of the former Soviet bloc, the article foregrounds complex—synchronic and diachronic—local responses to the shifting demands of secular and religious regimes, and highlights the social conditions and motivations generating those responses in looking for their underlying, long-term logic. Social anthropological research in the communities of the region known in the Russian language as Prichud'e (Peipsimaa in Estonian) suggests that over the period of the life of the last three generations, during which religion was subjected to severe political pressures, these communities developed a tacit strategy based on the compartmentalisation of religion by age and gender, which allowed them to maintain an Orthodox identity at the community level despite the demands of consecutive political regimes. While similar observations have been recorded in Old Believers' communities in Russia (Rogers 2009) and Romania (Naumescu 2016), here I propose to look at a mixed Orthodox and Old Believers' society whose main religious characteristic I denote through the working notion of 'priestless Orthodoxy'. My point is that it is a distanced attitude to the clergy, developed over centuries as a result of shifting politics towards Orthodoxy, that supported local ways of acting that contributed to these communities' unique sense of engagement with the material dimension of life, existing alongside their self-avowed secularity.

Theoretical Considerations: Deorientalising Orthodoxy

In this article I follow Chris Hann's line of argument that the relationship between Western social theory and Eastern Christianity is problematic in the sense that it both obscures and exposes the ethnocentric premises of the theory (Hann 2011). Eastern Christianity as an area of study remains under- and/or mis-represented in social scientific writings (Hann and Goltz 2010; Hann 2011; Lubańska and Ładykowska 2013), and its interplay with different fields of power, including that of the economy, remains understudied. This neglect extends beyond the ethnographic study of Orthodoxy, concerning this entire branch of Christianity more generally, with serious implications for anthropology and for social theory more broadly (Hann 2011; 2012).

Social theory owes much to Max Weber in this respect (Hann 2011; 2012). Weber's framework stresses the economic ethic (*Wirtschaftsethik*) of Protestantism as the key to the genesis of modernity, secularity and European exceptionalism, but an inadvertent result of this line of thought is an emphasis on Protestantism, which has exerted a long-term and widespread domination over anthropological reflections on religion. The 'Christian bias' embedded in the deep structures of anthropological theory (Cannell 2005; Robbins 2007) proves to be a "Protestant bias" (Hann 2007) and continues to distort the "anthropology of Christianity" (Cannell 2006; cf. Hann 2007; Lubańska and Ładykowska 2013) resulting in the above-mentioned general neglect of anthropology in favour of other branches of Christianity (Hann and Goltz 2010; Hann 2011; 2012; Zowczak 2000; Lubańska 2007; Lubańska and Ładykowska 2013). Under the heading of the 'anthropology of Christianity', one finds almost exclusively ethnographies of Protestant or Pentecostal movements from the post-colonial world (e.g. Cannell 2005; 2006; Robbins 2003a; 2003b; 2004; 2007; Keane 2007; Tomlinson 2006; Engelke 2006; Tomlinson and Engelke 2006).[2] Eastern Christianity seems excluded from many levels

---

2   However, some balance in the field has appeared lately. For example, the *Current Anthropology* Special Issue of 2014 (vol. 10) offers some fresh perspectives. Moreover,

of anthropological reflection, including from the deep structures of anthropological theorising.

In particular, the link between material/financial success and interiorised belief occupies a special position in anthropological/theoretical meta-representations. This coinage has a specific historicity. Weber's agenda consisted in the argument that the emergence and spread of capitalism relied on mobilising Protestantism's stress on hard work and productivity. The cornerstone of Weber's concept of work ethic was Luther's notion of work as vocation. The link between a Protestant ethic and economic success has been pursued by numerous authors since Weber to describe a distinctive evangelical spirit of American capitalism, and has established a firm representation for 'prosperity theology' (a.k.a. the health and wealth gospel) that links faith with financial success. Outside the US context, prosperity theology has been linked to the globalisation of charismatic Christianity (Coleman 2000), and described as a highly "portable", transnational entity that is easily adopted into new social contexts (Bielo 2007). Studies addressing 'Weber's question' in the Orthodox context are almost non-existent, with a few remarkable exceptions, such as Köllner (e.g. 2012). Another corollary of Weber's influence is the biased definition of religion, based on the Christian (or, more precisely, Protestant) idiom that anthropologists have at their disposal (Asad 1997; Cannell 2005). This means that they ideologically privilege a notion of religion that prioritises personal, private faith[3] over collective, public practice.[4] This makes them inherently discriminatory

---

it hosts at least three contributions investigating Eastern Christianity, in which the research agenda of the anthropology of Christianity (materiality, dis/continuity, theology-led kinds of social change) is applied (Hann 2014; Humphrey 2014; Keane 2014). However, the articles by Webb Keane (2014) and Caroline Humphrey (2014) are not based on original ethnographic research, which means that the demand for more anthropological research on Eastern Christianity applies *a fortiori*. This claim is consensually recognised within the anthropological milieu with an interest in the anthropology of Christianity (Boylston 2013), which established an electronic forum for intellectual exchange, namely 'New Directions in the Anthropology of Christianity' (formerly 'AnthroCyBib'; administered from the University of Edinburgh; https://www.new-directions.sps.ed.ac.uk/).

3   A feature which makes religion a 'portable' idea, easily exported mainly to the post-colonial world.

4   This leads inevitably to methodological failures in applying the anthropological conceptual apparatus to many other (not only non-Christian-derivative, but also non-Protestant-derivative) religions (see, for example, the category of 'belief', discussed by Rodney Needham (1972), Edward Evans-Pritchard, and Malcolm Ruel

toward religious traditions in which public manifestations of religion are privileged, such as Islam, which places emphasis on external, embodied behaviour (Asad 2003; 1997; Mahmood 2005), or Eastern Orthodox Christians. For the latter, religion: 1) is a core constitutive element of ethnic and national identity (Agadjanian and Roudometof 2005), which 2) relies heavily on the territorial spread of faith (which means that Orthodoxy remains a matter of birthright rather than personal belief, and that the globalisation paradigm produces remarkably different effects in these societies), and which 3) in some instances does not necessarily require belief in any form of divinity (Ghodsee 2009). Weber's influence thus remains fundamental in the way his thought constitutes anthropological common sense, and consequently, forms a methodological and theoretical impediment to the anthropological study of Eastern Christianity.

The issue of a meaningful definition of religion forms an especially fruitful direction of research, since still the most widespread construction is Clifford Geertz's universalisable definition of 1966 in which religion is separated from all forms of power. This contemporary hegemonic concept of religion has become "a modern Western norm", paradigmatic for contemporary social theory, whereas it is rather the product of a unique, Western European post-Reformation historicity (Asad 1997: 28), and as such lacks explanatory value for religions and societies which have never been subject to these historical processes. For example, Orthodox ecclesiology understands 'culture' and 'religion' as inherently related (Tataryn 1997), and thus offers an alternative to Western presuppositions of the nature of that relationship. In contradistinction to Western conceptualisations of personhood as a

---

(1982), and also, in a different vein, by Robbins 2007). The interiorised state that 'belief' denotes to certain Christians remains beyond the reach of ethnographers, who nevertheless tend to ascribe it to the members of religious communities that they study, often without empirical evidence. Hann argues against this evident ethnocentric distortion, calling for a more reflexive attitude with regard to the 'Christian' bias of the dominant European intellectual traditions: "Perhaps this criticism would be better formulated as the 'Protestantism of anthropology', since the liturgical traditions of the other branches of Christianity do not place the same one-sided emphasis on texts and interiorized belief [...] The basic challenge remains: how to understand the religions (or cosmologies, or simply world views) of other peoples, without distorting them through our own dominant conceptual prisms" (Hann 2012: 8).

liberal subject (autonomous, choosing, individualised) that remain the assumed unit of analysis in most social science, particularly in contemporary economics and political science, typical of Eastern Christianity is a relational person: a notion of personhood epitomised theologically as "being in communion" (Knight 2007; Zizioulas 1997; Chirban 1996; Agadjanian and Rousselet 2010). Casting the subject in social scientific terms, Gabriel Hanganu (2010), who engaged in an ethnographic investigation of theology and the materiality of icons in eastern Romania, found that Eastern Christians elaborate in their practices a peculiar version of "distributed personhood", which occupies an intermediary position between the notion of the individual as a self-contained unit and the various non-Christian forms of distributed personhood described by Strathern (1988). Hanganu's study enquires into many material, temporal and theological dimensions of Eastern Christians' "relational personhood".

Another Eastern Orthodox peculiarity is inherent in its theology of salvation, which developed outside the shadow of Augustine and the attendant debates on faith, good works and justification so prominent in the Christian West. With a much less negative and absolute view of the fall of man and original sin than in the West, theologians in the East (particularly Maximus the Confessor, and, later, Gregory Palamas) concentrated on the ways in which human beings could themselves participate in the process of self-transformation that would mitigate the effects of sin and lead to deification: returning to become one with God (Pelikan 2003: 10–16). On the practical level, such a conceptualisation triggers everyday responses very different to those suggested by Weber, as I hope to demonstrate in the following pages (but see also Rogers 2009; Ładykowska 2017). Such Eastern Orthodox peculiarities are often viewed in the West as Orthodoxy's inability to deal with religious pluralism or to accept the modern, liberal agenda with its emphasis on the rights of the individual. However, this 'East' versus 'West' tension is brought about by an essential discordance in ecclesiologies, and in definitions of person and community between the Western and Eastern Churches. This means that on one level they are a manifestation of a fundamental theological and ecclesiological position that cannot be 'corrected' by a simple acceptance of the principle of religious liberty (Tataryn 1997), as is often expected of these churches. This conflict also reflects the danger of approaching 'the East' in narrow, 'Western' terms: for this helps to perpetuate the principal premise that Orthodoxy has failed to develop the combination of political, legal and economic conditions that allow for a breakthrough to the increasingly secular modernity found in the West (Hann and Goltz 2010: 11). I argue here that it is yet another misrepresentation of Orthodoxy, appearing so only when seen through the lens of the narrow definition of modernity.

Indeed, modernity becomes a crucial issue in this debate. Even the multiple modernities (Eisenstadt 2002) paradigm presents a problem in this regard, as visible in the modest number of serious proposals discussing Orthodox Christian modernity (e.g. Agadjanian 2003; 2010; Makrides 2005; 2012; Stöckl 2006; 2011; Buss 2003). For such works either ask a question of whether and how Orthodoxy defines 'what it means to be modern' in its own terms, that is they argue for a *sui generis* Orthodox modernity, or they attempt to approach it through what they perceive as 'culturally normative', that is through the 'Western' mode of modernity and its terms. The latter approach reveals an inherent tension in basic tenets: Western modernity is defined by 'the breakthrough', whereas Orthodoxy defines itself through the "immutability of Tradition" (Agadjanian and Roudometof 2005: 11). This strained relationship unfailingly leads to negative conclusions, in which Orthodoxy's 'irrationality' is emphasised as responsible for its incompatibility with 'modernity' (as in Huntington's "clash of civilizations" theory, for example). 'Normative modernity' in these cases is conceptualised as 'rationalisation'. Another essentialising view of Orthodoxy, often invoked in order to defend it from the charge of its alleged incompatibility with modernity, highlights its intrinsically otherworldly orientation, meaning a less engaged attitude towards the material dimension of existence (cf. Kenworthy 2008). This otherworldly orientation includes a series of other essentialising categories allegedly inherent to Orthodoxy, such as a less individualistic attitude, a passive attitude towards the transformation of the world, sentimentalism, mysticism, asceticism, a strong communitarian spirit, social conservatism and anti-materialism (Makrides 2005: 183). Such a defence, however, despite its recognition for ethnographically recorded alternative notions of "rationalisation" and "modernization" (Makrides 2005: 198–200), in fact contributes to a reification of the conceptualisation of modernity as 'rationalisation' and 'progression', that is to the Western-centric perspective of modes of thought and action. This is not completely unfounded as Orthodoxy has developed a critical discourse on Western modernity, pointing to overall negative consequences of its development, such as secularisation, and then tries to solve these Western impasses by reference to Orthodoxy's own philosophical heritage. There is a pervasive discourse presenting Western Christianity as abandoning authentic Christian roots and thus currently experiencing this step's tragic consequences. Secondly, there has been a continuous influence exerted by the religious philosophical thought of nineteenth-century Russia, a current including the Slavophiles, which developed a strong anti-Western critique.

However, different levels of analysis allow for a variety of approaches. Historically speaking, despite the fact that Orthodoxy had many difficulties accepting 'modernity' because it arose from a geographical/ cultural/religious conglomerate of Western Europe, which was thought to have deviated from the true Christian doctrine and tradition preserved in the East, these countries have been not only continuously influenced by the "Western paradigm", but also expected to embrace it (Makrides 2013: 250). Orthodox societies which, based on different theological premises and with their own peculiar histories, may have produced an entirely different conception of religion or modernity, remain an unexplored, yet potentially promising area of study that can lead to the deconstruction of established definitions and notions. Thus, investigating alternative conceptions of religion does not only help to understand the political, legal and economic reasoning behind certain social developments which come under assault or critique from Western societal forces and policy-makers. It also sheds light on how our scientific vocabulary draws on concepts that rely on a specifically Protestant- (or Calvinist-) derivative soteriology and, as such, cannot be extrapolated to societies based on a different cosmological paradigm. Western social theory remains ethnocentric in the sense that it relies on categories originating from specifically Western currents of Christianity (Cannell 2005), while anthropology, itself a product of a "unique Western historicity" (Asad 1997), continues to be insufficiently reflexive towards its own origins. Orthodoxy, in this perspective, is an often-unremarked victim of orientalisation: it remains at the margins of anthropological reflection, both as an object of study and as a site from which anthropological definitions are formulated. Foreclosing Orthodoxy from both of these levels of anthropological interest culminates in the lack of an adequate framework for researching it (Lubańska and Ładykowska 2013).

Prichud'e

The research on which this article is based was conducted among Eastern Christians (both Orthodox and priestless Old Believers) of the region known in Russian as Prichud'e (Peipsimaa in Estonian). The region is composed of a chain of villages, of roughly comparable size (each numbering around 100 inhabitants), placed in a 20km-wide lane along the western bank of the Chudskoe/Peipus Lake. The villages of Logoza (in Estonian: Vene Lohusuu), Chorna (Mustvee), Raiusha (Raja), Kikita (Kükita), Tikhoka (Tiheda), Krasnye Gory (Kallaste), Rotchina (Rootsiküla), Nos (Nina), Malye and Bolshye Kol'ki (Väike ja Suur Kolkja), Sofiya (Sofia), Kazapel' (Vene Kasepää), Voronya (Varnja) and Kostina (Kirepi) are in the majority populated by Russian-speaking communities. Historical sources indicate that Orthodoxy was registered in this area as early as the late sixteenth century. Also, the Russian names of several of the villages listed above were already registered in the earliest available documents (mainly censuses) for the region dating from the late sixteenth to early-seventeenth centuries. During the Livonian war (1558–1582), Russia conquered this part of Estonia and established the Orthodox diocese of Jurjev-Viljandi.[5] In 1582, however, Tartu was conquered by Poles, and then later by Sweden. Due to the unfavourable conditions brought about by state regulations introduced following these conquests (supporting Catholicism and Protestantism, respectively), Orthodoxy was suppressed. Orthodox churches were closed, Orthodox priests were sent off to Russia, and the states' policies aimed at the reconversion of Orthodox believers to Catholicism or Lutheranism (Savikhin, Kasikov, and Vasil'chenko 2011: 119). As a result, Orthodox communities lived in isolation from mainstream Orthodoxy: without priests and without knowledge of the Nikonian reform (Savikhin, Kasikov, and Vasil'chenko 2011). These

---

5   During this period, a large number of Russians relocated to Prichud'e to take part in the construction of roads and bridges (Savikhin, Kasikov, and Vasil'chenko 2011: 119).

conditions not only made the local Orthodox communities more open to priestless Old Believer newcomers fleeing from persecution, but they also allow for a common framework through which both of these strands of Orthodoxy can be examined. Priestly Old Believers developed multiple hierarchies of ordained clergy separate from and critical of the mainstream Russian Orthodox Church. By contrast, priestless Old Believers were convinced that Patriarch Nikon's reforms had driven sanctity from the world and inaugurated the reign of the Antichrist. The ordination of new priests by bishops as a result became impossible, as did sacraments that required the participation of clergy. With the world in this state, priestless Old Believer theologians came to locate religious authority and its transmission increasingly in the collective decision-making capacity of the people themselves (Robson 1995: 25). This theological move lent a particular social shape to the kinds of Christian communities that sought salvation along the priestless Old Believer path. Most notably, it removed the authority of a specialist, ordained and self-perpetuating hierarchy regulating moral conduct. Residing side by side, both priestless Old Believers and Orthodox believers without churches and clergy not only continued to cultivate their faiths and identities, but also shared a common framework regarding the location of religious authority. I will illustrate this argument further on in the chapter. During the Great Northern War (1700–1721), Estonia became subject to Russia and as a result mainstream Orthodoxy received full privileges (Toom 2011).[6] Also, as part of the Russian Empire, it became the object of political interests connected to the expansion of that empire. As Paul Werth (1996) brilliantly illustrates, the extension of the empire implied a growing diversity of its subjects, a reported tenacity of indigenous beliefs and persistence of local identities, and consequent administrative concerns over their loyalty.

In response to this diversity, the second quarter of the nineteenth century witnessed the development of a new ideological formulation positing the existence of a peculiarly Russian spirit and set of morals that should serve as the basis for the Russian Empire's organic and distinct development. This new ideological formulation, promulgated

---

6   This fact has stimulated production of a large scholarship on the entanglements of Lutheranism and Orthodoxy in Estonia, a topic which remains beyond the scope of this article.

as Official Nationality in 1833, consisted of three principles: Orthodoxy, autocracy and *narodnost'* (a term usually translated as 'nationality'). Its exponents believed that these traits were deeply rooted in Russian history and defined Russia as a political entity and community. This emerging ideology asserted the need for a greater cultural and social unity of diverse, multiethnic and multireligious identities centred around these three principles. This shift necessitated greater administrative centralisation, and some fundamental transformations in the lives and attitudes of non-Russians. Russian administrators saw a specific need to inculcate among non-Russians a basic understanding of the Russian language, institutions and the morals and spirit on which they were founded. The empire's population—including Russian peasants—needed a certain basic knowledge in order to perform their assigned functions in society and to understand the broader social whole in which they were located, and whose interests they should serve. Thus, Orthodoxy was one of the basic principles included in Alexander I's and especially Nikolai I's mission of enlightenment and formation of an empire. In an institutional sense, the Orthodox Church's many local parishes served as a node of contact between the Russian state and the indigenous population. Thus, the Orthodox Church acted as a conduit for the ideas and conceptions that Russian administrators wished to foster in the subordinate population. The enactment of this policy meant a growing number of church buildings in newly acquired lands, including Prichud'e, where Orthodox churches began to be built around the 1820s. The construction of new churches in this period was an expression of the empire's Christianisation-cum-civilisation mission in the non-Christian edges of the empire, and it explicitly aligned modernity and progress with Orthodoxy (Jersild 1997; Jersild and Melkadze 2002; Manning 2008; Werth 1996).

While the reader may find the need to achieve this goal more obvious in areas such as the empire's eastern lands or the Caucasus populated by non-Christians, one must bear in mind that the church was part of the administrative apparatus in the Russian Empire and that, accordingly, it performed administrative functions. Modernity was a key concern of the growing state, and Orthodoxy occupied a principal position in this project. Throughout the nineteenth century until 1905, the Russian Empire witnessed a whole array of changes in the policies concerning religion (e.g. Werth 1996) and serfdom. Then came the revolution with its entirely new vision of modernity. This period marked antireligious campaigns and imposed dramatically new configurations in the arrangement of class, land, property and labour. However, despite the imposition of anti-religious policy, I believe that it is possible to argue that underlying structures of Orthodox community life persisted. The example of Prichud'e provides an exceptional but illustrative case of the continued role of Orthodox and Old Believer practices in preserving community identities.

The Prichud'e region has been the central focus of attention of a number of Estonian and Russian researchers (e.g. Jaanus Plaat, Tatjana Shor, G. Ponomarieva, Irina Külmoja, Kristin Kuutma, Fedor Savikhin, Aarne Kasikov, Evgenii Vasil'chenko, A.A. Ageeva, or the pioneering E.V. Richter and A. Moora, to name but some of the authors who have produced an enormous amount of literature over the last century). The main object of their interest was Old Belief rather than the Orthodox faith, with the prominent exception of the work of Patriarch Aleksii II (1999), who focused on the fate of the Orthodox Church structures in the region.[7] These studies primarily concentrate on: 1) the periodisation and routes of migration of this population(s); 2) linguistic issues; 3) the Old Believers' subculture, mentality, folklore, folk religion and customs. Especially the issue of the origins of this Orthodox population (have these populations appeared on what is today Estonian soil from Russia, fleeing from the persecutions of Old Belief, or from the western parts of historical Livonia?) seems to be very salient, as is perfectly understandable given the highly politicised question of contemporary Estonian (ultimately EU)-Russian relations.

The guiding question is whether this population thrived as a result of the schism of the seventeenth century (e.g. Richter 1976 and her followers), which would mean that the Orthodox are the descendants of Old Believers, or much earlier, as is suggested by sources from 1582 when the region was administered by the Polish King Batory (Savikhin, Kasikov and Vasil'chenko 2011), which would mean that favourable

---

7   It should be stated that in Estonia there are two main Orthodox Churches: the Estonian Apostolic Orthodox Church, an autonomous church subordinate to the Ecumenical Patriarchate of Constantinople, and the Estonian Orthodox Church of the Moscow Patriarchate, a semi-autonomous diocese of the Russian Orthodox Church. The Orthodox communities of Prichud'e belong to the latter.

conditions for Orthodox settlement already existed earlier and persisted until the time of the immigration of the Old Believers (e.g. isolation from mainstream Orthodoxy and the state ban on priests). A number of these studies have been carried out in an archaeo-graphic manner, which means that their guiding question is the preservation of Old Believer traditional culture. These studies usually assume a once strong, systematic and coherent Old Belief, and set out to measure the level of traditional culture still remaining in the locale. Thus, there is little analytic room in these studies for lived practice or literally for anything other than the preservation of this tradition or its demise. Eschewing such a research agenda, on the basis of the picture sketched above I intend to make a point that so far has been omitted from the literature. Namely, I propose to look at both communities as similarly centred around Orthodox values and concerned with the preservation of their faith in the face of dramatic political, structural and social changes. That they are able to succeed in this, to some extent, is due to their distanced relationship with the clergy and a shared, specific—and tacit—policy of the rythmisation of their religious and economic lives.

Priestless Orthodoxy

The Orthodox parish of *Pokrova Presviatoi Bogoroditsy* (The Protection of Our Most Holy Lady) in the village of Nina, for example, was described in a chronicle (*letopis'*) maintained by consecutive parish priests in the period 1824–1927. Parts of this document have been published (Danilevskii 2018). The chronicle not only contains quite rich information about ritual life, but also constitutes a kind of diary of these clergymen's largely unsuccessful attempts to become part of the village community. Written through the prism of an outsider, almost always dealing with the organisation of liturgy and more concerned with their relation to their hierarchs than to their flock, the chronicle nevertheless sheds some light on local interrelations between the Orthodox and Old Believers. For instance, on 7 December 1923,[8] the parish received an order to begin performing liturgy according to the New Style, following the official

---

8 Estonia was at this time already an independent state, following the 1920 Treaty of Riga. It was, however, a turbulent time and legislation was still subjected to negotiation on the path to full independence from the previous hegemon.

switch from the Gregorian to the Julian calendar adopted during the All-Orthodox Congress in Constantinople. This rule was supposed to come into force from 14 October, which is the Day of Pokrova, in the name of which the parish is consecrated. This move, introducing a substantial change in ritual life, was highly controversial: it triggered a high level of discontent among believers. A reaction must have been expected, as potential dissent was threatened with extremely severe punishment. Insubordinate priests were to be deprived of the right to perform liturgy and to keep their posts. Parishioners who resisted respecting this decision and incited disorder or performed illegal actions of their own will were to be punished not only by the church authorities, but also by state authorities. Rebellious parishioners were to be considered apostates, and to be deprived of the right to participate in sacraments and prayers and, should they not repent, of the right to a Christian funeral. Parishes without parishioners (as a result of such behaviour) were to be removed, with church buildings being closed and shifted with all their assets into the property of the closest functioning Orthodox parish. In the chronicle, the then parish priest expresses his anxiety over the necessity to perform liturgy during the upcoming Christmas and the celebration of the Baptism of Jesus (*Kreshchenie Gospodne*/Jordan) on a new date, which parishioners "did not accept at all". During the actual liturgy in the church, only ten people were present. The culmination of tension came with the official (New-Style) celebration of *Kreshchenie Gospodne*, the date of which corresponded with that of the Old-Style Christmas Eve.

The procession into the symbolic water of the Jordan gathered only a small number of people, while the remaining inhabitants of the village stood aside and just watched the "familiar ritual" with interest, but without participating. The resolution of this conflict was incited by an Old Believer deputy, P. Baranin, who came to Nina with a political lecture. Baranin, an active member of the priestless Old Believer community, had established his political agenda in independent Estonia around the issue of the separation of church and state, arguing for the full autonomy of the Russian parishes in Prichud'e (Danilevskii 2018: 267). Asked to express his opinion on the situation with regard to the church calendar, the deputy responded that, as an independent community, Old Believers enjoy freedom from the authorities in this respect and there is no pressure to intervene in their religious life. The audience became excited and turned to the priest, who was present during the meeting, asking for his decision with reference to the switch to the New Style. When he answered that he would comply with the new church rules, the priest caused uproar. Parishioners called him a betrayer of Christ, and told him that they would replace him. Over the following months the situation simmered down somewhat, but the approach of Easter sparked fresh discussions. The bishop received a letter from the Nina Parish Council with a question as to how to proceed with the calendar during Easter. The chronicle mentions that a large number of such requests were sent from across the entire region. The church hierarchies, afraid of a radicalisation of discontent, agreed to make concessions: they did not protest against celebrating Easter in 1924 according to the Old Style, and later they left this decision in the hands of parishes.

This historical account demonstrates clearly that the principle of *poslushanie*—obedience—typically indicating the locus of authority in Orthodox communities, may locally be, at least at times, reversed. This picture teaches us that power relations may be reversed and that the religious authority of the priest can be compromised in the name of the authority of tradition. This situation occurred in this particular village, because of the presence of Old Believers and the familiarity of Orthodox parishioners with their Old Believer neighbours' ways of organising religious hierarchies and the rights that this implied. The next section aims to illustrate that such inspiration goes beyond the structures of the church itself, and that other forms of social activity may be subject to similar influences.

Work and Prayer

My research has revealed some peculiarities that are common to both Orthodox and Old Believer villages. Historically, the main economic activities in the region have been fishing and farming (mainly onions). Before the Soviet period there was a fishermen's *artel'* (a kind of cooperative), providing employment for male members of the community. Women were busy with growing vegetables. With the rise of collectivisation, *kolkhozes* and *sovkhozes* were established, but working in these was not considered prestigious. Families adopted a tactic of delegating men for collective work, while women performed only minimal compulsory duties to the *kolkhoz* in order to reserve time to be able to take care of the household, a highly valued activity. That this was a deliberate move is attested to by a development of the 1970s, when the *kolkhoz* made available small plots of arable land for private use. From this moment, under the conditions of the Soviet planned economy, men continued to work in the *kolkhoz*, while women began a semi-official but full-scale entrepreneurial activity of growing vegetables (very much in demand on the Soviet-era food market), distributing them to Leningrad and its vicinities, and selling them for a market price. This move contributed to the accumulation of wealth of all the families, with women being the central agents of this change. With perestroika, the material status of these families deteriorated; but by the time of my fieldwork (2014–2019) these villages were again materially flourishing, benefiting from a growing tourism industry which again relied on women's engagement.

A significant element here is that these economic activities, both those that are profit-oriented and those performed as a part of socialist duty, are undertaken by a middle generation (of men and women) that at this period in their life are not concerned with parish life (even though local churches remained open during the entire Soviet period). Today, all the women involved in these activities during Soviet times are elderly, and are now committed Orthodox and Old Believers. Their today middle-aged children, meanwhile, remember being actively involved in ritual life in their childhood, but nowadays define themselves as "workers, not believers". While the pervasive discourse is that of a "dying village, where only the elderly generation remains", ethnographic observation reveals that the majority of the current middle-aged generation maintains very close relations with their parents, and despite the fact that they locate their main employment beyond Prichud'e, they actually continue to live in the village on some basis. In so doing, they are part and parcel of the life of a parish whose existence, as I was repeatedly told by all generations alike, continues to determine the identity of the village. On the basis of this historical analysis of the biographies of various village inhabitants, my argument is that there is an underlying logic that compartmentalises and separates, but also ultimately connects the spheres of economy and religion between different genders and age cohorts within this community. Despite it appearing that at some stages of their lives community members are focused uniquely on economic matters, the overall aim of these behaviours is to maintain the collective, Orthodox identity. This argument takes some inspiration from the work of Douglas Rogers (2009), who, nevertheless, attempted to escape the questions of the relationship between religion and economy that have been guiding my research. Rogers combined archival and fieldwork methodologies in studying an Old Believer community in the Urals. Employing an 'ethical' framework, Rogers discovered that these Old Believers appear to have maintained ethical continuity throughout the most dramatic changes of Soviet atheistic rule.

According to Rogers, this was possible thanks to what he calls an "ethical repertoire", ranging from work to prayer, that allowed different age cohorts of subsequent generations to engage in different domains of social life for over three centuries without the necessity of abandoning their faith altogether. The community members were

> by turns, serfs on a feudal estate, peasants in a thriving merchant town, exemplary Soviet state farmers, and shareholders in a struggling post-Soviet agricultural enterprise. Each of these organisations of labour, land, and money, and of state power and rural landscape, has generated ethical expectations and aspirations every bit as powerful as—if also often in conflict with—the precepts and practices of Old Belief (Rogers 2009: xi)

By creative responses to the civil regulations of subsequent regimes and the compartmentalisation of religion by age and gender, they have managed to ensure that their faith endured despite unfavourable conditions. Rogers calls this a tradition of "differing ritual participation", and argues that, "generation became a key category for the formation of different kinds of ethics and subjectivities [...]: deferring ritual participation until late in life mapped a distinction between prayer and work as fields of ethical practice onto a social distinction between older and younger generations" (Ibid.: 46).

The separation of worldly affairs—reserved for younger and middle age community members—and of ritual practices (including the spiritual development of one's soul and an interest in salvation), reserved for those of older age, helped these Old Believers adapt to the demands of subsequent civil regimes, while reproducing religious practices through the activities of the very young and the old. This practice, called *obmirshchenie*, allowing for "temporary secularisation"

(Naumescu 2016) and thus successful reproduction of tradition within a world at odds with the precepts of their faith, is typical for Old Believers. Prichud'e, however, developed historical conditions in which the effect of this entanglement of economy, religion, age and location of religious authority resonates beyond the community which engendered it. In the exceptional situation of Prichud'e, the differences between Old Believers and Orthodox beliefs in fact facilitate the overall continuity of the village's identity.

Conclusion

The combination of anthropological and historical approaches in my study enables an elucidation of how priestless modes of Orthodoxy, which developed in an earlier period, interacted with subsequent pro- and anti-Orthodox political regimes, and how they coped under these shifting regimes of regulations. My argument in this article is that there is an underlying logic that compartmentalises the spheres of economy and religion between gender and age cohorts that aim at maintaining a collective, Orthodox identity. This collective identity is strongly rooted in the history of the region, where specific regimes and oppressive politics imposed on Orthodox communities inspired creative responses allowing them to preserve continuity of tradition in the face of shifting visions of modernity. The church and its hierarchies are secondary to the success of this strategy. Rather, it is the cohabitation of two strands of Orthodoxy, which in these specific conditions have allowed mutual imports, that has further structured the economic and religious lives of each. Whereas elsewhere, Orthodox and Old Believer strands stand in marked contrast, in the Prichud'e case, Old Believer distance from church organisation of religious life has also informed the preservation of these villages' Orthodox identity.

References

Aleksii II, Patriarch. 1999. *Pravoslavie v Estonii*. Moscow: Tserkovno-nauchnyi tsentr 'Pravoslavnaia entsiklopediia'.

Agadjanian, Alexander. 2003. Breakthrough to Modernity, Apologia for Traditionalism: The Russian Orthodox View of Society and Culture in

Comparative Perspective. *Religion, State & Society*, 31 (4), 327–346, https://doi.org/10.1080/0963749032000139617.

Agadjanian, Alexander. 2010. Liberal Individual and Christian Culture: Russian Orthodox Teaching on Human Rights in Social Theory Perspective. *Religion, State & Society* 38 (2), 97–113, https://doi.org/10.1080/09637491003726570.

Agadjanian, Alexander and Kathy Rousselet. 2010. Individual and Collective Identities in Russian Orthodoxy.I In: Chris Hann and Hermann Goltz (eds). 2010. *Eastern Christians in Anthropological Perspective*. Berkeley, CA; London: University of California Press, pp. 311–328.

Agadjanian, Alexander and Victor Roudometof. 2005. Introduction: Eastern Orthodoxy in a Global Age—Preliminary Considerations. In: Victor Roudometof, Alexander Agadjanian and Jerry Pankhurst (eds). 2005. *Eastern Orthodoxy in a Global Age: Tradition Faces the Twenty-First Century*. Walnut Creek: Altamira Press, pp. 1–26.

Asad, Talal. 1997. *Genealogies of Religion*. Baltimore: John Hopkins University Press.

Asad, Talal. 2003. *Formations of the Secular: Christianity, Islam, Modernity*. Stanford: Stanford University Press.

Bielo, James S. 2007. "The Mind of Christ": Financial Success, Born-again Personhood, and the Anthropology of Christianity. *Ethnos* 72 (3), 315–338, https://doi.org/10.1080/00141840701576935.

Boylston, Tom. 2013. Orienting the East: Notes on Anthropology and Orthodox Christianities. *Anthrocybib: The Anthropology of Christianity Bibliographic Blog*, http://anthrocybib.net/2013/05/26/orienting-the-east/?preview=true%26amp%3Bpreview_id=1534%26amp%3Bpreview_nonce=3d1d152ef4.

Buss, Andreas E. 2003. *The Russian-Orthodox Tradition and Modernity*. Leiden: Brill.

Cannell, Fenella. 2005. The Christianity of Anthropology. *Journal of the Royal Anthropological Institute* 11 (2), 335–356, https://doi.org/10.1111/j.1467-9655.2005.00239.x.

Cannell, Fenella. 2006. Introduction. The Anthropology of Christianity. In: Fennella Cannell (ed.) 2006. *The Anthropology of Christianity*. Durham, NC; London: Duke University Press, pp. 1–49.

Cannell, Fenella (ed.) 2006. *The Anthropology of Christianity*. Durham, NC; London: Duke University Press.

Danilevskii, A. A. 2018. Letopis' Nosovskoi Pokrovskoi Tserkvi: 1917–1927. In: A.A. Danilevskii and S.N. Dotsenko (eds) 2018. *'Svoi' vs 'Drugoi' v kul'ture emigratsii. Sbornik statei*. Moscow: Flinta/Nauka, pp. 206–281.

Eisenstadt, Shmuel N. 2002. Multiple Modernities. In: S.N. Eisenstadt (ed.) 2002. *Multiple Modernities*. New Brunswick; London: Transaction Publishers, pp. 1–29.

Engelke, Matthew. 2006. Clarity and charisma: On the uses of ambiguity in ritual life. In: M. Engelke and M. Tomlinson (eds) 2006. *The Limits of Meaning*. Oxford: Berghahn, pp. 63–83.

Forbess, Alice. 2005. *Democracy and Miracles: Political and Religious Agency in a Convent and Village of South Central Romania*. Unpublished doctoral thesis, London School of Economics and Political Science.

Geertz, C. 1968[1966]. Religion as a cultural system. In: M. Banton (ed.) 1968. *Anthropological Approaches to the Study of Religion*, pp. 1–46.

Ghodsee, Kristen. 2009. Symphonic Secularism: Eastern Orthodoxy, Ethnic Identity and Religious Freedoms in Contemporary Bulgaria. *Anthropology of East Europe Review* 27 (2), 227–252.

Hann, Chris. 2007. The Anthropology of Christianity per se. *Archives européennes de sociologie* 48 (3), 383–410.

Hann, Chris. 2010. Tattered Canopies Across Eurasia: New Combinations of the Religious, the Secular, and the (Ethno-)national after Socialism. *Cargo* 8 (1–2), 4–26.

Hann, Chris. 2011. Eastern Christianity and Western Social Theory. *Erfurter Vorträge zur Kulturgeschichte des Orthodoxen Christentums* 10, 5–32.

Hann, Chris. 2012. Personhood, Christianity, Modernity. *Anthropology of This Century* 3, http://aotcpress.com/articles/personhood-christianity-modernity/.

Hann, Chris. 2014. The heart of the matter: Christianity, materiality, and modernity. *Current Anthropology* 55 (10), S182–S192, https://doi.org/10.1086/678184.

Hann, Chris and Hermann Goltz. 2010. Introduction: The Other Christianity? In: Chris Hann and Hermann Goltz (eds). 2010. *Eastern Christians in Anthropological Perspective*. Berkeley, CA; London: University of California Press, pp. 1–29.

Harakas, Stanley. 1992. *Living the Faith: The Praxis of Eastern Orthodox Ethics*. Minneapolis: Light and Life Publishing Company.

Humphrey, Caroline. 2014. Schism, Event, and Revolution: The Old-Believers of Trans-Baikalia. *Current Anthropology* 55 (10), S216-S225, https://doi.org/10.1086/678476.

Keane, Webb. 2007. *Christian Moderns: Freedom and Fetish in the Mission Encounter*. Berkeley: University of California Press.

Keane, Webb. 2014. Rotting bodies: the clash of stances toward materiality and its ethical affordances. *Current Anthropology*, 55 (10), S312–S321, https://doi.org/10.1086/678290.

Kenworthy, Scott. 2008. To Save the World or to Renounce It: Modes of Moral Action in Russian Orthodoxy. In: Mark D. Steinberg and Catherine Wanner (eds) 2008. *Religion, Morality, and Community in Post-Soviet Societies*.

Washington, DC; Bloomington: Woodrow Wilson Center Press; Indiana University Press, pp. 21–54.

Köllner, Tobias. 2012. *Practising Without Belonging? Entrepreneurship, Morality, and Religion in Contemporary Russia*. Berlin: Lit-Verlag.

Lubańska, Magdalena (ed.) 2007. *Religijność chrześcijan obrządku wschodniego na pograniczu polsko-ukraińskim*. Warszawa: IEiAK UW; DiG.

Lubańska, Magdalena and Agata Ładykowska. 2013. Prawosławie— „Chrześcijaństwo Peryferyjne"? O Teologicznych Uwikłaniach Teorii Antropologicznej i Stronniczości Perspektyw Poznawczych Antropologii Chrześcijaństwa'. *Lud* 97, 195–219, https://doi.org/10.12775/lud97.2013.00.

Ładykowska, Agata. 2017. Prawosławie, Ekonomia I Weber: Związki Nieoczywiste. *Etnografia Polska*, 61(1–2), 105–124, https://rcin.org.pl/Content/65945/WA308_85282_P326_Prawoslawie-ekonomia_I.pdf.

Mahmood, Saba. 2005. *The Politics of Piety: The Islamic Revival and the Feminist Subject*. Princeton: Princeton University Press.

Makrides, Vasilios N. 2005. Orthodox Christianity, Rationalization, Modernization: A Reassessment. In: Victor Roudometof, Alexander Agadjanian and Jerry Pankhurst (eds) 2005. *Eastern Orthodoxy in a Global Age: Tradition Faces the Twenty-First Century*. Walnut Creek: Altamira Press, pp. 179–209.

Makrides, Vasilios N. 2012. Orthodox Christianity, Modernity and Postmodernity: Overview, Analysis and Assessment. *Religion, State & Society* 40 (3–4), 248–285, https://doi.org/10.1080/09637494.2012.760229.

Meyendorff, John. 1984[1979]. Teologia bizantyjska. *Historia i doktryna (Byzantine Theology: Historical Trends and Doctrinal Themes)*, trans. from English by Jerzy Prokopiuk. Warszawa: Instytut Wydawniczy Pax.

Mintz, S. 1985. *Sweetness and Power: The Place of Sugar in Modern History*. New York: Viking.

Naumescu, Vlad. 2016. The end times and the near future: The ethical engagements of Russian Old Believers in Romania. *Journal of the Royal Anthropological Institute* 22 (2), 314–331, https://doi.org/10.1111/1467-9655.12379.

Needham, Rodney. 1972. *Belief, Language, and Experience*. Oxford: Blackwell.

New Directions in the Anthropology of Christianity. University of Edinburgh, https://www.new-directions.sps.ed.ac.uk/.

Pelikan, Jaroslav. 2003. *The Christian Tradition: A History of Doctrine. Vol. 2: The Spirit of Eastern Christendom (600–1700)*. Chicago; London: The University of Chicago Press.

Robbins, Joel. 2003a. What is a Christian? Notes toward an anthropology of Christianity. *Religion* 33 (3), 191–199, https://doi.org/10.1016/S0048-721X(03)00060-5.

Robbins, Joel. 2003b. On the paradoxes of global Pentecostalism and the perils of continuity thinking. *Religion* 33 (3), 221–231, https://doi.org/10.1016/S0048-721X(03)00055-1.

Robbins, Joel. 2007. Continuity Thinking and the Problem of Christian Culture: Belief, Time, and the Anthropology of Christianity. *Current Anthropology* 48 (1), 5–38, https://doi.org/10.1086/508690.

Robbins, Joel. 2014. The Anthropology of Christianity: Unity, Diversity, New Directions. An Introduction to Supplement 10. *Current Anthropology* 55 (10), S157-S171, https://doi.org/10.1086/678289.

Robson, Roy. 1995. *Old Believers in Modern Russia*. De Kalb: Northern Illinois University Press.

Rogers, Douglas. 2009. *The Old Faith and the Russian Land: A Historical Ethnography of Ethics in the Urals*. Ithaca; London: Cornell University Press.

Ruel, Malcolm. 1982. Christian as believers. In: J. Davis (ed.) 1982. *Religious Organization and Religious Experiences*. London: Academic Press. Reprinted in: M. Lambek (ed.) 2002. *A Reader in the Anthropology of Religion*, Oxford: Blackwell, pp. 99–113.

Stöckl, Kristina. 2006. Modernity and its Critique in 20th Century Russian Orthodox Thought. *Studies in East European Thought* 58 (4), 243–269.

Stöckl, Kristina. 2011. European Integration and Russian Orthodoxy: Two Multiple Modernities Perspectives. *European Journal of Social Theory* 14 (2), 217–234, https://doi.org/10.1177%2F1368431011403462.

Strathern, Marylin. 1988. *The Gender of the Gift*. Berkeley: University of California Press.

Tataryn, Myroslaw. 1997. Orthodox ecclesiology and cultural pluralism. *Sobornost Incorporating Eastern Churches Review* 19 (1), 56–67.

Tomlinson, Mathew. 2006. The limits of meaning in Fijian Methodist sermons. In: M. Engelke and M. Tomlinson (eds). *The Limits of Meaning*. Oxford: Berghahn, pp. 129–146.

Tomlinson, M. and M. Engelke (eds) 2006. *The Limits of Meaning*. Oxford: Berghahn.

Toom, Tarmo. 2011. Orthodox Church in Estonia. In: John Anthony McGuckin (ed.) 2011. *The Encyclopaedia of Eastern Orthodox Christianity*. Oxford: Wiley-Blackwell, pp. 226–228.

Weber, Max. 2001[1905]. *The Protestant Ethic and the Spirit of Capitalism*. London; Chicago: Roxbury Publishing Company.

Zowczak, Magdalena. 2000. *Biblia ludowa*. Wrocław: Funna.

5. The Moral Economy of Consensus and Informality in Uzbekistan[1]

Tommaso Trevisani

Moral Economies in Post-socialist Eurasia

The concept of moral economy has been popular among anthropologists of post-socialist societies, especially for addressing moral claims and commentaries of those disenfranchised by the expansion of the market principle. Typically, following Thompson's (1963) original usage of the concept, the focus of these studies has been on the revival of older moral economies among communities marginalised by the demise of socialism, either by looking at how those dispossessed by post-socialist reforms invoke values and principles that challenge reform outcomes and question their morality (Hann et al. 2003), or on how, leaning on Scott's (1976) understanding of the concept, local strategies are set up to react against new forms of land dispossession (as in Gambold-Miller and Heady 2003, on Russia) or labour exploitation (Kofti 2016,

1   An early draft of this paper was presented at a workshop of the Industry and Inequality group (2012–2015) at the Max Planck Institute for Social Anthropology in 2013. I wish to express my deep gratitude to all participants for feedback, criticism and comments received, especially to Catherine Alexander, Chris Hann, Jonathan Parry, James Carrier for providing written feedback. An improved draft was presented at a conference organized in Stockholm in June 2015 by the George Washington University's Central Asia Program (CAP) and the Swedish Institute of International Affairs. M. Laruelle and T. Dadabaev are warmly thanked for this opportunity. Furthermore, I wish to thank Laura Adams, Niccolò Pianciolla, Riccardo Cucciolla, Marco Buttino for their advice and for feedback on different versions of the paper. The final draft has greatly benefited from the comments of this volume's anonymous reviewers. Fieldwork was funded by Gerda Henkel Foundation and Stiftung Wissenschaft und Politik, Berlin.

https://doi.org/10.11647/OBP.0282.05

on Bulgaria). But the emergence of new, distinctively pro-market, post-socialist moral economies has also been observed: Susanne Brandtstätter (2003), for instance, reports on how in south-east China's context of economic boom, values became revitalised in order to stabilise newly volatile social interactions and trust in institutions was ignited "bottom-up" by recourse to non-market economic actions that energised communities' sociality and rituality. By contrast, in the cotton-growing oasis of Khorezm in Uzbekistan, those in power have attempted, by manipulating older ideas of the moral economy, to mitigate the tensions triggered by impoverishment and polarisation, and to strengthen rural communities' acceptance of decollectivisation. Yet, despite persistent appeals to social harmony and symbolic redistribution, commodification and disintegration have grown as a consequence of increasing disparities between reform winners and losers since the end of collective agriculture (Trevisani 2011; Hann 2019: 129–166). Whether old or new, re-surfacing or newly emerging, post-socialist moral economies point to the moral dis-embedding of markets (Polanyi 1957) and to attempts by local communities and governments at handling the rift between market and society opening up with the "transition" to capitalism in the former socialist world (Hann 2002; Götz 2015).

Lamenting inaccurate, inflationary usage of the term, Chris Hann (2018) has recently cautioned against the concept of moral economy. He has argued that while useful to problematise the moral embeddedness of economic action, the concept turns hollow when abstracted from concrete settings that are best studied ethnographically. Instead, he pledges to ground moral economies by tracking dominant values through history, i.e. by looking at their concrete reconfigurations in social relations across time. In the Hungarian case study that he presents, the central value of material work retains appeal and meaning across the epochs and systems. This explains why recently introduced workfare policies are welcomed by the rural poor in Hungary, even if they are a palliative measure against their growing problems. Some scholars have seen in workfare a form of labour dispossession originating in the context of neoliberal austerity and labour precarisation, and one that is often condemned and contested by its recipients (Standing 2011; Wacquant 2012). By contrast, Chris Hann observes how, paradoxically, the introduction of *"közmunka"* in Hungary, (Hann 2018: 237)—a workfare scheme coupling manual work and welfare in the context of low employment and welfare shrinkage—is welcomed by the rural poor because it appears moral and meaningful even though it goes against their class interests, since it resonates with the locally rooted notion of "work as a value". This value, Hann argues, can be, at best, instrumentalised by reactionary politicians, but never totally ignored, since it remains constitutive of moral communities across time. In the Hungarian case we have an example of how a new "moral economy" (although Chris Hann is sceptical of the phrasing) brings together populist elites and rural poor against the "dominant form" (236) of EU-mediated market integration, resulting in an increasingly illiberal and pro-populist market economy model. Accordingly, workfare in Hungary testifies to the resilience of the central value of work in society, while populism's appeal is rooted in criticism against the dominant form of integration and qualifies for Chris Hann as a "countermovement" in the sense of Karl Polanyi.

Seen from another corner of former socialist Eurasia, Chris Hann's Hungarian case study on the workings of the moral dimension of political economy offers intriguing lines for comparison. Due to its different political and economic framework, neoliberal workfare à la *közmunka* does not exist in Uzbekistan. But there are similarities with the traditionally commended, communal duty service known in Uzbekistan as *hashar* (see for instance Wall 2008: 149–152). *Hashar* is a form of non-remunerated voluntary community service work, widespread in the traditional Islamic neighbourhoods of the *mahallas*, Central Asia's urban residential communities (Rasanayagam 2011a) and part of the "older moral economy of the mosque" (Hann 2011: 115–116) in Central Asia's oasis cultures. Typically, it encompasses work of the type that in rural Hungary could pass as *közmunka* (upkeep of streets and canals, renovating communal infrastructure, etc.). *Hashar's* very existence, coupled with the fact that the state in Uzbekistan lacks financial means and is able to guarantee only abysmal social subsidy, forestalls the very possibility of a workfare system comparable to those of more developed market economies. And yet, as in the Hungarian case, so too in Uzbekistan we can observe local convergences of interests and values between populist elites and ordinary citizens materialising in particular moral economies. In Hungary, this convergence results in hegemonic populist discourses successfully deflecting the "blame" for newly created economic problems from national elites to supra-national entities. In Uzbekistan, the sodality of authoritarianism and informality sustains the hegemony of national(istic) discourses and fosters the compliance of the new middle classes with the authoritarian regime.

In both settings, and against the grain of Thompson's original usage, a moral economy perspective can shed light on the connections between illiberal politics, economy and populism through values across history. In addressing these relationships, the role and meaning of moral economies can shift over time and space, even within the same political framework. So, for instance, in Uzbekistan: whereas my research in Khorezm highlighted how communities' and power holders' interests and values were drifting apart despite mutual invocations to a common moral economy, research later conducted on newly emerging, middle-class sensibilities in another part of Uzbekistan, the Ferghana Valley, pointed in the opposite direction (Trevisani 2014). Over the fieldwork, local discourses signalling compliance with the course of the authoritarian regime had emerged as a topic that caught my attention. While this "consensus" is ambiguous, unstable and a manifestation of particular, heterogeneous social segments, it also signals the existence of an underestimated and often-overlooked legitimacy of the autocratic ruling elites among a significant part of the population, the growing middle strata. With an interest in the material conditions and moral reasoning underpinning people's contradictory political sentiments under a harsh authoritarian regime, I would here like to pay attention to how people's place in the informal economy shapes their attitudes towards the state. More specifically, I will argue that authoritarianism and informality mutually reinforce each other when their sodality is reinforced by a shared vision of the moral economy.

Informal Economy in Uzbekistan

Anthropologists have used the concept of the informal economy (Hart 1973) to address economic activities outside the formally contractualised and regulated sector. Rasanayagam has adopted it to describe how in post-Soviet Uzbekistan boundaries between the formal and the informal economy have become blurred, if not in fact meaningless, since informality, as compared to the situation before independence, is no longer counterbalanced by a "formal counterpart" and "has become the rule" (2011b: 683), the normal way of conducting life and business.

While the informal sector existed and even thrived in the Uzbek SSR, he concludes that after the collapse of the USSR a more general informalisation of the state, society and lifeworlds (682) has occurred in Uzbekistan. Classic examples for such informalisation could be seen in the restaurant owner forced into illegality as a consequence of regulatory ambiguity that makes him become easy prey to racketeering officials; or the teacher unable to sustain his family by a meagre income that during the Soviet Union used to be satisfactory, and who, nowadays, in order to sustain a modest living, additionally to his salary takes bribes from pupils and works in agriculture. Such examples abound in Uzbekistan since the informalisation of economic practices has risen to become an all-important form of integration (Rasanayagam 2011b).

During the Soviet Union the second (shadow or illegal) economy (Grossman 1977; Humphrey 1983; Ledeneva 1998) that revolved around the diversion and redistribution of manipulable resources was part of the "historic compromise" between the Soviet power holders and a populace refraining from voicing political claims in exchange for decent living standards (Cook 1993). Soviet power holders accrued "a legitimation based on popular consensus and acceptance of, or at least indifference to, the rulers' chosen course" (132). This consensus was based on the relative affluence and large availability of formal jobs, basic goods and social entitlements, and around the predilection of sectors of strategic importance, such as the military or heavy industry workers, who received special treatment and privileges.

In Uzbekistan this late Soviet historic compromise had its own nuances. Here, as Lubin (1984) shows, the native population did not wish to enter the officially privileged and better-paid economic sectors because the informal possibilities to private gain entailed in the less prestigious and lower-paid sectors made them more attractive than the officially privileged ones. Much of people's material conditions came to depend on informal and illegal mechanisms. Generalised collusion in these practices had a depoliticising effect on people, reinforcing their "consensus" with the status quo. The cotton sector, representing the economic backbone and the major drive for modernisation of this more backward Soviet republic (by comparison with the more industrialised European core), has been of special significance also in regard to the spread of informal and illegal practices. Centred around fraudulent overreporting of cotton harvests and private appropriation of collective resources, these practices came to public notoriety with the cotton scandal of the perestroika years, when investigations disclosed systematic collusion of party officials, ranging from top republican levels down to *kolkhoz* enterprises, and resulted in a "purge" and a reshuffle of the republican political establishment (Rumer 1991; Cucciolla 2017).

Although economic informalisation had been already a characteristic of the late Soviet years, in the early post-Soviet period people's relation towards the informal sector changed significantly. Under the new conditions of shortage and contraction of the socialised sector, people had to struggle for their livelihoods. Their reliance on informal sources of income had become existentially crucial in a situation of need and deprivation at a time when formal-sector jobs were no longer providing liveable salaries. The old system, in which consensus was sustained through collusion in the informal economy, also underwent a radical transformation by adapting to the economic shortage and to the reorganisation of the economic structure from the all-Soviet to the national economy framework. But far from meaning the end of the formal economy and of the state's grip on the informal sector, I observe how the informal economic sector nowadays can be viewed as instrumental in sustaining the compliance of the middle strata with the dominant political order. In what follows, I want to scrutinise this relationship with a moral economy perspective. Unlike Hungary, where the convergence of interests and values between populist elites and ordinary citizens reverts around the value of manual work, in Uzbekistan we witness the centrality of the informal economy in shaping the moral framework in the relationship between the authoritarian state and its citizens.

The "Uzbek Path", Informal Economy and Middle Strata

After the end of the Soviet Union Uzbekistan did not follow the Washington Consensus or "shock therapy to the market"-type of liberalisation policy. Instead, by prioritising political control and stability over economic growth and structural reforms, it opted for a very gradual evolution of the political and economic system with a partial and piecemeal introduction of market reforms stylised by the government as the "Uzbek path" to the market (on this for instance:

Gafarli and Kasaev 2001). With this model the government aimed at following the economic trajectories of developmental states such as South Korea (Harvey 2005), but results lagged behind expectations: Corporations and foreign capital have been mostly scared off by an unfavourable investment climate, the chosen path to economic self-sufficiency and re-industrialisation outside the WTO framework did not lead to an economic performance able to raise the living standards of a rapidly growing population, and also forced many to migrate for labour. Despite reform reluctance and attempts to screen off globalisation from the country, its typical effects, such as the dissolution of Soviet-protected salaried work, the growth of a massive labour migration, and the rise of nationalism, have occurred regardless (Bazin 2009).

At the onset of independence, a façade of liberal institutional set-up and democratic power divisions was adopted but, in substance, the centralised power of the Soviet-era command hierarchy was preserved and even strengthened. The new national elites, now liberated from Moscow's oversight, enjoyed unrestrained power. Under the strong hand of the first president, Karimov, the opposition was outlawed and meaningful political dialectic blocked (Fierman 1997), the only veritable opposition remaining consisting in grassroots Islamic activism voicing criticism of the former Soviet establishment. Islamic grassroots movements outside the official political spectrum posed a challenge to the newly independent political establishment in the early post-independence period, but this political Islam was eventually surmounted thereafter, and in the aftermath of 9/11 secular authoritarian regimes in the region further consolidated their domestic power by soliciting Western security support in the war on terror on the grounds of a grossly exaggerated, internal "Islamic threat" (Khalid 2007).

Unwilling to open up to (and marginalised by) international markets, the authoritarian government's domestic economic policy has been the decisive factor in the definition of economic and social relations in the country. The cotton sector (and agriculture more broadly) remained the object of heavy government intervention as it maintained a central role in the economy to fund a more diversified and urban-based economy. In the initial years of independence agriculture was rearranged around import substitution (wheat) and cash crop export (cotton). The rural sector remained heavily taxed through the imposition of unfavourable procurement prices, leaving behind severely impoverished rural communities (Kandiyoti 2003), so that rural wealth was syphoned off to the growing cities, in which services- and trade-based sectors gradually advanced and over time surpassed in importance the role of cotton for the overall economy.

As elsewhere in neoliberal and post-socialist reform settings (cf. Harvey 2005), in Uzbekistan the privatisation of state and collective assets has been orchestrated by power holders mostly to meet the self-serving interest of the new elites. The state kept a strong control over the channelling of the sources of wealth accumulation. Despite this, and although the possibilities of entrepreneurial success were being rigged and biased in favour of the elites and their affiliates, the very possibility of freely engaging in individual entrepreneurial activity, especially encouraged by a government eager to emulate the success of Asian Tigers, set free a growth of trade, bazaar economy, entrepreneurialism and brought a people previously employed in regular work or in collectivised agriculture to the new, non-regulated and chaotic entrepreneurship of the market era. Mirroring broader post-socialist patterns, the social sector was significantly defunded and social inequalities increased sharply. But the growing inequality also opened up an often-overlooked space in between the newly rich and newly poor, occupied by those who were able to navigate with some success the challenges and opportunities offered by Uzbekistan's road to national independence: the new middle strata (Trevisani 2014). This trend can be exemplified with the urban transformation that occurred in Namangan, a city that I have repeatedly visited for fieldwork between 1997 and 2009.

Over the years of independence, this city in the Ferghana Valley had greatly enlarged its surface. New neighbourhoods, peripheries, bazaars, transport infrastructure, high-rise buildings, and shops had reshaped the cityscape and conferred to it a more modern urban outlook. Soviet Namangan in the year 1973 counted 194,000 inhabitants and 31 large factories which employed 17,200 industry workers as of 1975.[2] This

---

2   Namangan's factories were mostly in the light industry sector. The shoe and
     textile factories, meat factory, and food processing factories were among the most
     important employers in the city. However, its industry also included a chemical
     plant, construction material processing factories and two power stations (O'zbek
     Sovet Enziklopediyasi, 1976: 527–528).

means that although industry was a significant employer at that time, the city's primary vocation has never been an industrial one and there can be said to be some continuity between the Soviet and the post-Soviet employment structure. The Soviet textile industries attracted Russophone workers relocating from Europe, while local (Uzbek Muslim) residents preferred employment in administration, social services, education, trade, and the 'domestic sector' (*maishni xizmat*—something close to petite bourgeoisie employment—services, handicraft etc.), as well as in the administration of the cotton produced in the city's agricultural hinterland.[3] After independence, when factories closed down, the *promzona* (Namangan's industrial district) decayed and the jobs in the light industry (textile, food processing) disappeared. Public sector jobs also dramatically worsened and lost their attraction. Those who were left behind without a job, or with a job too bad to earn a living, were absorbed by the informal sector in myriads of ways, in sectors including trade, handicraft, construction and transport, operating virtually unreported and untaxed outside the capture of the state. The Slavic former industrial workers left, but the city's population, sustained by the higher birth rates among the titular nationality, grew nonetheless (the city' population more than doubled in between 1973 and 2008). Uzbeks making their living in the reformed public or the informal private sector gradually reshaped the post-Soviet city: like many other Central Asian cities, Namangan had developed divided between a traditional, Uzbek-speaking area composed of *mahalla* neighbourhoods and a predominantly Russian-speaking, modern, Soviet sector referred to as *mikroraion*, an apartment block community built of multi-storey, prefabricated buildings. In the *mikroraion* district, after the mass-departure of the Russophone inhabitants, many of the new residents had moved from the nearby rural districts into the city, taking up jobs in the public sector: university, college, and school teachers (*domlas*), medical staff, police, etc. Roads had become busier with *marshrutka* buses and private cars than ever. The city's commercial, educational, administrative, and leisure opportunities increasingly draw people from the rural districts for day-trip matters to the city. In the old city, the

---

3   For comparison, according to Abdullaev in 1975 more people were employed in trade and catering alone (18,400) than those in industry, a tendency that would increase year by year until the end of the Soviet Union (Abdullaev 1995: 134).

*mahalla*s around the main bazaar are now full of little *zehxona*, sweatshops and craft shops dealing with textiles, handicrafts and utensil supply, often developing in-house, within the walls of residents' traditional *hovli* houses (the traditional, large houses with internal courts, suited to multi-generational and multi-nuclear families). More than aspiring to a public-sector job or education, nowadays the *mahalla*'s youth is attracted by the better possibilities for earning money prospected by the bazaar. In the former colonial city, once the city's Soviet and now post-Soviet administrative centre, where the main government buildings are located, little *dukkon*s (shops) such as service and copy shops, travel bureaus, etc., have appeared in large numbers. In this changed urban setting, ordinary people's struggle for livelihoods have become more cut-throat and competitive, but spaces for economic success and development have also opened up, and the situation for urban citizens looks less bleak and difficult than in the rural areas.

In this transformed urban landscape, the middle strata, a socially heterogeneous group straddling the private and the public employment sector and situated in between the impoverished and the newly enriched urban elites, has risen and adapted to the changed economic and political environment. By looking at their moral stances and political sensibilities, and at how they navigate livelihoods in an authoritarian context, I found that the terms of the moral economy of the urban middle strata had developed differently from those observed before in rural Khorezm.

Andijan and Its Consequences

The Ferghana Valley is a region renowned for its religious zealotry and acrimonious relationship with independent Uzbekistan's secular leadership. Over the early years of independence, the region had witnessed grassroots protests for moral renewal and re-Islamisation against the secular government of the newly independent state. Most notably, the movement "Adolat" (justice), active in the early 1990s in Namangan, was pressing for sharia-based rule and challenging the secular government with an Islamic anti-corruption rhetoric, which elevated the city to a symbol of the confrontation between the post-Soviet government and local Islam. Rooted in the Islamic spring of the late perestroika years, the movement captured public interest and sympathies among the Muslim majority but lacked coherent goals and profile and failed to seize power and to affirm itself as a meaningful alternative to the secularised national order propagated by the post-Soviet government. Over the 1990s the government eventually mastered the challenge to its power monopoly in this city and imposed severe controls on the region, but tensions lingered on. The region continued to attract particular concern of the government's security arm and became a social and political test bench for the young independent state confronting mass impoverishment, social polarisation and potential instability.

In May 2005 tensions culminated in the "Andijan events" when a popular rally of people protesting against the incarceration of a pious group of entrepreneurs known as "Akromiya" accused of sedition by the government ended in a bloody repression (see on this: Ilkhamov 2006; Liu 2014). The group's mixing of economic and philanthropic accomplishments made it widely popular, but its success was also the reason it became a thorn in the side of the government. Adopting a religious ethic, its local popularity resonated as a form of socially-minded, moral entrepreneurship. Although the Andijan uprising was a desperate attempt by ordinary people to voice their dissatisfaction against the inefficiency and the corruption of the government officials, it was not questioning the "system" as such. In May 2005 protesters gathered on the main square to direct the attention of the president to the city's problems in protest against the city authorities, but government overreaction turned the peaceful sit-in into a massacre in which hundreds were killed by the indiscriminate use of force (Human Rights Watch 2005). The protest was preceded by a nation-wide introduction of new taxation, licences and control measures targeting the informal sector and perceived as unjust and too vexing. At stake were the attempts by the government to bring the flows of the informal economy back under state control by introducing new regulation. These measures not only greatly affected the profits of small traders and entrepreneurs, but also increased the discretionary power of corrupt officials over them. The more general issue underlying the Andijan protests revolved around the relationship between powerholders and entrepreneurial middle strata, as the latter were struggling with their businesses while resisting state recapture. Andijan 2005 left a deep scar in Uzbek society, after which diplomatic relationships with Western democracies deteriorated and the country entered a period of asphyxiating repression that lasted until the death of President Karimov in 2016. With their uncompromising attitude state authorities powerfully demonstrated their firm will to regain state capture over the informal sector. We shall see below how this change in attitude also altered the terms of the tacit Soviet-era compromise or "trading" of informality for political quiescence.

The post-Andijan tensions permeated fieldwork in Namangan in 2009. These tensions were lingering between the struggling middle strata, trying to sustain everyday life with their informalised livelihoods, and a government eager to get a hold over the informal economic processes. Over fieldwork in Namangan, on my daily itinerary to the city's main bazaar, the bad condition of the road was the daily topic of conversation in the *marshrutka*s (minibuses operating as collective taxis on fixed routes). After finding out that *marshrutka* drivers of this route would regularly gather informally to discuss their problems, I also learned that one day drivers resolved, after meeting at the Friday prayer in their *mahalla* mosque, to take the problem in their own hands and, knowing that the city government would not intervene to improve road maintenance, to call for a *hashar* for the renewal of the road. Privately organised public transport with *mashrutka*s had emerged as an important employment sector in Uzbekistan after independence (see: Sgibnev 2014). Despite state attempts at regulation (for example, by introducing flat-rate licences for drivers, etc.), it remained highly informal and variegated. Some individuals in Namangan were said to own dozens of cars and hire drivers, and while some were individual drivers on leased cars, others again were occasional drivers that after work used their own vehicle to earn extra money as part-time drivers. The drivers' *hashar* started successfully and money was being raised. But the petitioning was blocked by the authorities and its organisers were admonished. Checks by the traffic police became more frequent on this road and some cars of known drivers would get checked and fined more assiduously than others. After Andijan, this and similar cases of grassroots activism were feared by city authorities for their political potential and strictly forbidden. The road was not renovated. The *hashar* was called off and drivers acquiesced. But soon thereafter, the city officials granted the drivers of this particular fixed marching route the right to a fare increase.

Such increases had given voice to protests by angry residents in the past, and could even be taken back by authorities, fearful of the voice of the street. But in the tense post-Andijan climate this and similar government efforts to prevent Andijan-type social entrepreneurship "from below" attest to the changed situation. The city residents were made to pay for one category's dissatisfaction by the government's permitting of a fare increase. Here and in similar cases, professional categories (informal or formal) were rewarded for their acquiescence. Drivers stopped the *hashar* out of fear of losing everything, but, in the end, they perceived to have made a gain by refraining from pushing too hard against the city authorities. By so acting, drivers were acknowledging that the informal and precarious nature of their livelihoods did not allow them to voice stronger demands, and also, that informality, the new normal in economy, is profitable to the extent and in the ways that the power holders allow it to be so.

Navigating Everyday Informality in the Ferghana Valley

Uzbekistan is known for being a difficult place for conducting anthropological fieldwork (see for instance: Zanca 2011). Since 1997 I have been observing the evolution of independence in everyday life in Uzbekistan over various fieldwork periods. But in 2009 my last sojourn in Ferghana Valley's Namangan region ended before time when I was halted by the police on the grounds that I stayed overnight in a village I was invited to for a wedding. When a police car picked me up at 5.30 in the morning after the wedding celebration from the house of my embarrassed host, I was taken by surprise. The policemen politely escorted me back to town. At their headquarters, I was reprimanded and my passport confiscated until the payment of a fine of ca. 1000 USD, supposedly for the breach of Uzbek migration law. The same officials who knew about my valid permit to do research on weddings and about my research trips to villages over the previous months suddenly saw me as a criminal offender. I had to sign a handwritten letter declaring my "guilt" and pay the fine or face deportation and the denial of a visa in the future. I left the country a week later, penniless but freely, and with guarantees of open doors to future trips. Nonetheless, I was denied a visa without any reason until 2019, when I eventually re-entered the country, now ruled by a different president, without the need for a visa.

For an innocuous visit to a wedding to turn into a heavily fined breach of the migration code several things had to happen first. 1) A few weeks before my inviting institution, the French research institute IFEAC, had been closed down in Tashkent following diplomatic friction between the presidents of the two countries. 2) Days before my finding, my local mentor, a university teacher working for the government and monitoring my activities (knowing my whereabouts, introducing me to people, etc.), had unequivocally signalled to me that my ethnographic work on the (embarrassing because poor?) village realities that he was putting before my eyes was offending his national feelings. 3) The landlord of the rented apartment in which I lived and was bound to by official registration, a woman related to the city's ruling establishment, had requested the apartment back before the end of the rent for hosting—of all things—a wedding feast (to which I was not invited). This circumstance induced me to go to the village instead, just on the day before I got caught "in flagrante delicto".

Far from being an isolated case among foreign researchers in those years, the episode is nonetheless instructive. However sad and disappointing, it gave me the opportunity to see with my own eyes what Uzbeks knew from their own lives, namely that abiding by the law, even for the well-intentioned, is an arduous undertaking and offers little protection from arbitrary rules and the whims of moody officials. Western observers tend to see the regime's stability based on fear and coercion and to dismiss the national ideology as mere propaganda and to regard people supporting it merely as the regime's thugs. For Rasanayagam (2011a), for instance, the national ideology is a hollow instrument to legitimate authoritarian rule, a mere tool of control, not something people would actually believe in or seriously engage with. Such positions find validation in widely documented narratives of criticism, anger and deep frustration with an essentially oppressive regime (Ilkhamov 2001; Zanca 2011; Liu 2012). And yet, when learning about my mishap my friends and acquaintances in Namangan invited me to show sportsmanship and not to take it personally. Such occurrences resonated with their everyday experience of dealing with an intrusive, extractive state, that many understood nonetheless as a precondition for their livelihoods and as a "necessary evil". My interlocutors in Namangan, more often than not, saw their government as a guarantor for stability, progress and for their perspectives of a better future.

The vicissitudes of Akram (a pseudonym) in securing his livelihood make for a good example for how people in Uzbekistan engage in livelihood strategies straddling the formal/informal divide and yet justify the political order as something necessary, although flawed and corrupt, thereby developing *an attitude of implicit consensus with the system.* After study at the Namangan university where his father was a teacher (*domla*), he abandoned the prospect of a university career illustrated by his father, deeming himself not suited to it. After marrying a girl from the neighbourhood, he started working under his father-in-law in the warehouse of a public company specialised in road construction. This Soviet-era enterprise was not doing well financially and seemed not to prospect a career, but far more lucrative than his modest salary as a junior worker was the money that Akram made by selling Soviet-era mechanical equipment and supplies from the company stock at the bazaar. In a pattern reminiscent of post-socialist privatisations elsewhere, the company heads and their associates appropriated the assets of the public company with the connivance of government officials who were giving their assent and taking advantage from it. Although in our conversations he condemned the corruption of "those up", he did not see himself as acting immorally, because he saw what he did in the company as something inherent to the nature of his job—"this is how all these companies work". In his job, Akram's familial affiliation to senior company officials was more important than his formal employment as a junior worker. After equipment and machinery were sold out the company closed down and Akram began to work temporarily for a low salary as a teacher in the village school where his older brother was the school director. At that time, he would say that he worked as a teacher, while in reality more than ever being involved in business outside the classroom. He was making the real money by growing beetroots on a sizeable plot informally rented from a farmer in the village. After the village's *kolkhoz* farm had been closed down, the land remained in public ownership but long-term tenure rights were granted to farmers (most of them former *kolkhoz* senior staff—directors, agronomists, heads of brigades, etc.) who got valuable land for agricultural use from the state without having to pay for ownership. Instead of paying a rent for tenure, farmers were bound by their leaseholds to grow state mandated crops (cotton) on the largest share of their plots, but they were also left enough land to grow their own crops or to informally sublet land to local villagers for cash or for a share of the harvest. Land subletting is illegal, strictly speaking, but here, as in Khorezm (Trevisani 2011), it was an informal practice tolerated by local authorities to reward farmers for their loyalty and for the cotton plan fulfilment. Such informal deals could last for a season or more and Akram started this economic venture by informally renting land from a farmer along with a friend. Together, they hired daily labourers, purchased agricultural inputs and, after compensating the farmer with a share of the crop for the use of the plot, they shared the profits from the sale of the harvest at the bazaar. Later on, Akram started in parallel another business with another friend from the *mahalla*. It consisted in importing gas cylinders from Russia, a lucrative trade since in Uzbekistan LPG cars' popularity was growing (gas being cheap in Uzbekistan—a natural gas exporter—while imported petrol was getting more expensive). Bulk purchase and wholesale were in cash and on the spot. The procurement through Kyrgyzstan involved bribes for smuggling the cylinders over the border on a lorry and costs for recon travels to cities in Siberia. (For these trips Akram relied on networks and knowledge established in his youth as a labour migrant when working in different odd jobs obtained through acquaintances from his village.) In the village, the gas cylinders would be stored in a privately owned cattle-shed once owned by the *kolkhoz*. Their distribution in the regional bazaars involved other informal payments and intermediation, and was accomplished through friends in the *mahalla*.

Akram's "enterprise" was totally informal, its business model based on trustful handshakes. Facilitated by a web of friends and acquaintances and kinship, it thrived in the grey zone between the formal and informal economy, and was shaped by formal rules and their circumvention. His livelihood efforts demonstrate a fluid and overlapping set of informal strategies that illustrate the pervasive informalisation (Rasanayagam 2011b), yet what attitudes, moral and political, did this all produce in him?

Rationalising the "Dominant" Form of Integration

Akram's livelihood allowed for average means, but these were never a reason for complaint. He would always say about himself that he had everything, that he was happy with his life and the opportunities that *mustaqillik* (independence) had opened up to him. His three sons were growing up and their expensive *to'y*s (life cycle celebrations, a social obligation that weighs on parents who typically will save money over years to have it spent over one lavish feast) would be provided for by him, and thanks to the support of friends and relatives. His criticism wasn't directed against national independence, but against the systemic corruption of the powerful public officials that came with it. He would talk badly about the public prosecutors, the money-extorting police and the university teachers, who in his view were all corrupt and drunkards (and bad Muslims). To him, the low appeal of the public sector was not only because those who work there were seen by him as immoral, exploiting their positions for their own interests, but also because their low salaries made it arduous for them to live without stealing. In his view, "work for the state" (*davlat ishi*), as opposed to "work for oneself" (private business) was conducive to an immoral life. He saw himself as "free" (*"hech kimga bo'ysunmayman"*—"I don't have to obey to anyone"), whereas the *domla*s and those who "work for the state" must obey their superiors and embrace a sinful, corrupt existence.

Akram, who was in his first university year in the period of Adolat, and whom I have known since 1997, in a conversation in spring 2009 confessed to me that in his youth he had had critical thoughts about the regime but that he had reconciled with the social order and with the president. Unchecked criticism would only lead to anarchy. In his opinion, people in Andijan had been misled. Retrospectively, recalling memories of the people rallying on the square in front of the *hokimiyat* (city government building) in Namangan in 1992, he thought of them as a "herd of sheep" (*"poda"*)—"they were not thinking by themselves, whoever might come and say something, that's what they would be doing." In his narrative, the president was a very acute thinker, who foreigners from the West failed to understand:

> The relationship among our countries has been cooling down? The nature of commerce is interest, and not good deeds, and if foreigners want to invest in our country, it is for profit, not for our well-being. But the president does not want to sell out the country. We'll do it our way. It will take longer [i.e., to reach development], but we'll do it.

While Akram "muddles through" with different informal employments and entrepreneurial activities, he maintains a happy-go-lucky take on the economic problems of existence and views his real wealth and safety in his family and web of friends (*inoq*) and relatives, which make his life rich and fulfilling. A sense of frustration about the increasingly difficult livelihood struggle, the loss of formal securities and protected employment which came with the Soviet Union, was easier to find among the representatives of generations older than Akram's. By contrast, Akram's moral reasoning around the informalisation of livelihoods and around the political and economic framework that made it possible, emphasised a contentedness for entrepreneurial freedoms and the securities of having a strong fulfilment from his local (rooted in family and friends in the *mahalla*) and national sense of belonging. Such and similar narratives by people who had entered adulthood over the years of independence (and were not alienated by economic failure and hardship!) attest to an acceptance of the current situation, but also to a moral numbness and collusion with the "dominant" form of integration, an unwillingness to challenge the given order and a readiness to come to terms with it as best as possible.

Authoritarian Mode of Integration

Evaluating the level of consent under repressive conditions is always problematic and not just in the case of Central Asian authoritarian countries (Matveeva 2009). Some help can be found in the historiography of Italian fascism, where intense debating on the nature and the social backing of the regime in the so-called pre-war "years of consent" (De Felice 1974) has resulted in a distinction between *consent* and *consensus* (Morgan 1999; Kim 2009). While the narrower notion of consent applies with reference to the appraisal of a government by its political constituencies, the more encompassing notion of consensus has its roots in the Gramscian notion of hegemony and addresses more broadly how social stability and cohesion can be created and maintained through measures that work at the level of ordinary people's attitudes and everyday practices (see: Berezin 1997; Passerini 1987). The distinction between consent and consensus helps address contradictory subjectivities, since a lack of consent does not necessarily translate into an absence of consensus and political disaffection with the status quo can coexist in the same person with the sustaining of beliefs and practices that support it. This distinction is apt in the repressive environment of the Ferghana Valley, where people like Akram could morally distance themselves from a corrupt political order but at the same time recognise its necessity and sustain it, or in other words, distance themselves from "consent" but practice "consensus". In fascist Italy the middle classes were a heterogeneous group, with uncertain class boundaries and unsteady political inclinations. They were disparate in their social and economic interests and only unified in their quest for order and stability. Nevertheless, they were of crucial importance to the regime, and yet their support was neither unambiguous nor unconditional, a reason why the state had to adopt a plurality of rhetoric and political strategies to keep its hegemonic grip on them (Berezin 1997). The state incorporated them ideologically, through an ideology of class "harmony", and practically, through the doctrine of "corporatism", by which professions, economic sectors, interest groups and virtually all organised activity in the public sphere were organised in confederations, top-down modelled on the artisanal guilds (de Grazia 1981).

The post-Soviet Uzbek state is confronted with similar problems and the solutions adopted are also similar. Soviet organisations and institutions often changed in name only in post-Soviet Uzbekistan, while the government has resorted to a plurality of context-specific strategies to recapture the informal sector and to bring it under its oversight. After independence, the type of command structure that organised the once inflated and state-subsidised socialised sector has been maintained in a more dilute form, but now the power holders faced the problem of how to keep the ranks of the command-administrative system built in Soviet times under these new, more informalised and less attractive conditions. Under the long presidency of Karimov, the state strengthened ways to maintain a workable command hierarchy through more indirect levers.

Public employees have comparatively low salaries but often they have the security of life-long employment. Their jobs are also becoming more prestigious, since the re-strengthening of the public sector confers more importance on those public officials who can exert power in their workplaces. But, as often lamented by public sector workers: "work for the state never ends", additional tasks, extraordinary assignments, the "cotton duty",[4] obligations towards the superiors, and the dedication to

---

4   At the time of my fieldwork, it consisted in the monitoring of the cotton harvest, when public sector workers, officials, and students were called to abandon their tasks, relocate to the cotton fields and help with the harvest by either picking cotton or monitoring those picking it.

a demanding work sociality that can be at times pleasant and fulfilling, and at others a burden, are the unofficial price for the rewards that public sector employment can entail. The possibility of taking bribes, moonlighting or exerting influence, which can turn public sector jobs into powerful, remunerative positions, is not evenly distributed and is reflected in a workplace hierarchy in which inequalities in wages, formal rights and other, more informal entitlements have also grown.

Outside the realm of public employment, private entrepreneurship underwent a similar process and faces similar dilemmas. In agriculture, for instance, the state has retreated from the production process after decollectivisation, but it has long maintained control over retail, credit, inputs, and has thereby retained the ability to steer the sector through indirect levers (Trevisani 2011). At the intermediate level of the production hierarchy, cotton is attractive to farmers not because of its low procurement prices but because it offers securities and stability within the framework set by the state. Within this formal framework farmers can manipulate agricultural resources to their advantage and use land more profitably on the side to the extent that government officials let them do so. Analogously, in the bazaars, although more market freedoms have been introduced, the state keeps a cap on the possibility of profit making by introducing high taxes and many rules and licences that hamper business. Their exemption, or discretionary application or verification by enforcement organs, plays a crucial role in the profitability of a business, and marks the difference between a successful and an unsuccessful entrepreneur.

As in Akram's case, the middle strata navigate this system with ambivalence, on the one hand lamenting corruption, and on the other accepting, even internalising, the rules of the game. In both public and private sectors, whether one turns out to be a "winner" or a "loser" (Hann et al. 2003) depends on one's individual capacity to work out the available conditions. After the 1990s, the second decade of independence has been one in which informal livelihoods have been increasingly re-formalised by a more alert and capillary presence of the state in the economic domain. The Soviet state saw the informal sector as undermining its power over the economy (as most vividly exemplified with the case of the "cotton scandal"); in post-Soviet Uzbekistan the state has re-integrated the private sector, which is no longer parasitic to state capture as it used to be in Soviet times. Nowadays the state "squeezes" the private sector to pursue its interests and priorities. Its taxation supports the national budget, an infrastructure modernisation programme creating jobs, and the financing of a no longer all-enveloping, but nevertheless newly bolstered, public sector.

The middle strata, in this context, be it those who "work for the state", or those "who work for themselves", are those to whom the regime confers or allows to occupy an intermediate position in the new social hierarchy. Middle strata might complain about increasingly difficult livelihood struggles, unfair treatment, an exploitative and repressive environment. At the same time, many benefit from the relative securities and certainties that the state has to offer to those who cooperate. The gains and opportunities provided by the informal economy became more attentively monitored by the authorities. Access to these informal gains (i.e. the possibility of making them) has become an informal compensation by which the regime secures the cooperation or loyalty of its low- and middle-level affiliates in the public and private sectors. By co-opting people through mechanisms grounded in a manipulative use of the informal economy, the regime shapes the "consensus" of a significant segment of the population. Mabel Berezin (1990) has written that the Italian middle classes were "created constituencies", fable, heterogeneous constituencies created by the political economy of the corporatist state. By comparison, Uzbek middle strata are no less heterogeneous and unstable. They have emerged from the political economy of the independent state, one in which the role of informality continues to be central, both for the public and the private sectors.

A Moral Economy of Consensus and Informality

In this paper I have attempted to examine the moral and political sensibilities of the middle strata in Uzbekistan in the decade that began after Andijan 2005 and ended with the Karimov presidency in 2016 from a moral economy perspective. Since the beginning of the new presidency under Karimov's successor Shavkat Mirziyoyev, the country seems to be moving towards an expansion and better protection of market freedoms for the entrepreneurial individual (Schmitz 2020). This process is just beginning and at this stage it raises many questions that future studies will need to address empirically. But going back to the Karimov era, we can say that the creation of a politically opportunistic and unstable social constituency, shaped by the relationship between authoritarianism and informality, can be viewed as one of the legacies outlasting this period. We have seen that although informal practices have become more pervasive, informalisation did not level out formal rules. The government's attempt at re-capturing the informal sector has seen the middle strata internalising peculiar values and habits that were formed under protracted years of "consensus" and that have increased their adaptiveness to the authoritarian informal economic framework that has emerged after independence.

A comparison of the Uzbekistan case with Hann's work on Hungary is instructive. In both cases we see strong reactions to the market in the form of right-leaning populisms and authoritarian countermovements (against which Polanyi at his time was already warning). In both cases, they have emerged as a reaction to dominant forms of global market integration that have been marginalising ordinary citizens in weaker national economies. But on closer scrutiny, the local convergences of interests and values between elites and ordinary citizens develop in different directions in Uzbekistan and in Hungary: Hungary accounts for a case in which pre-existing values (material work) that resonate with local legacies and deep-rooted understandings of community life are recuperated and instrumentalised by populist elites for modern workfare policies managing the rift between market and society in a way that sits well with the elites; in Uzbekistan, we see how the integrative force of the informal economy is demiurgic in shaping new values and attitudes in society and, by extension, creating a new social stratum, that of the "new Uzbeks" (Trevisani 2014). A lesson from this exercise in comparison could perhaps be, as Chris Hann (2018) suggests, that the moral dimension of the political economy matters more than ever. As he draws our attention to how populisms tap into historically shaped values that resonate with people's lived experiences and moral horizons, he also invites us to address the question of peoples' contradictory consciousness in relation to authoritarian and populist post-socialist systems with a perspective that puts the moral dimension of the economy at the centre of our analysis.

References

Abdullaev, Olimjon. 1995. *Namangan Viloyati. Tabiati, Aholisi, Xo'jaligi* [Namangan Region: Its environment, population, economy]. Namangan: Namangan viloyati noshirlik bo'limi.

Bazin, Laurent. 2008. Some Responses to Globalisation in Uzbekistan: State Authoritarianism, Migrant Labour and Neo-Traditionalism. *Anthropology of the Middle East* 3 (1), 10–27, https://doi.org/10.3167/ame.2008.030103.

Berezin, Mabel. 1990. Created constituencies: The Italian Middle Classes and Fascism. In: R. Koshar (ed.) 1990. *Splintered Classes: Politics and the Lower Middle Classes in Interwar Europe*. New York: Holmes and Mayer, pp. 142–163.

Berezin, Mabel. 1997. *Making the Fascist Self: The Political Culture of Inter-war Italy*. Ithaca: Cornell University Press.

Brandtstädter, Susanne. 2003. The Moral Economy of Kinship and Property in Southern China. In: Chris Hann et al. (eds) 2003. *The Postsocialist Agrarian Question: Property Relations and the Rural Condition*. Münster: Lit Verlag, pp. 419–440.

Cook, Linda J. 1993. *The Soviet Social Contract and Why It Failed: Welfare Policy and Workers' Politics from Brezhnev to Yeltsin*. Cambridge, MA: Harvard University Press.

Cucciolla, Riccardo M. 2017. *The Crisis of Soviet Power in Central Asia: The 'Uzbek Cotton Affair' (1975–1991)*. Unpublished doctoral dissertation, IMT School for Advanced Studies Lucca.

De Felice, Renzo. 1974. *Mussolini il duce. Gli anni del consenso 1929–1936*. Torino: Einaudi.

Fierman, William. 1997. Political Development in Uzbekistan: Democratization? In: Karen Dawisha and Bruce Parrott (eds) 1997. *Conflict, Cleavage, and Change in Central Asia and the Caucasus* Cambridge: Cambridge University Press, pp. 360–408.

Gambold-Miller, Lisl and Patrick Heady. 2003. Cooperation, Power, and Community: Economy and Ideology in the Russian Countryside. In: Chris Hann et al. (eds) 2003. *The Postsocialist Agrarian Question: Property Relations and the Rural Condition*. Münster: Lit Verlag, pp. 257–292.

Götz, N. 2015. 'Moral economy': Its conceptual history and analytical prospects. *Journal of Global Ethics* 11 (2), 147–162, https://doi.org/10.1080/17449626.2015.1054556.

Gafarli, M. and A.C.H. Kasaev. 2001. *Rivojlanishning O'zbek Modeli: Tinchlik va Barqarorlik—Taraqqiyot Asosi* [The Uzbek Model of Development: Peace and Sustainability—the Basis for Development]. Tashkent: O'zbekiston.

Gramsci, Antonio. 1971. *Selections from the Prison Notebooks*, translated by Q. Hoare and G. Nowell Smith. London: Lawrence & Wishart.

Grossman, Gregory. 1977. The second economy of the USSR. *Problems of Communism* 26, 25–40.

Hann, Chris. 2002. Farewell to the socialist 'other'. In: Chris Hann (ed.) 2002. *Postsocialism: Ideals, Ideologies and Practices in Eurasia*. London; New York: Routledge, pp. 1–11.

Hann, Chris et al. (eds) 2003. *The Postsocialist Agrarian Question: Property Relations and the Rural Condition*. Münster, Lit Verlag.

Hann, Chris. 2011. Smith in Beijing, Stalin in Urumchi: Ethnicity, political economy, and violence in Xinjiang 1759–2009. *Focaal-Journal of Global and Historical Anthropology* 60, 108–123, https://doi.org/10.3167/fcl.2011.600109.

Hann, Chris. 2018. Moral(ity and) Economy: Work, Workfare, and Fairness in Provincial Hungary. *European Journal of Sociology* 59 (2), 225–254, https://doi.org/10.1017/S000397561700056X.

Hann, Chris. 2019. *Repatriating Karl Polanyi: Market Society in the Visegrád States*. Budapest; New York: Central European University Press.

Hart, Keith. 1973. Informal income opportunities and urban employment in Ghana. *Journal of Modern African Studies* 11, 61–89.

Harvey, David. 2005. *A Brief History of Neoliberalism*. Oxford: Oxford University Press.

Human Rights Watch. 2005. 'Bullets Were Falling Like Rain': The Andijan Massacre, 13 May 2005, *Human Rights Watch Report* 17.5D (2005), https://www.hrw.org/reports/2005/uzbekistan0605/uzbekistan0605.pdf.

Humphrey, Carolyn. 1983. *Karl Marx Collective: Economy, Society and Religion in a Siberian Collective Farm*. Cambridge: Cambridge University Press.

Ilkhamov, Alisher. 2001. Impoverishment of the Masses in the Transition Period: Signs of an Emerging 'New Poor' Identity in Uzbekistan. *Central Asian Survey* 20, 33–54, https://doi.org/10.1080/02634930120055442.

Ilkhamov, Alisher. 2006. 'The Phenomenology of 'Akromiya': Separating Facts from Fiction. *China and Eurasia Forum Quarterly* 4, 39–48.

Ledeneva, Alena. 1998. *Russia's Economy of Favours: Blat, Networking, and Informal Exchange*. Cambridge, Cambridge University Press.

Liu, Morgan. 2012. *Under Salomon's Throne, Uzbek Visions of Renewal in Osh*. Pittsburgh: University of Pittsburgh Press.

Liu, Morgan. 2014. Massacre through a Kaleidoscope: Fragmented Moral Imaginaries on the State in Central Asia. In: Madeleine Reeves, Johan Rasanayagam and Judith Beyer (eds) 2014. *Ethnographies of the State in Central Asia: Performing Politics*. Bloomington: Indiana University Press, pp. 261–284.

Lubin, Nancy. 1984. *Labour and Nationality in Soviet Central Asia*. Princeton: Princeton University Press.

Kandiyoti, Deniz. 2003. The Cry for Land: Agrarian Reform, Gender and Land Rights in Uzbekistan. *Journal of Agrarian Change* 3 (1–2), 225–256, https://doi.org/10.1111/1471-0366.00055.

Khalid, Adeeb. 2007. *Islam after Communism: Religion and Politics in Central Asia.* Berkeley: University of California Press.

Kim, Yong Woo. 2009. From Consensus Studies to History of Subjectivity: Some Considerations on Recent Historiography on Italian Fascism. *Totalitarian Movements and Political Religions* 10 (3–4), 327–337, https://doi.org/10.1080/14690760903268907.

Kofti, Dimitra. 2016. Moral economy of flexible production: Fabricating precarity between the conveyor belt and the household. *Anthropological Theory* 16 (4), 433–453, https://doi.org/10.1177/1463499616679538.

Matveeva, Anna. 2009. Legitimising Central Asian Authoritarianism: Political Manipulation and Symbolic Power. *Europe-Asia Studies* 61 (7), 1095–1121, https://doi.org/10.1080/09668130903068624.

Morgan, P. 1999. The Years of Consent? Popular Attitudes and Resistance to Fascism in Italy 1925–1940. In: Tim Kirk and Anthony McElligott (eds) 1999. *Opposing Fascism: Community, Authority and Resistance in Europe.* Cambridge: Cambridge University Press, pp. 163–179.

Namangan oblasti. 1976. *O'zbek Sovyet Entsiklopediyasi*, vol. 7. Tashkent: O'zSSR Fanlar Akademiyasi, pp. 527–533.

Passerini, Luisa. 1987. *Fascism in Popular Memory: The Cultural Experience of the Turin Working Class.* Cambridge: Cambridge University Press.

Polanyi, Karl. 1957. The Economy as Instituted Process. In: K. Polanyi, C.M. Arensberg and H.W. Pearson (eds) 1957. *Trade and Market in the Early Empires: Economies in History and Theory.* Glencoe: Free Press, pp. 239–270.

Rasanayagam, Johan. 2011a. *Islam in Post-Soviet Uzbekistan: The Morality of Experience.* Cambridge: Cambridge University Press.

Rasanayagam, Johan. 2011b. Informal economy, informal state: The case of Uzbekistan. *International Journal of Sociology and Social Policy* 31 (11–12), 681–696, https://doi.org/10.1108/01443331111177878.

Rumer, Boris. 1991. Central Asia's Cotton Economy and Its Costs. In: William Fier (ed.) 1991. *Soviet Central Asia: The Failed Transformation.* Boulder: Westview Press.

Scott, James. 1976. *The Moral Economy of the Peasant: Rebellion and Subsistence in Southeast Asia.* New Haven, CT: Yale University Press.

Schmitz, Andrea. 2020. *Die Transformation Usbekistans: Strategien und Perspektiven, SWP Studie 13.* Berlin: Stiftung Wissenschaft und Politik.

Sgibnev, Wladimir. 2014. Urban Public Transport and the State in Post-Soviet Central Asia. In: K. Burrell and K. Hörschelmann (eds) 2014. *Mobilities in*

Socialist and Post-Socialist States. London: Palgrave Macmillan, https://doi. org/10.1057/9781137267290_10.

Standing, Guy. 2011. *The Precariat: The New Dangerous Class*. Edinburgh: A&C Black.

Thompson, Edward P. 1963. *The Making of the English Working Class*. Harmondsworth: Penguin.

Trevisani, Tommaso. 2011. *Land and Power in Khorezm: Farmers, Communities, and the State in Uzbekistan's Decollectivisation*. Berlin: Lit Verlag.

Trevisani, Tommaso. 2014. The Reshaping of Cities and Citizens in Uzbekistan: The Case of Namangan's "New Uzbeks". In: Madeleine Reeves, Johan Rasanayagam and Judith Beyer (eds) 2014. *Ethnographies of the State in Central Asia: Performing Politics*. Bloomington: Indiana University Press, pp. 243–260.

Wacquant, Loic. 2012. Three Steps to a Historical Anthropology of Actually Existing Neoliberalism. *Social Anthropology* 20 (1), 66–79, https://doi. org/10.1111/j.1469-8676.2011.00189.x.

Wall, Caleb. 2008. Working in Fields as Fieldwork: Khashar, participant observation and the tamorka as ways to access local knowledge in rural Uzbekistan. In: Caleb Wall and Peter Mollinga (eds) 2008. *Fieldwork in Difficult Environments: Methodology as Boundary Work in Development Research*. Berlin: Lit Verlag, pp. 137–160.

Zanca, Russell. 2011. *Life in a Muslim Uzbek Village: Cotton Farming after Communism*. Boston: Wadsworth Cengage Learning.

6. The Moral Dimension of (Un)Employment

Work and Fairness in an Eastern German Town

Katerina Ivanova

Introduction

In this chapter I focus on the connection between work as value and material economy of employment in an industrial town in Saxony. I am drawing on the ethnographic data that I gathered during one year of fieldwork in 2018–2019 in Zwickau as well as on historical material. My research in Zwickau has been focused on the transformations in its automotive industry and social structure. During socialist times, the town became famous for being the birthplace of Trabant—an iconic East German car. Unlike many other towns in former East Germany, Zwickau has retained its automotive industry since the reunification in 1989. Thanks to Volkswagen's extensive investment, the car production there continued, keeping thousands of jobs in the region. The recent shift towards electric vehicle production, however, poses some new challenges for the production site and for the locals. During my fieldwork, I was following social networks and relationships in Zwickau, talking to former and current automotive industry workers, trade union activists, local politicians, and other locals.

The rich industrial history of Zwickau, with its continuities and changes, makes the town an exceptional site for studying work and industrial labour in particular. By looking at a moral dimension of employment throughout time, I aim to examine the embeddedness

https://doi.org/10.11647/OBP.0282.06

of certain policies and discourses of (un)employment in the long-standing local traditions regarding morality of work. Employment, being a remunerated form of work, has inherited the moral significance of work in general, as employment and unemployment are framed in moral terms in both official discourse and everyday communication. In the following chapter, I will explore the moral meaning of work in the Zwickau region over time, and the ideas that might have influenced it, including the Protestant ethic, nationalist ideology and socialism as well as the material conditions under which they developed. By recognising the moral dimension of the economy, as suggested by Hann (2018: 231), in the sense of a collective and systemic basis for long-term shared values, I strive to analyse both moral values and material economy in their simultaneity and complexity.

Work as a Moral Value before Socialism

Zwickau, which is located in Saxony at the foot of Erzgebirge mountain range, was a centre of Zwickau coal mining district (Zwickauer Steinkohlenrevier), where black coal has been extracted for almost 800 years since the tenth century and up until the resources were exhausted in 1979. It was thanks to black coal mining that the industry of Zwickau flourished, especially since the beginning of the wide use of steam engines. The Zwickau machine factory, rope factory and the whole automotive industry owe their existence to the coal mining industry. Before industrialisation the town was famous for wool weaving and silver mining.

Some of the oldest German industrial worker biographies were also found in this region. For example, the biography of Carl Neumann, written down and published by his brother-in-law and a pastor Tobias Leberecht in 1853, tells a story of a worker in an industrial town (Fischer 1972). A half-orphan Carl Neumann learns to be a carpenter from his uncle, then marries and takes over a small indebted house and a business from his father-in-law. After he loses his small business, he moves to a Saxon factory town, rents a place for his family and works as an errand boy in a sugar factory. Thanks to his strong faith, skills and hard work (*Tüchtigkeit*) he moves ahead on the social ladder and becomes a respected craftsman (*Meister*), buys a house and gains the economic freedom that he would have probably never achieved before the age of industrialisation (Fischer 1972: 294). The biography was an instructive story of social descent and ascent from petty bourgeois, to de-classed worker and then to middle-class craftsman. In this story, the two virtues, faith in God and hard work, being strongly intertwined, stood at the core of personal evolution. The positive image of the worker in this and similar biographies was created through the narrative of taming the 'inner beast', or the allegedly anti-social and undisciplined nature of the working class, by turning to God (Jensen 2005: 542).

Another similar social mobility was described in a famous worker's biography of a coal miner (*Bergmann*), published in 1906 by Friedrich Naumann. The miner, Franz Louis Fischer, was a son of a small mine owner, who was impoverished and committed suicide, when Franz was a child. Franz, after being a bell ringer, an errand boy and a shepherd boy, became a coal miner in 1870 (Emmerich 1975: 386).

He later became a miners' representative and from 1886—a milk trader. In his biography, special attention is drawn to the 'civil virtues' (*Bürgerliche Tugenden*), most of all diligence (*Fleiß*) (Sinjen 2013). Fischer noted proudly that he inherited those virtues from his father and grandfather, and that his whole family worked like "bees" (*wie die Bienen*) through good and bad (Sinjen 2013). Both biographies, although it was claimed they had been written by the workers themselves, were written down and published by two pastors. Friedrich Naumann, who told the story of Fischer the miner, was a social thinker, theologist and a politician, who stood at the origins of the liberal democratic party (the modern FDP). Naumann published workers' biographies through his interest in the 'social question', which he hoped would be solved in non-Marxist terms. Therefore, it is difficult to judge the extent to which the opinions voiced in these biographies were truly those of the workers and protagonists of each story. But if we were to treat them as valid sources of information, we could mark a strong connection between religiousness and work, as well as their affinity with the 'Protestant ethic', especially in its Calvinist expression, as discussed by Weber, which emphasises diligence, discipline and thriftiness. According to this ethic, the working man fulfils his calling in the world through hard work, and work is seen as a goal in itself. In these writings we can see how idleness (*Nichtstun*) is presented as dangerous for the soul. Both biographies present hard work as a moral virtue, which eventually raises those who exhibit it up on the social ladder. Naturally, the class struggle is absent in these writings and a worker is presented as a majorly middle-class subject. Here, it is, perhaps, also important to mention that Zwickau became a hotspot for the Reformation when Thomas Müntzer, a rebellious Protestant preacher and a leader of the peasant uprising of 1525, came there in 1520 to preach in St. Mary's Church, and later in St. Katharine's Church. It has also been theorised that Müntzer's preaching was strongly influenced by a tense socio-economic situation in Zwickau at the time, where the gap between the rich and the poor was particularly noticeable in the context of the cloth-making industry (Scott 1989). Rapid industrialisation made nineteenth-century Saxony a space where the tensions of modernity were particularly noticeable.

The impoverished working class became associated with various 'social ills', such as alcoholism, criminality, prostitution, child labour, high child mortality, etc. (Jensen 2005). At the same time, some literature began to appear which might be roughly considered early working-class ethnography, influenced by social democratic ideas: *Drei Monate Fabrikarbeiter und Handwerksbursche: Eine Praktische Studie*, written in 1891 by a priest, Paul Göhre, who went on to work in a factory for three months and described his experiences, and *3 ½ Monate Fabrik-Arbeiterin* by Minna Wettstein-Adelt, published in 1893. With its growing urban working class, Saxony was at that time becoming a cradle for early workers' movements, in which the textile industry around the Chemnitz area played an especially important role. The five-month strike of the Crimmitschau (a small town north of Zwickau) textile workers in 1903 for the reduction of working hours is especially worth noting. Although ultimately ending in the defeat of the workers, the strike had some long-lasting effects on wider industrial relations in the region and resulted in the creation of employers' associations. The end of the nineteenth century introduced the German 'founding father' Otto von Bismarck's answer to the 'social question', in the form of health, accident and pension insurance for all workers, a development which is often considered to mark the beginning of the German welfare state. Although some forms of state-provided insurance already existed by then, the recipient of such benefits was redefined: it was no longer 'the poor' but 'the worker', which unintentionally contributed to the differentiation of the working class (Kocka 2016: 400). The state's social insurance system was also meant to contribute to the processes of nation-building, strengthening the state and preventing the spread of socialist ideas.

Bismarck's simultaneous introduction of a social welfare system for the workers and the attempts to suppress the social democratic movement through *Sozialistengesetze* (laws against socialists) became known over time as the policies of 'carrot and stick'. The fact that the social welfare system was a conservative, rather than leftist, project constitutes one of the particularities of the German case (Kocka 2016: 404). Saxon social democrats were also gaining power, as in the Reichstag elections of 1874, when six representatives of the Social Democratic Workers' Party of Germany (*Sozialdemokratische Arbeiterpartei Deutschlands*) entered the Reichstag. After the 1903 Reichstag elections, when the Social Democratic Party of Germany (*Sozialdemokratische Partei Deutschlands*, the SPD) won twenty-two of the twenty-three constituencies, the land became known as the 'Red Kingdom'. These developments in Saxony led to some unrest among the conservatives, whose response came in the form of a new, restrictive, three-class franchise election system (*Dreiklassenwahlrecht*) adopted in 1896 for the Landtag elections. Voters were divided into three groups depending on their tax payments, and their votes varied in weight accordingly. Due to their lower incomes and taxes, social democratic voters' votes were weighted rather low. In 1909, despite 54% of the voters supporting socialist candidates, the SPD received only 39% of the votes, because most of their voters only had one vote (Retallack 2019: 29). Saxon conservatives also strove to signal that Saxony had to endure the democratic pressurescoming from Baden, Württemberg and Bavaria, which threatened the whole German Reich (Retallack 2019: 37). The antisocialist political groups and the opponents of the "bloody revolution" defended their ideologies by framing democracy and equality as something foreign to culturally defined "Germanness" (Retallack 2019: 36), which might have made Saxony an especially fertile ground for nationalist political developments later on. Apart from being framed as 'civil virtues', *Fleiß* [hard work] and *Arbeit* [work] were later on increasingly associated with Germanness within the nationalist ideology. Within the process of the so-called *Nationalisierung der Arbeit* [nationalisation of work], work was cast as a German virtue, whereas laziness signalled a foreign, 'non-German' spirit (Brückner 1998: 61).

Work, regarded strictly in the sense of wage labour, has also been promoted as an exclusively male task, as campaigns against the working women and the 'double earner' (*Doppelverdiener*) families took place in 1933–1934 (Buggeln, Wildt 2014: XI). 'Freedom to work' turned into 'duty to work', which was presented in the propaganda as an 'honour to work' (Buggeln and Wildt 2014: XII). Work, especially manual work, was associated with purifying and educational functions.

This ideology found its terrifying expression in the unfree labour and the concentration camps, where manual work was supposed to educate and 'raise' the opponents of the regime. *Arbeit macht frei* ['Work sets you free'] was the ironically dark slogan at the gates of some Nazi concentration camps. On 15 July 1925 Hitler delivered a speech to an audience of about 3500 in Zwickau, where he also emphasised the importance of work for German identity, as he talked about the inability of Jews to perform productive work. About 20,000 unfree labourers, including those sent from the concentration camp Flössenburg, worked in Chemnitz and Zwickau Auto Union (the predecessor of Volkswagen's subsidiary, Audi) plants in Saxony. The use of unfree labour by Auto Union also received a lot of criticism in the Sachsenring newspaper during the GDR period. Ironically, the link between the two continued as it became clear that Volkswagen had received goods produced by unfree labourers in GDR prisons.

Work and Employment in the 'Workers' and Peasants' State'

In the post-war years the economy of the SBZ and then later the GDR retained some of the elements of Nazi wartime economy, such as the workbook (*Arbeitsbuch*), fixed wages and forced labour (*Arbeitseinweisung*). Not so far from Zwickau, in Erzgebirge, Wismut AG was mining ore to produce uranium. In 1951 the paper factory in Crossen, north of Zwickau, was expropriated and used for the processing of uranium. Wismut was especially known for the use of forced labour, poor and dangerous working conditions, as well as constant policing from the side of the armed Soviet forces (Hoffmann 1999).

With time, however, the company relied less and less on forced labour, as the relatively high wages and good supply of consumer goods for the uranium miners attracted workers, despite working conditions that were still extremely harsh. Tough working conditions, high pressure on workers, and the constant raising of work targets caused dissatisfaction and unrest among workers in the GDR. Despite the June 1953 'New Course' policies, which were supposed to reduce pressure on workers, an uprising broke out on 17 June, and was forcefully suppressed. As a result of the uprising, surveillance and control over workers was severely increased. However, the uprising succeeded in a way, in that it caused the state power to take the satisfaction of the workers on the shop-floor more seriously, as it also undermined the self-image of the GDR as the workers' state. The economy of Zwickau at the time was mainly based on mining, the textile industry and the automotive industry. In 1977, after almost 800 years of extraction, coal mining stopped because resources were exhausted. The automotive industry proved to be most resilient industry in the region, remaining crucial for the livelihoods of its inhabitants since it began in 1904, when August Horch opened his first car factory in town. In 1958 the former Horch and Audi plants were united under the name of *VEB Sachsenring Automobilwerke Zwickau*. As we discuss the socialist era, we can turn to the personal experiences of my informants, many of whom were Sachsenring workers during the GDR period. In the GDR, employment was guaranteed by the state, even though the state sometimes had difficulties in fulfilling this guarantee, especially in the post-war period. It was not only a constitutional right but also a duty (Jancius 2006; Rudd 2006). A significant part of socialist ideology revolved around work and its meaning for being human. This socialist obsession with work, although a characteristic feature of the GDR, was far from a new phenomenon in eastern Germany. The idea of work as a duty towards the community and an ultimate virtue had deep religious underpinnings in the Protestant ethic. In this sense, work as a moral virtue was a shared concern of both the state and religion. However, despite these shared values, in the early years after the 1949 foundation of the GDR, the state's policy towards the church was rather hostile. At that time, 81.9% of the population were Protestants, whereas by 1986 this number had dropped to 23% (Cordell 1990). In the later census of 2011, the population of Zwickau, in particular, was registered as mostly (about 75%) atheist, with 21.7% being Protestants. Although the church has suffered significant losses in membership due to aggressive policies of secularisation, it has still managed to coexist with the state for a rather long time. The strategy that made this possible was what the evangelical church termed itself "a church in socialism", as opposed to a church alongside, or against socialism (Cordell 1990).

Despite the seemingly conflictual relationship between the Protestant Church and the socialist state, they did share similar stances on certain moral issues. These included anti-fascism, the ideals of peace and community, framing economic matters in terms of morality (Graf 1994) as well as humanism, equality and solidarity (Pollack and Richter 2012). Contrary to Weber, some have argued that Protestant ethics had the potential to give rise to socialism as much as it facilitated capitalism due to its dual focus on individualism and social accountability (McCormack 1969). Indeed, I would argue that by adapting to the socialist reality, the church in the GDR did not necessarily have to betray Protestant principles. In other words, the idea of the 'church in socialism' is far less contradictory than it may seem. The shift towards post-materialistic values in the West and the rise of secular ecumenism in the 1970s resulted in the critique of capitalism as well as the re-evaluation of socialist systems among theologists in the West (Pollack and Richter 2012). As argued by Peperkamp (2010), an emphasis on humanity (*Menschlichkeit*) was something that characterised the understanding of religiosity among her East German informants, and was also in line with the values officially promoted by the state, such as justice and equality. Also, for a state dealing with the problems of declining work ethic and alcoholism, the church's emphasis on work ethic as well as its position as a provider of social welfare were rather appealing (Goeckel 1988).

Although Marx has famously claimed that communism should realise the principle "From each according to his ability, to each according to his needs", the socialist states have often claimed a different principle: 'From each according to his ability, to each according to his work (*Leistung*)'. As argued by Mladenov (2017), state socialism and early capitalism shared the same principle of commodification of labour, according to which the only way to sustain oneself was increasingly to become wage labour. Although the ideal of public ownership of enterprises was meant to reduce the alienation of the workers, in reality, the means of production was controlled by the state, or the elites, rather than the workers. This commodification of labour led to the spread of productivism—a cultural-material mechanism that reduces humans to resources (Mladenov 2017: 1120).

However, one could argue that the work in state socialism was less 'alienating' due to its deep intertwinement with the social fabric. In the GDR, the factory would seep into all spheres of life, including the private sphere: health, leisure and family life were all closely connected to the workplace. And the larger the enterprise, the more its influence would spread beyond the formal work. As Berdahl (2005: 241) observes, the workplace in the GDR was not only the centre of everyday sociality, but it was also a symbolic space of social membership and national belonging. "Our factory was our family", many former Sachsenring workers say. According to Thelen (2005) personal networks in the workplace developed as an outcome of both economic constraints and as a part of the official policy, whereas trust within those networks developed as a by-product. As has been discussed in some studies (Friedreich 2007; Kohli 1994), strong workplace relationships and informal relationships within the socialist brigades also strengthened the bargaining power of workers on the factory floor. Sachsenring employees also enjoyed many advantages in that the enterprise had its own kindergarten, polyclinic, and sports teams and provided good holiday spots (*Ferienplätze*) on Lake Balaton or in Erzgebirge. These advantages, which went far beyond financial compensation, constituted the so-called *Zweite Lohntüte*, or 'social wage'. One former Sachsenring engineer, as we talked about how work had changed after the shift to a market economy, drew my attention to the difference between the two concepts of *Job* and *Arbeitsplatz* [workplace]. A job for him was something temporary and alienating, whereas the workplace was associated with permanence and a deep sense of personal connection. For him, a job belonged to capitalism, whereas the workplace belonged to socialism. Some, however, found the growing 'flexibility' and diversity at work rather liberating and emancipating. As long as it did not mean losing one's job, flexibility could be seen as a learning opportunity and a tool against the deskilling of the workers. In return for more flexibility and skills, which made the rotation of the tasks within the team possible, the workers received better payment in the new market economy. Andreas, a sixty-year-old former Sachsenring shop-floor worker, who transferred to Volkswagen overnight, remembered the transition from Sachsenring to VW as an interesting and eventful time and talked about the rigidity of the working roles in the GDR more sarcastically than nostalgically:

> In the GDR times you mostly did the same job, there was little flexibility. I attached the front left wheel. And some did that their whole life long. It doesn't matter if it's a front-left or back-right [wheel]: you put a wheel there, tighten the four screws, bend—and that's it. Or for example in Sachsenring there were nicknames for certain colleagues, depending on their occupation. There was one, they called him the 'fuel tap' [*der Benzinhahn*], I don't even know what the guy's name was. This colleague pre-assembled the fuel taps, and he did it in our shift his whole life. That was the 'fuel tap'.

Some, however, found ways to bring some diversity into their working routine. Jens, another former Sachsenring shop-floor worker, was a highly skilled welder, working as a 'Jumper' (*Springer*), which meant that, unlike most of his colleagues, he was trained to work at multiple stations and was ready to 'jump in' where he was needed. He also took pride in being able to challenge himself this way:

> The work was very diverse. But they would always ask you. Not like 'you have to do', but 'would you do that?'. Everything on a voluntary basis, not like a must. But I never said no. No, because I have to say honestly, I actually enjoyed it. I didn't want to do the same work every day. So I did that... And also the salary was higher if you were the '*Springer*', because you were highly skilled.

Car industry workers' privileged position, compared to, for example, textile workers in Zwickau was evident not only in the pay they received but also in their position in the context of the shortage economy. Easier access to one of the most valuable goods in the GDR—Trabi spare parts—granted them power on the informal exchange market and privileged access to high-value consumer goods, such as meat or furniture. The high demand for the car also made the work more meaningful and made the workers feel like they were a part of an important mission. The workers knew about the multiple flaws of Trabant cars, as well as their inferiority compared to Western cars. However, the choice on the 'market' was rather limited, and in this context, Trabi was a highly desired commodity. Wartburg, which was produced in Eisenach, was seen as a better alternative, but also a rather costly one. Furthermore, the inferiority of the Trabi, in the eyes of all of my informants, had no bearing on their skills or ability to work hard. Rather, the flaws were blamed on the shortage of materials and the difficult decision-making process in the planned economy. Therefore, despite the criticism of the product they produced, the workers could maintain a certain pride in their work. In fact, other studies (Lüdtke 1994) have also discussed the fact that the ability to produce *at all* under poor working conditions, within the shortage economy and the slow, inefficient decision-making of a centralised economy was itself a source of particular pride.

As Jens told me proudly,

> In the peak times, we made 603 cars per day! Ok... But all the parts had to be there. For example, all of those electronic parts were from the suppliers. And they had to be here. There was always a problem of shortage—shortage of skilled workers and shortage of materials. But like I said, in the peak times we produced 603 cars in two shifts.

In large enterprises like Sachsenring there was a constant *Fachkräftemangel* [lack of skilled workers], which also made the workers feel important and needed. To reflect that, one of the slogans of the time read "Alles was jung ist und Hände hat nach Zwickau, an den Trabant" (All that is young and has hands—to Zwickau, to (work on) Trabant). The competition among the enterprises for the workers not only strengthened their bargaining power, but also contributed to their sense of self-worth and pride, which made the experience of excess labour after 1989 especially painful. The high symbolic status of the workers was also supported by state ideology. Work, and especially factory work, was mythologised as a heroic act, and workers—as heroes (*Helden der Arbeit*). This expression reflects the generally militarised rhetoric surrounding work (Kohli 1994: 42). In the early years of the GDR, the state sought its legitimacy in the rhetoric of anti-fascism. This was especially vivid in Sachsenring's newspaper *Die Kurbelwelle* in the 1950s, which used anti-fascist and anti-war language to condemn the founder of the Audi and Horch plants in Zwickau, August Horch, who was accused of collaborating with the Nazi regime by producing military equipment and forced labour. "The 'fine locksmith's apprentice' August Horch [...] who supported the great genocide of our history by all means"—read one of the headlines of *Die Kurbelwelle* at the time. In later years this source of legitimacy was not as pronounced, but certain parts of the discourse persisted. Here is how Andreas, whom I mentioned earlier, described this ideologisation of work to me:

> So in the Sachsenring it was always said—"boys, watch out, we have to build more cars for peace again today [laughs]. And we did it, we built one more car for peace. Although we had the timing out of sync, today we built more cars for peace... Then from 01.01 [the day of his transfer to Volkswagen] nobody could say anymore 'we need a car because of peace', but rather: guys, we have to push it, we need the cars. The *customers* need the cars! Not like in the GDR times.

As one study carried out in the 1970s shows, the proud status of a worker was so highly valued socially, that almost everyone from a shop floor worker to the plant manager was willing to identify himself with the working class (Engler 1999). Because of this high status of workers in the GDR, it has been called an *arbeiterliche Gesellschaft* [workers' society] (Engler 1999), or, as my informants often said not without a degree of irony, an *Arbeiter-und-Bauern-Staat* [Workers' and peasants' state]. The symbolic and ideological primacy of the workers did not necessarily bring privileged status in terms of access to material goods or political power. However, in the case of the car industry in Zwickau, the 'working class people' enjoyed certain better opportunities (in terms of education or holiday spots, for example), and high wages. As we discussed the events of the Peaceful Revolution, Jens told me: "they made one mistake—they held the worker too 'small'. If the worker had more freedom, there would be no protests." He then told me about the difficulties of going abroad and exchanging the money. For him, the whole process was humiliating. It was perhaps also the gap between ideological pathos and praise of the worker on the one side, and the lack of freedom and political power on the other, that largely contributed to the dissatisfaction.

In the two sections above I have discussed the development of work as a moral value in and around Zwickau both before and during the GDR period. I started by presenting some early workers' biographies, in which the Protestant ethic represented the morality of work, glorifying it as an end in itself, as a purifying force and as a tool for self-realisation. Hard work has also been framed in nationalist discourses as a German virtue. At the same time, another, lesser-known side of the Protestant ethic is social accountability, i.e. the idea of work as duty towards the community was developed in Nazi Germany in less attractive ways. In socialism, the notion of work as a duty towards the community was articulated through the ideological heroisation and glorification of work. Workplaces in the GDR, due to their extensive involvement in all spheres of life, also became spaces of social and national belonging, once again connecting work to community and nation. As I have shown, despite the complicated relationship between the church and the state in the GDR, some Protestant ideas proved to be rather compatible with the socialist system (such as work discipline and social welfare). On the basis of historic and ethnographic material, I emphasise the continuity, rather than disruption and change, of work as a moral value over time in the Zwickau region, challenging the binary divisions between capitalism and socialism, individualism and collectivism, secular and religious. In the next section, I will discuss how the material conditions around work changed after the German reunification and transition to the market economy. I argue that the way that challenges of the labour market after 1989 and the subsequent employment policies were received by the people 'on the ground' should be discussed in the context of the importance of work as a moral value, deeply rooted in local history.

Zwickau Labour Market after 1989

After German reunification in 1990, the fate of Sachsenring was in the hands of Treuhandanstalt, which divided it into twenty-six enterprises, closed down most of them and privatised the rest. By the end of 1994, Treuhandanstalt had 12,354 VEBs in its portfolio, of which 3,718 were shut down. As some of my interlocutors in Zwickau believed, many enterprises were prematurely closed down in order to either speed up the privatisation process or to kill off the competition for Western companies. The textile industry in the Zwickau region was often mentioned as an example of such a sell-out. Some of the enterprises, like Sachsenring, went through a long cycle of new investments and bankruptcies. Surviving enterprises, which were assessed as profitable, were privatised by mostly Western investors. In some cases, the enterprises were sold for a symbolic amount of one mark. Under the circumstances of such a shock therapy, more than one million people lost their jobs after the reunification and the real unemployment has been estimated as reaching 40% in the early 1990s (Turner 1998). As Mau (2019: 151) put it, many of the *Werktätige* [working people] turned into *Untätige* [idle people]. Unemployment spread unequally among different groups according to qualifications, age and gender (Trappe 2006). For example, among those who were between fifty and sixty-five years old at the time of the Wende, more than one million people were forced into *Vorruhestand* [early retirement] (Mau 2019: 155). The early retirement often led to material, social and cultural dispossession. Due to the premature end of their working lives, the pensions of these early-retired were low, their social networks were broken, and their sense of self-worth was threatened. As a result, many of the early-retired see themselves as the actual losers of transformation (Mau 2019: 155).

The fact that the new society of which they became members tolerated unemployment came as a shock to many (Rudd 2006). The state found itself unable to fulfil the promise of *blühende Landschaften* [blooming landscapes], as it became clear that the economic disparity between the East and the West would persist for many years to come. This failed promise, the *Ausverkauf* [sell-out] and closing of the enterprises, as well as activities carried out by Treuhand in general, sparked a number of protests and factory sit-ins all over eastern Germany (Böick 2011). Here is how one of my informants, a former accountant at Sachsenring, described the situation at the time:

> Millions, millions were unemployed [after the *Wende*]. And there were no jobs. Many people didn't really like to work. And, such people, they thought when the West comes, and we will get the Western money (*Westgeld*), and then 'the fried ducks' will fly in our mouths without having to work for it. They didn't expect that one has to really work (*rabotten*) so that he can live. And those people were the first on the street, unemployed. Some people were naive (*blauäugig*), they let themselves be blinded, main thing—Western money. And then they were on the streets.

Employment at Sachsenring also dropped tremendously from 11,500 people in 1989 to 6,500 in 1991 and 2,200 in 1992. As the anxieties concerning layoffs piled up, the workforce organised a protest in order to urge Treuhand to set up an employment and training agency, or in fact to come up with any solution that would take care of the soon-to-be-laid-off workers. After a number of conflicts, strikes and sit-ins, as well as support from then Saxon Minister-President Biedenkopf, despite Treuhand's unwillingness to do so, the *Sächsische Aufbau- und*

Qualifizierungsgesellschaft (SAQ) was founded. At its initiation, SAQ took over 3,600 employees and 550 trainees and was considered a successor of Sachsenring's work council and IG Metall (Swain 2002). SAQ provided re-training programmes for the workers and was supposed to help them find subsequent re-employment. The attitudes towards SAQ among the research participants in Zwickau were quite ambivalent. Active union members from IG Metall would say that it played a crucial role in mobilising the workers. The managers and engineers argued that it was a useless organisation, which promoted the inaction of the workers on the labour market, had a demoralising influence on them, and did not really help them find a new job. Some of my interlocutors even went so far as to say that SAQ was used as a scheme for a subsidy fraud. The workers who went through training at SAQ mostly neither praised nor condemned it.

One of my informants, Elke, a former shop-floor worker, who had just finished her apprenticeship at Sachsenring in 1990 and ended up being employed at SAQ, saw it as quite a positive development. It not only helped Elke in some practical matters, but, as she got pregnant in the meantime, it provided a sort of bridge, a safety net that gave her time to adapt. She explained that it was very important for her psychologically that she did not just start getting the unemployment benefits, but still felt like she was working, and it allowed her to stay embedded in social networks at work. Almost all of my informants would agree that the training that SAQ provided was rather pointless in terms of employment and was mainly meant to keep the workers off the streets. Keeping them off the streets basically meant preventing both unemployment and protests. "These training companies mushroomed all over and got a lot of funding, SAQ as well. And they offered pointless training, which mostly brought nothing. The people didn't find jobs through that. Pointless, because there were no jobs here... All enterprises were closed off", said Mrs Schulze. Employment at SAQ was mostly seen by the 'outsiders' as a sort of a useless mock-labour (Rajković 2017).

The next crisis after the *Wende* was caused by the reforms of Agenda 2010, connected with one of the most substantial cuts to the social security system in German history. The reform included such neoliberal measures as the loosening of job security and the decrease of social costs to the employer at the expense of the employees. Schröder himself described the reform as one that would "reduce the state benefits, promote individual responsibility and request more personal contribution from each individual".

In 2004, the reform sparked protests against *Sozialabbau* (social cuts) all over Germany. The protests were carried out on Mondays and were called *Montagsdemos*, which was criticised by the government as an inappropriate analogy with the peaceful revolution of 1989. In my fieldsite in Zwickau, the protests against Hartz IV started in August 2004, and during some over 4,000 people gathered on the main square. The protests continue even fifteen years later, as the local MLPD (*Marxistisch-Leninistische Partei Deutschlands*) leader still stands with between seven and ten people in front of the shopping mall, Arcaden, in the Old Town of Zwickau almost every Monday at 5p.m. When I first encountered the protesters, they were holding a poster which declared "Wir wollen Arbeit, von der wir leben können! Keine Almosen! Weg mit Hartz IV—das Volk sind wir!" ["We want work, from which we can make a living! Not charity! Away with Hartz IV—we are the people!"]. Later, their leader told me that they had started the demonstrations with the trade unions. However, the trade union almost immediately distanced itself from MLPD, and since then there had been two separate Monday demonstrations in Zwickau. In November 2004 the trade unions stopped their demonstrations under some pressure from SPD. The results of Agenda 2010 are mostly considered a success because unemployment in Germany did gradually fall from 10.5% to an average of 5% in 2019, and the economy has steadily grown since then, although causality is not transparent in this case. The unemployment rate mostly declined in the East, which could also be partially explained by the fact that some of the long-term unemployed, who lost their jobs during the *Wende*, retired. The reform was also blamed for its negative consequences, such as growing inequality and poverty. It has led to a stronger stigmatisation of the unemployed in public discourse and caused a boom in the temporary employment business (*Leiharbeitsfirmen*). People prefer temporary employment (even with poor working conditions) to the idea of becoming a Hartz IV recipient, which is seen as both morally and financially problematic. Indeed, to many of my interlocutors in the field, receiving benefits was considered shameful:

> I would say, if you want money from the state, then you should please sweep the streets, or clean windows, or go to some firm, or build

the streets. But no, they [the unemployed] don't want to! And they keep receiving their benefits. That is why we still have thousands of unemployed in Zwickau.

In March 2019 I attended a 'conversation at the kitchen table' (*Küchentischgespräch*) in Zwickau which was organised by SPD, the party which was primarily responsible for Hartz IV, as a part of a campaign for the Landtag elections. The name of this event was 'What comes after Hartz IV?', and the clear suggestion of the party was the *Bürgergeld*, or basic income. The format of this discussion allowed the public to sit in a pub, at the 'kitchen table', with the politicians and to ask them questions. Although it turned out to be rather a matter of politician's monologues than a discussion, some people managed to ask their questions and share their concerns. One of them, a young woman in her thirties, was a single mother of two and a former bank employee, who left her job to engage in volunteering in the area of female unemployment. She started her speech with the phrase "I am very nervous because I want to come out (*mich outen*)—I am a Hartz IV receiver". She went on to talk about the stigmatisation and the shame that she was subjected to. "We are not all lazy or incapable. There is a story behind each one of us", she said with her voice shaking.

The stigma and the tragedy behind unemployment seems to be strongly connected with the deeply-rooted moral values which I discussed earlier in relation to early workers' biographies, and which are also connected to the perception of work in Protestantism. Falling out of working life was considered not only shameful, but also destructive for the soul and one's mental health. The 2004 reforms seem to have capitalised on these traditional narratives of work as an instrument of moral growth. Despite some attempts to establish a countermovement (such as the Monday demonstrations against the Hartz IV reforms), the protests have failed to appeal to the general public, who instead reached a general consensus in agreement with state policies.

Moral Dimension of Work

Despite continuing interest in the entanglement and interplay of the spheres of economy and morality, the concept of *moral economy* has received a fair amount of criticism recently. Although not invented by Thompson (1971), the term moral economy was introduced into widespread academic use in his article, 'The moral economy of the English crowd in the eighteenth century'. The term has since then 'migrated' from history to political science through the writings of Scott (1976), and to sociology and anthropology (Edelman 2012: 59). However, rather than promoting a dialogue by moving across the boundaries of separate disciplines, the concept has contributed to a certain "division of labour" between studies focused on either economy or morality (Hann 2016: 4). In his critique of the concept, Chris Hann (2018) makes a case for dropping the term 'moral economy' altogether in favour of the *moral dimension* of economy, a term he borrows from sociologist Amitai Etzioni. Hann suggests that recognising the moral dimension of economy as opposed to 'moral economy' would help in overcoming the division between economy and morality. In this chapter, I have followed Chris Hann's (2016: 7) suggestion that we should recognise "a moral dimension in the sense of a collective and systemic basis in long-term shared values", which captures both the dynamic nature of morality and economy, and the resilience of some long-term, dominant values. I am focusing here on the moral dimension of work as a central activity for economies everywhere (Hann 2018: 7). Industrial work is of particular interest in this regard, as it became separated in time and space from the rest of peoples' lives and was associated with the economic sphere (Parry 2005: 142). E.P. Thompson (1967) has contrasted the rhythm of the factory and its abstract clock-time with work on the fields, which is governed by the rhythms of nature and characterised by short periods of intense labour alternating with long periods of idleness. In contrast to pre-industrial work, where one was directly in contact with the results of his work, industrialisation turned labour into a "fictitious commodity" (Polanyi 2001), which was to be sold to a capitalist in return for money, which further separated work from other domains of life. The word 'fictitious' implied that labour (man), just like land (nature) and money, was never 'produced' with the intent that it be sold as a regular commodity for the price of wages or rent (Polanyi 2001: 136–137).

The distinguishing feature of the work ethic in modern capitalism is increasing flexibility. Flexibility has become a measure of one's value as a worker, as the burdens of market uncertainty are transferred onto wage earners or the state (Boltanski and Chiapello 2007: 218). To accommodate fluctuating demand, part-time and temporary employment have increasingly become the norm among workers. Although Volkswagen in Zwickau has abstained from employing a temporary workforce since the emissions scandal in 2016, its multiple suppliers in the region do employ temporary workers through temporary employment agencies. The combination of two types of workforce within one enterprise causes division between the workers, one of the reasons being their unequal treatment although they are often are equally qualified and perform the same tasks. Without temporary workers, flexibility within Volkswagen factories is achieved via different means, but often also at the expense of the workers, who need to transfer to a different team, intensify their labour, or work overtime to compensate for the changes on the market. Uncertainty has also become a more tangible threat to the workers in Zwickau since the factory has been set to shift solely to the production of electric cars, as many of the workers fear that the demand will not be sufficient to keep the plant running in the long term. I have argued in this chapter that compliance with the commodification of the labour market and neoliberal social policies was achieved not only due to economic conditions, but also due to the embeddedness of such policies within the system of values concerning morality and work. In this chapter, I have attempted to show certain continuities of such values in the region since early industrialisation, through socialism and in the modern context. Focusing on the moral dimension of (un)employment in Zwickau allows us to identify the moral grounds, informing both economic and political decisions. In line with Hann (2018), I have sought to connect the development of certain moral sentiments with changes in the material economy. By doing so, I have attempted to explain the attitudes towards work, employment and compliance with certain employment policies in an eastern German industrial town and their connection to the morality of work in a late-capitalist context.

In his analysis of work as a moral value in provincial Hungary, Hann (2018: 249) argues that the government's *közmunka* workfare policy is endorsed at the local level because it is embedded in long-term moral values, such as a pre-industrial Christian ethic of work as an end in itself, and the ethics of socialist industrialisation, which was focused on the glorification of work as a state ideology. He also shows how the idea of work's moralising influence is used by populist politicians to legitimise workfare policy as a way of dealing with the perceived 'moral deficit'

among the Roma population and justifying negative attitudes towards
the new category of migrants—refugees. In this chapter, I have pointed
out several similarities between the two cases of rural Hungary and an
industrial town in Saxony. The prevalence of the Weberian type of work
ethic is one of them. Aside from hard work, craftsmanship and manual
skills are especially valued within this Christian work ethic. In the Saxon
case, hard work also constitutes an important aspect of national identity,
and it was central to the process of nation-building. The centrality of
work under socialism, similarly to rural Hungary, was quite in line with
the previous moral narratives concerning work in the region. Although
in reality the organisation of work in socialism was often ridiculed
for its sluggishness, frequent pauses and informality, which were also
denounced by my informants in Zwickau, none of my informants
confessed to being guilty of such idleness themselves. Rather, they
would still talk about work as value, not in the sense of a sacrifice, but
as an enjoyable and honourable activity in itself. As in the Hungarian
case, work as a moral value is also used in anti-migrant rhetoric in
order to divide people into groups of 'deserving' and 'undeserving'.
Deservingness among my informants in Zwickau was mostly focused
on productivity and hard work—qualities they believed they had but
felt the need to defend due to the discourse of sluggishness surrounding
the discussions of work in East German factories.

Conclusion

Despite dramatic changes which occurred in the economy of the region,
certain moral values and discourses around work persisted over time
and left their mark on issues of employment. As in Hann's (2018)
analysis of provincial Hungary, recognition of moral dimensions allows
us to uncover certain consistencies beneath the ever-changing and fluid
economic life in Zwickau. The changes to the labour market since 1989
have posed for a challenge to the workers in Zwickau. Initially, the wave
of unemployment swept many off their feet and the long-term moral
value of work as a duty towards the community was shaken. First,
unemployment stood in the way of individuals' ability to contribute to
society through work. Second, on a more practical note, with workplaces
being central to most social relations during socialism, losing one's job

often meant being cut off from one's social networks and communities. Many found themselves in a moral dilemma: they had to work to stay a part of the community, but had no opportunity to find employment. Temporary employment measures such as SAQ assisted some workers in material terms, but did not manage to cover the moral vacuum that the loss of employment created. In order to be morally respectable, work had to be meaningful and useful, and taking courses on constructing a resume were not seen as such. Fear of the moral descent associated with unemployment pushed some into conforming to the rising flexibility and precarity.

Although they were initially met with a certain resistance, the social welfare cuts which came with the Hartz IV were ultimately accepted by the public. I argue that the failure of the protest might be connected with the embeddedness of the reforms' rhetoric in long-term, shared values concerning work, which dictated that one must only be rewarded according to his individual contribution and effort (*Leistung*). These values were also cemented within socialist ideology in the form of *Leistungsprinzip*. As I have shown in this chapter, the morality of work in Zwickau included both work as a duty towards the community and as an individual responsibility. Rather than being an inherent feature of either a capitalist or socialist system, these values remained central in the long term and constituted the moral dimension of work in the region.

References

Berdahl, Daphne. 2005. The Spirit of Capitalism and the Boundaries of Citizenship in Post-Wall Germany. *Comparative Studies in Society and History* 47 (2), 235–251, https://doi.org/10.1017/S0010417505000125.

Boltanski, Luc and Eve Chiapello. 2007. *The New Spirit of Capitalism*. London; New York: Verso.

Böick, Marcus. 2011. "Aufstand im Osten"? Sozialer und betrieblicher Protest gegen die Treuhandanstalt und Wirtschaftsumbau in den frühen 1990er-Jahren. In: Dieter Bingen, Maria Jarosz and Peter Loew (eds). 2011. *Legitimation und Protest. Gesellschaftliche Unruhe in Polen, Ostdeutschland und anderen Transformationsländern nach 1989*. Wiesbaden: Harrassowitz, pp. 167–185.

Brückner, Wolfgang. 1998. *"Arbeit macht frei": Herkunft und Hintergrund der KZ-Devise*. Opladen: Leske+Budrich, https://doi.org/10.1007/978-3-322-92320-2.

Cordell, Karl. 1990. The Role of the Evangelical Church in the GDR. *Government and Opposition* 25 (1), 48–59.

Edelman, Marc. 2012. E.P. Thompson and Moral Economies.I In: Didier Fassin (ed.) 2012. *A Companion to Moral Anthropology*. New York: John Wiley & Sons, pp. 49–66, https://doi.org/10.1002/9781118290620.ch3.

Emmerich, Wolfgang (ed.). 1974. *Proletarische Lebensläufe. Autobiographische Dokumente zur Entstehung der zweiten Kultur in Deutschland, Bd. 1: Anfänge bis 1914*. Reinbek bei Hamburg: Rowohlt.

Engler, Wolfgang. 1999. *Die Ostdeutschen: Kunde von Einem Verlorenen Land*. Berlin: Aufbau Verlag.

Fischer, Wolfram. 1972. *Wirtschaft Und Gesellschaft Im Zeitalter Der Industrialisierung: Aufsätze, Studien, Vorträge*. Göttingen: Vandenhoeck & Ruprecht, https://doi.org/10.13109/9783666359514.

Friedreich, Sönke. 2007. Die Alte Arbeit Und Ihr Ende: Erfahrungen Aus Zwei Systemen in Den Schilderungen Der Arbeitswelt Ehemaliger Angehöriger Der DDR-Automobilindustrie. In: Manfred Seifert, Irene Götz and Birgit Huber (eds). 2007. *Flexible Biografien? Horizonte Und Brüche Im Arbeitsleben Der Gegenwart*. Frankfurt: Campus Verlag, pp. 193–213.

Goeckel, Robert F. 1988. Church and Society in the GDR: Historical Legacies and "Mature Socialism". *International Journal of Sociology* 18 (4), 210–227.

Götz, Norbert. 2015. 'Moral Economy': Its Conceptual History And Analytical Prospects. *Journal Of Global Ethics* 11, 147–162, https://doi.org/10.1080/174 49626.2015.1054556.

Graf, Friedrich Wilhelm. 1994. Eine Ordnungsmacht Eigener Art. Theologie Und Kirchenpolitik Im DDR-Protestantismus.I In: Hartmut Kaelble, Jürgen Kocka and Hartmut Zwahr (eds). 1994. *Sozialgeschichte Der DDR*. Stuttgart: Klett-Cotta, pp. 295–321.

Gudeman, Stephen. 2008. *Economy's Tension: The Dialectics of Community and Market*. New York; Oxford: Berghahn Books.

Hann, Chris. 2016. The moral dimension of economy: work, workfare, and fairness in provincial Hungary. *Max Planck Institute for Social Anthropology Working Papers, 174*, https://pure.mpg.de/rest/items/item_2353110/component/file_2353109/content.

Hann, Chris. 2018. Moral(ity And) Economy: Work, Workfare, And Fairness In Provincial Hungary. *European Journal Of Sociology* 59, 225–254, https://doi.org/10.1017/s000397561700056x.

Hoffmann, Dierk. 1999. Die Lenkung Des Arbeitsmarktes in Der SBZ/DDR 1945–1961: Phasen, Konzepte Und Instrumente. In: Peter Hübner and Klaus Tenfelde (eds). 1999. *Arbeiter in Der SBZ-DDR*. Essen: Klartext, pp. 41–80.

Jancius, Angela. 2006. Unemployment, Deindustrialization, and "Community Economy" in Eastern Germany. *Ethnos* 71 (2), 213–232, https://doi.org/10.1080/00141840600733694.

Jensen, Birgit A. 2005. Bawdy Bodies Or Moral Agency? The Struggle For Identity In Working-Class Autobiographies Of Imperial Germany. *Biography* 28, 534–557, https://doi.org/10.1353/bio.2006.0013.

Kocka, Jürgen. 2016. Bismarck Und Die Entstehung Des Deutschen Sozialstaats. *Francia. Forschungen Zur Westeuropäischen Geschichte* 43, 397–408.

Kohli, Martin. 1994. Die DDR Als Arbeitsgesellschaft? Arbeit, Lebenslauf Und Soziale Differenzierung. In: Hartmut Kaelble, Jürgen Kocka and Hartmut Zwahr (eds). 1994. *Sozialgeschichte Der DDR*. Stuttgart: Klett-Cotta, pp. 31–61.

Lüdtke, Alf. 1994. "Helden Der Arbeit"—Mühen Beim Arbeiten. Zur Mißmutigen Loyalität von Industriearbeitern in Der DDR. In: Hartmut Kaelble, Jürgen Kocka and Hartmut Zwahr (eds). 1994. *Sozialgeschichte Der DDR*. Stuttgart: Klett-Cotta, pp. 188–213.

Mau, Steffen. 2019. *Lütten Klein: Leben in Der Ostdeutschen Transformationsgesellschaft*. Berlin: Suhrkamp.

McCormack, Thelma. 1969. The Protestant Ethic and the Spirit of Socialism. *The British Journal of Sociology* 20 (3), 266–276, https://doi.org/10.2307/588952.

Mladenov, Teodor. 2017. From State Socialist to Neoliberal Productivism: Disability Policy and Invalidation of Disabled People in the Postsocialist Region. *Critical Sociology* 43 (7–8), 1109–1123, https://doi.org/10.1177%2F0896920515595843.

Parry, Jonathan. 2005. Industrial Work. In: James G. Carrier (ed.) 2005. *A Handbook of Economic Anthropology*. Cheltenham & Northampton: Edward Elgar Publishing, pp. 141–159.

Peperkamp, Esther. 2010. Between Menschlichkeit And Missionsbefehl: God, Work, And World Among Christians In Saxony. In: Esther Peperkamp and Malgorzata Rajtar (eds). *Religion and the Secular in Eastern Germany, 1945 to the Present*. Leiden: Brill, pp. 107–124, https://doi.org/10.1163/ej.9789004184671.i-224.40.

Pollack, Detlef and Hedwig Richter. 2012. Protestantische Theologie Und Politik in Der DDR, *De Gruyter Oldenbourg* 294.3, 687–720, https://doi.org/10.1524/hzhz.2012.0026.

Polanyi, Karl. 2001. *The Great Transformation: The Political and Economic Origins of Our Time*. Boston: Beacon Press.

Rajković, Ivan. 2017. For an Anthropology of the Demoralized: State Pay, Mock-Labour, and Unfreedom in a Serbian Firm. *Journal of the Royal Anthropological Institute* 24 (1), 47–70, https://doi.org/10.1111/1467-9655.12751.

Retallack, James. 2019. „Rotes Königreich" Oder Hort Des Konservatismus? Sachsen Im Späten Kaiserreich.I In: Konstantin Hermann, Mike Schmeitzner and Swen Steinberg (eds). 2019. *Der Gespaltene Freistaat. Neue Perspektiven Auf Die Sächsische Geschichte 1918 Bis 1933*. Leipzig: Leipziger Universitätsverlag, pp. 27–41.

Rudd, Elizabeth. 2006. Gendering Unemployment in Postsocialist Germany: 'What I Do Is Work, Even If It's Not Paid. *Ethnos* 71 (2), 191–212, https://doi. org/10.1080/00141840600733686.

Scott, James C. 1976. *The Moral Economy Of The Peasant: Rebellion And Subsistence In Southeast Asia*. New Haven: Yale University Press.

Scott, Tom. 1989. *Thomas Müntzer: Theology and Revolution in The German Reformation*. London: Palgrave Macmillan, https://doi.org/10.1007/978-1-349-20224-9.

Sinjen, Beke. 2013. "Prosa Der Verhältnisse": Die Entdeckung Der Erzählliteratur Durch Die Arbeiterbewegung (1863–1906). Unpublished doctoral thesis, University of Exeter, https://ore.exeter.ac.uk/repository/handle/10871/14937.

Swain, Adam. 2002. Broken Networks and a Tabula Rasa? "Lean Production", Employment and the Privatisation of the East German Automobile Industry.I In: Al Rainnie, Adrian Smith and Adam Swain (eds). 2002. *Work, Employment and Transition: Restructuring Livelihoods in Post-Communism*. London: Routledge, pp. 74–96.

Thompson, Edward P. 1971. The Moral Economy of The English Crowd in The Eighteenth Century. *Past & Present* 50 (1), 76–136, https://doi.org/10.1093/past/50.1.76.

Trappe, Heike. 2006. Lost in Transformation? Disparities of Gender and Age.I In: Martin Diewald, Anne Goedicke and Karl U. Mayer (eds). 2006. *After the Fall of the Wall: Life Courses in the Transformation of East Germany*. Stanford: Stanford University Press, pp. 116–139.

Turner, Lowell. 1998. *Fighting for Partnership: Labor and Politics in Unified Germany*. Ithaca: Cornell University Press.

7. Beyond Blue Eyes?

Xenophobia on the Eastern Margins of the European Union[1]

László Fosztó

Introduction

A distant observer of Romanian public events during the past decade could easily conclude that these years were complicated by political and social crises and that the population of this country has gone through a rather difficult period. It is rather telling that there were eleven prime ministers in and out of office between 2010 and 2020. Joining the European Union has proved to be a mixed blessing for Romania. While mass demonstrations, government crises, and moral panics unfolded almost without interruption, the overwhelming majority of Romanians have continued to express trust and positive attitudes towards the institutions of the European Union, even if they concur that these institutions are not interested in their opinion (Alexe 2019).[2] Most domestic commentators also agreed that 'joining the club' was the best possible geo-political trajectory for Romania. The sceptical

1   László Fosztó is Senior Researcher at the Romanian Institute for Research on National Minorities (ISPMN). During the completion of this chapter he benefited from a grant from the Romanian Ministry of Education and Research, CNCS—UEFISCDI, a project hosted by the Babeș-Bolyai University, number PN-III-P4-ID-PCE-2020-0338, within PNCDI III. The author would like to thank Agnieska Pasieka and Juraj Buzalka for their support and patience.

2   The 2020 Eurobarometer showed that around 60% of Romanians express trust in the European institutions which rates among the highest scores: https://ec.europa.eu/commfrontoffice/publicopinion/index.cfm/Survey/getSurveyDetail/yearFrom/1974/yearTo/020/surveyKy/2262.

outsider might maintain that the process of being absorbed into the larger political and economic structures had immediate negative effects, and that the transformations also entail significant, longer-term socio-political costs.

There are obviously immediate hardships related to massive population movement across open EU borders. Romanian labourers increasingly took up jobs abroad which, even if they promised higher wages, caused family ties to suffer from the separation, and consequently the work experience and job expectations of different generations diverged. There are other problems that spring from joining the common market. But the promise of a common socioeconomic space remained unfulfilled and the success was clouded by a sense of non-belonging. While these issues might be much less obviously connected with the aftermath of 'Europeanisation', they reared their ugly head very soon. Experiences of mobility were not always positive, and despite the nominal equality offered by the common EU citizenship, socio-cultural divisions became more salient than before. Being stigmatised and rejected abroad, or returning to an increasingly divided home society, was a common experience for many migrants. While ideas of (Western) civilisation, efficiency, progress, and wealth were hegemonically consolidated in the public sphere, increasing numbers of Romanians felt that they had fallen short of achieving their aspirations.

Mass migration from Romania began earlier following the change of the regime, but its negative effects peaked in this period. The Romanian countryside began to lose some of its most productive and mobile young inhabitants during the first decades of post-socialism, but even these migrants had some difficulties 'fitting in' in the destinations. After Romania's 2007 accession to the EU even the most underprivileged, including the large Romani population, could afford to try their luck abroad. The media headlines in the destination countries carried news of 'invasion of beggars, and criminals'. And Western governments took heavy-handed actions: most notably, the Italian coalition led by Berlusconi enacted a Nomad Emergency Decree (2008), which targeted inhabitants of the camps where Eastern European migrants were clustered (inhabitants were fingerprinted and selected prior to deportation), the Sarkozy administration in France started outright evictions and 'voluntary repatriations' of the Romanian Roma (2010). These policies not only violated EU citizenship prerogatives for free movement but also contributed to the heightening of anti-Roma sentiment, both in the host countries and at home.

The European Commission decided to act on this issue, urging nation-states to step up their efforts for the social inclusion of Roma populations, yet the local effectiveness of the European Framework on Roma Integration (2011–2020) to this day remains debatable. The main conclusion was that nation-states should take greater responsibility for the social integration of their Romani citizens (or at least keeping them home as much as possible), and report back annually to the commission on the progress achieved in improving their situation. Even if self-monitoring of the member states was regularly optimistic, the EU's own Agency for Fundamental Rights (FRA), in charge of monitoring, promoting, and protecting human rights, produced a report showing little evidence of progress. Michael O'Flaherty, the acting director of the FRA, in his introduction to this report, warned:

> The inability—or unwillingness—to address anti-Gypsyism in order to ensure equal opportunities for Roma is unacceptable. But an important opportunity lies ahead, as the 2011 EU Framework for National Roma Integration Strategies completes its cycle in 2020 and the EU will soon need to review it. Our analysis makes clear that the process of Roma inclusion cannot continue as 'business as usual'. It requires an honest and open debate on failures and a renewed stronger political commitment to fulfil the promise of the EU Framework "to make a tangible difference to Roma people's lives" (FRA 2018: 3).

At the moment of the publication of that report, the new 'policy cycle' was already on its way and placed the concept of anti-Gypsyism (a concept coined to describe manifestations of anti-Romani racism) at its core. The new EU Roma strategic framework for equality, inclusion and participation was published in October 2020 with detailed guidelines and an ambitious portfolio of indicators for progress.[3] It is anybody's guess how member states will adjust and implement their own policies to achieve these 'tangible differences'. In this chapter I argue that while focusing on and taking action against stigmatisation or other negative attitudes as vehicles of Roma exclusion is a necessary move, it is unlikely to be sufficient to tackle the broader problems in the regional socio-

---

3   https://ec.europa.eu/info/publications/new-eu-roma-strategic-framework-equality-inclusion-and-participation-full-package_en.

political landscape, including the rise of populist politics, increasing xenophobia, and more general social (dis)integration. The ability to understand and address xenophobia and anti-Gypsyism will be much enhanced if we look beyond legal definitions of human rights, without falling back on cultural explanations, or simply blaming it on racist attitudes of individuals. We need to address the socio-economic structures including the historical patterns of social interactions, inquire into the challenges brought about the European integration, and value opportunities, whilst also seeking to limit the disintegrative potential of the common market. In my argument I go back to the work of Karl Polanyi (Polanyi 1944), in an attempt to follow a recent call for "repatriating Polanyi" to Central-Eastern Europe (Hann 2019).

The empirical examples I present come from Transylvania and the issues I address are broad themes recurrently discussed by Chris Hann, to whom this volume is dedicated. The structure of the chapter is the following: the first section is a brief literature review on the role of ethnicity in the political economy of Romania, the second is a sketch on how a Polanyian approach might describe the persistent and emerging ethnic divisions in Romania, showing how ethnic diversity is embedded in economic relationships. While ethnicity was and remains an important part of the social fabric, it provides local modes for interaction which offer a buffer to local communities and through which exclusionary political rhetoric cannot easily penetrate and exacerbate xenophobia. Then in the third section, before concluding, I present some case studies of recent events.

Ethnicity, (Dis)Embeddedness, and the Roma

Ethnic categories have played an important role in the socio-economic organisation of Eastern European societies throughout different historical periods. In this section I will look at some of the rather abundant literature (although this will not be an exhaustive overview) and show how elements of a Polanyian analysis can be connected to existing models. The new mobility of the poor within the EU also renewed theoretical discussions of ethnicity, race, mobility, and social exclusion of certain EU citizens. Many recent analyses blame the continued exclusion of the Roma within the EU on the "racialisation" of the poor both at home (Vincze et al. 2019) and during the migration process (Yıldız and De Genova 2019). In these arguments ethno-racial categories are seen as products of socio-economic processes (and not as the root causes of exclusion). Therefore, they need to be analysed as part of the political economy of the society in which they appear and persist.

Structurally similar arguments have been around for some time, at least since the work of Nicolae Gheorghe and Sam Beck (Gheorghe 1983; Beck 1989) who described the process of racial exclusion as part of the historical processes and political economy of the Romanian principalities. Gheorghe and Beck not only identified roots of racism against the Roma in the economic history of premodern times, but also articulated a critique of the existing system for not being able to address the persistent "Gypsy problem" in the late socialist Romania (Beck 1985). Rather than being remains of the ancient past, socialist systems (or at least the Romanian version in its late phase) actively produced ethnic differences rather than integrating the members of society based on the "socialist citizenship" they professed.[4] At the official level, Roma, unlike other "cohabiting nationalities", did not receive any legal recognition during socialism. Their recognition instead emerged through institutional acts intended to deny and suppress their cultural presence (Fosztó 2018). The economic potential of the late socialist state sharply decreased during the 1980s and integrative efforts gave way to strict surveillance and obsessive xenophobia by the regime. In the late days of socialism, Romania was unable to offer positive responses to the existing cultural diversity of its population. The regime actively reproduced ethnic divisions and increasingly anti-Gypsy attitudes (Beck 1984). One could describe this period of desperate attempts at redistribution of decreasing resources, coupled with surveillance and oppression leading to alienation and xenophobia, as the disembedding effect of an excessive central-command economy, which can cause damage similar to the disruption brough about by the 'free-market', as Polanyi has argued (Hann 2009). The socialist transformation of the Romanian economy (collectivisation and industrialisation) and society (regional and local planning, the so called 'systematisation', destruction

---

4   Katherine Verdery (1991), approaching the issue from a different perspective, demonstrated how nationalism was an immanent part of the Romanian socialist regime.

of villages in order to create urban agglomerations, etc.) produced population displacement and enforced forms of mobility which created need, and called for a 'counter movement' similar to 'market-based' modernisations.

After the fall of socialism, 'market relations' were reintroduced to Romanian society, but ethnic divisions did not disappear. Democratic elections brought to the surface political divisions along ethnic lines (most saliently in the case of ethnic Hungarians) and the Roma continued to endure ethnic disadvantage and stigma. Romania's more state-controlled (neo-patrimonial) transition was ultimately more prolonged, and probably less painful, than for those countries that swallowed the bitter pill of the neoliberal solution such as privatisation of industry and services. Even so, as a large comparative research project led by Iván Szelényi has shown, by the end of the first decade of post-socialism, new patterns of social exclusion had emerged alongside the consolidation of the market economy (Ladányi and Szelényi 2006). Roma in Romania, similarly to other Romani populations in the region, were suffering even worse forms of exclusion than before. By this time the project of the European Union was being touted as embodying the 'Four Freedoms' (free movement of goods, capital, services and persons). Romania joined the EU and completed its transition to more neoliberal forms of integration, while the outlook for the Roma was negative (Sigona and Trehan 2009) and even extended new forms of xenophobia at a larger scale (Stewart 2012). The exclusion suffered by Roma is not exclusively a problem of their home societies, as illustrated by the moral scandal at the sight of Roma beggars on the streets of Western European cities. As Keith Hart, talking about beggars, observes: "they infringe the dominant narrative of responsibility and autonomy: they provide a bad symbol of the free-market society that must be presented as inevitable"(Hart 2016: 247).

In the next section I will review some of the regional and socio-ethnic divisions in Romania. These divisions are neither new, nor are they the consequence of EU accession. They have persisted and been reproduced throughout history since the Middle Ages; they are not only a legacy of the past but are also constitutive of existing solidarities and divisions in the present. They have roots in historical forms of integration and provide embeddedness at both local and regional levels. These forms of integration are far from vanishing or being replaced by ideologies promoted by the (capitalist or socialist) nation-state, so it is unsurprising that they are also re-emerging in the new context.

"The Two Romanias" and Emerging New (Dis)Integration

The maps showing the results of the first post-socialist election renewed arguments that in fact there are 'multiple Romanias'. The formula postulating the existence of "the two Romanias" goes back to intellectual discussions in the interwar period (see Butoi 2014 for the case of Mircea Vulcănescu), and the idea that more than one Romania exists had a clear undertone of social critique, and usually emerged from desires and appeals to dissolve regional, ethno-social and other divisions in favour of a more unitary, socially even, and economically just national society. Still, the divisions have proved stubborn, and many would argue that they are a constitutive part of this society. These structures persist due to the unequal levels of development in different regions and for different social groups, which in turn are rooted in the peripheral integration of the country in European capitalist markets during the nineteenth century (Stahl 1980). To phrase it in Polanyian terms, ethno-social divisions are the main form of embeddedness of Romanian economic relations. After the fall of the socialism, divisions between Transylvania and the rest of the country became more salient, but a general rural / urban divide was also quite apparent. Each consecutive election reminded commentators of the persistence of these divisions, which also largely corresponded with political attitudes.

Historically, the 'first of the Romanias' was shorthand for the cosmopolitan urban centres, which were home to large numbers of ethnically non-Romanian inhabitants (mainly Jewish, Greek, Armenian, Hungarian and German minorities). The 'second of the Romanias' denoted the rural and 'backward' majority of Romanian peasants, whose existence was dominated by religion and tradition. The presence of 'foreigners' in the cities fuelled ideologies which presented modernisation or progressive politics as alien to the 'national soul', which was considered more characteristic of the villages. This backward-looking discourse became a popular tool of the extreme right, which culminated in the legionary movement, and harnessed strong support from students and young urban intellectuals. The cities became battlegrounds for interwar national policies to take modernisation further alongside Romanisation. The Romanisation of the cities acquired a renewed momentum during the late socialist industrialisation. This period also saw an increase in the emigration of Romania's remaining Jewish and German populations, and as a result Romanian cities are much more ethnically homogenous today, even if some regional differences remain. The most intense transformation of the Romanian countryside happened during the early socialist period, in the collectivisation of agriculture (Kligman and Verdery 2011). While the process was, to many villagers, painful if not disastrous, it did not result in the more cohesive and unitary rural Romania that had been hoped for. In both the urban and rural transformations, one could easily identify state-driven efforts to increase centrality and redistribution, which aimed not only at a more economically equal but also a more ethnically homogenous population. However, redistribution (and regional investment) was not channelled evenly and certain regions were 'left behind'. The most conspicuous point of difference on the map remains the largely rural area of eastern Transylvania, the Szeklerland, where two thirds of the 1.2 million ethnic Hungarians live. With an unfavourable landscape for intensive agriculture, mountainous and with temperatures much lower than the country average, Szeklerland has become known in public discussions as an ethnic enclave in Romania's least developed region. Certainly, most inhabitants of the region do not share this view.

Conversely, they are proud of their particularities, and would argue that the maintenance of historical, social, and ethnic structures are the region's main resources. From an inhabitants' perspective, Szeklerland continues to be a stronghold of the Hungarian ethnic identity and locally rooted social structures, and this region is the primary constituency for Hungarian ethnic votes in national and European elections. Since the fall of socialism unemployment was high and outmigration from the region also intensified. During the early first years of post-socialism, Hungary was a popular destination. Today, Western EU member states (Austria, Germany, etc.) are much more attractive for financial reasons. The role of the Hungarian state has undergone a series of transformations thanks to the renewed waves of investment (both financial and ideological) during the Orbán governments of the past decade. Inhabitants of the region follow Hungarian-language media (made in Hungary), and are also consumers of global culture. Members of the younger generations (those who grew up after conscription was abolished) regularly speak better English than Romanian. Each summer, poor grades in the school leaving exam, particularly in Romanian language and literature, renew debates on the inefficiency of teaching of the 'national language' in the Szeklerland.

The recent dynamics among German ethnic citizens are even more intriguing. The remaining ethnic community is relatively small (about 36,000), however native German-language education flourishes in the former Saxon cities and towns.[5] Most of the students in these schools are of ethnic Romanian origins (or are local Hungarians in the case of the Swabian region of Satu Mare / Szatmár). There is an ongoing reinvention of 'Germanness' in the absence of ethnic Germans (Oltean, Anghel, and Schuster 2017; Cercel 2019). As a result of this process, there are close to one thousand high-school (lyceum) graduates each year who have followed a full German curriculum. Schooling children in German could be seen as a pragmatic decision by parents who want to equip their children with language skills and a valuable diploma for accessing the job market in Austria or Germany, but in fact many of these graduates do not leave the country. They are increasingly securing jobs in new local associations and businesses, which are flourish thanks to the investments pouring in from Germany.

In the adoption (at least partly) of an affiliation to German culture, a broader integrative process is underway. Parents invest massively in elaborate school leavers' ceremonies, and whole families increasingly participate in the general renaissance of local rituals connected to Saxon traditions. This reinvented Germanness is embedded in and supported by the Lutheran Church. Many old Saxon church buildings are renovated with donations from and voluntary participation of returning migrants, or the (at least temporarily) remigrating children of those who left Romania in the late socialist period. The whole process can be understood as taming market forces and re-embedding the process

---

5   In the academic year 2019–2020 there were about 15,000 students enrolled in primary school (Grades 1–8), and an additional 3,500 in high school (Grades 9–12). http://www.fdgr.ro/ro/statistici/612; http://www.fdgr.ro/ro/statistici/613.

within a more 'Europeanised' Romania. The embedding process is also hosted and indirectly supported by the public schools designed for the German ethnic minority.

Roma are not clustered in a particular region, unlike the minorities discussed previously; they live all over Romania, although there is a relatively larger proportion of Roma in Transylvanian counties. In terms of the urban-rural divide, a slight majority of Roma still live in villages or small towns as opposed to cities. This demographic aspect is significant, since historically the economic practices of Roma society have always been embedded in exchanges with non-Roma neighbours (most often local peasants). Because they have been excluded from owning land, they have rarely developed a 'rooted' local agriculture, and Roma groups have most often specialised in mobile services and trading in goods which were not produced by peasant society. The Romani conception of self-sufficiency prioritises the cultivation of social relations with members of the majority society as opposed to an ideal of economic autarchism through agriculture (see Brazzabeni, Cunha, and Fotta 2016).

The traditional spread of Romani groups can also be explained in terms of their enhanced interaction with non-Roma populations. Territorial separateness most often takes the form of segregated settlements in proximity to the majority. Today, these settlements are characterised by a lack of infrastructure, overcrowding in poor housing conditions, overpolicing, and difficulties in accessing public services. Even if some urban Roma settlements take the form of urban ethnic ghettoes, most impoverished areas are ethnically mixed, with Roma and non-Roma living side by side. These settlements are often stigmatised as 'Gypsy neighbourhoods' or 'țigănie'. Social exclusion, economic disadvantage and racialised identity are all imposed on inhabitants of these segregated settlements and the main channel by which families can escape exclusion is to move out of the segregated settlement. Due to this ethnic stigma and racial exclusion, Romani ethnicity is underreported in the census (official figures show 621,500 Roma vs. an estimated 1.8 or 2 million population). Their dispersal all over the country means a wide diversity of Roma groups. Some of these groups are more assimilated, whilst others continue to maintain their own approaches to community integration. Many Roma are bilingual (speaking Romani and Romanian equally well), yet several other communities speak additional languages. Hungarian (in Transylvania) or Turkish (in the South) are most frequent, but because of the recent migration and return, speakers of Spanish, Italian, or English are not rare either. The example of Szeklerland and the (historically) German regions shows that ethnic categories are not only a part and product of the economic structures, but they also maintain the social embeddedness of economic relations. Ethnicity and language skills are salient human categories and skills in Eastern Europe (as well as elsewhere). The dynamics of these categories are diverse and particular to the particular group. For instance, in Szeklerland we see a history of social closure , while in the case of the renaissance of Germanness, this group is seen as prestigious and worthy of repopulation, while in the case of the Roma we see a variable and resourceful combination of different social skills, and an ability to live in a wide variety of regional and social configurations.

Roma political parties (traditionally allied with the socialists) harness few votes and do not make great efforts to reach out to the ethnic community. But a large number of short livedassociations, foundations, and NGOs who claim to work with and for the benefit of the poor Roma. State support, and more recently, funds from the EU or the EEA and Norway Grants, are channelled through the civic sector. Some of these organisations disappear as soon as projects end and funding dries up, while many others continue to respond to the community's needs even in situations where public services provided by the state should already be in place. The state apparatus has also developed local and regional structures for addressing the needs of the Roma (there are Roma experts in each county's local government, and local mediators for health and education, etc.). In Polanyian terms, one could argue that this is a beneficial process as the redistributive efforts of the state are seeking to embed its workings in local relations, however there are also examples of the opposite: there is an ongoing centralisation of institutions on the promise of increased efficacy (and subordination to ethno-political goals) at the expense of local embeddedness. The territorial offices of the National Agency for Roma were dissolved, and the associated posts were relocated to the central office, located in Bucharest, in 2018. Obviously, ethnic categories are not the only categories that articulate the political-economic space: they act in conjunction with other social categories. Ideological divisions are present, and the Social Democratic Party (PSD—the reformed heir of the Communist Party), the largest parliamentary party, is usually central to the political arena. PSD has deep roots in the rural regions, and mainly dominates in the southern and eastern parts of Romania. Another permanent presence on the scene is the Liberals who exist in various different guises (PNL, PD, ALDE). The extreme right of the political spectrum has been virtually uninhabited for at least a decade since the Greater Romania Party (GRP) failed to enter Parliament in 2008 and subsequently faded into insignificance Some of its most vocal politicians were absorbed into mainstream parties.[6] In addition to the main parties, different forms of protest movements entered the political arena during this period: from the more ecologically inclined (protesters against mining in Roșia Montana), through to proponents of civic radicalism and those demanding stronger anti-corruption measures (i.e. Save Romania Union).

The connection between ethnic and ideological divisions seems conjunctural. None of the mainstream parties has a clear positive agenda related to ethnic or national minorities, nor are their agendas consistently nationalistic in orientation. On the contrary, most Romanian parties readily enter governing coalitions with the Hungarian ethnic party, the DAHR (Democratic Alliance of Hungarians in Romania). Even if outright far-right arguments rarely surface in mainstream politics, elements of xenophobic discourse are always at hand. Some of the top ranked and most popular politicians come from ethnic minority backgrounds (German, Hungarian, Tatar, or even Palestinian from Syria).[7]

---

6   For example, former president of the youth organisation and spokesperson of the Greater Romania party Lia Olguța Vasilescu entered the Social Democrat Party, was elected as a senator, became the Mayor of Craiova, and later even served as Minister of Labour (2017–2018).

7   To name a few of the most visible: Klaus Iohannis is a 'West-oriented and liberal' Transylvanian Saxon who is serving his second term as President of Romania. Ludovic Orban is another prominent liberal (Prime Minister between November 2019 and December 2020), born in Brașov to an ethnic Hungarian father and Romanian mother. Despite her name, Laura Codruța Kövesi, head prosecutor of the National Anticorruption Directorate (2013–2018) who has since acted as European Chief Prosecutor (from late 2019) is an ethnic Romanian who married and later divorced a Hungarian, but kept his name. There are many Hungarians in high public office, and a few Roma, such as former State Secretary in the Ministry

Ethnic stigma is used largely opportunistically, and xenophobic arguments are spearheads of political arguments. Even if this practice is not without its dangers, the xenophobia rarely penetrates local ethnic relations. The socio-economic context for ethnic relations embeds interactions in the historically established pattern. The fragility of ethnic peace is apparent (at least in the upper echelons of politics). One can follow the recurrent anti-Semitism (mainly in the forms of Holocaust denial and the cult of 'interwar heroes'), or instances of anti-Hungarian and anti-Gypsy rhetoric. In early 2020 both the acting (Klaus Iohannis) and the previous (Trăian Băsescu) presidents were fined by the National Council for Combating Discrimination for anti-Hungarian and anti-Gypsy speech respectively.[8] Some politicians stir domestic and diplomatic outrage with anti-German remarks (i.e. associating Klaus Iohannis with the national-socialist regime) and posting Hitler-moustached representations of the President on social media.[9]

These attempts to denigrate the President and stigmatise Germans proved to have little effect. Quite the opposite: the renaissance of Germanness is visible in the growing numbers of local councillors and even mayors elected by those towns where the number of Germans had decreased in the past decades. The consequences of emphasising ethnic categories (and those populations who identify with these categories) are far-reaching. At the level of human labour, which Polanyi identifies as one of the fictitious commodities, ethnic categories act as social anchors. They also shape the political sphere, for example the Hungarian party routinely relies on ethnic votes (even if there are signs of decline in the trend of ethnic Hungarians voting as a block). It also has broader

---

of European Funds Ciprian Necula, or Valeriu Nicolae, former State Secretary in the Ministry of Labour. There are also others, like Raed Afarat, a Syrian-born Palestinian physician who studied in Romani during late socialism, stayed in the country, and became popular as the founder of a medical emergency service (SMURD). He was briefly in the Ministry of Health, then continued to serve as State Secretary in several consecutive governments. Another Muslim politician served as Ministry for Development and Vice-Prime Minister in a socialist government: Sevil Shhaideh (née Geambec) is an economist of Dobrudjan Turkish and Crimean Tartar origins, married to a Syrian businessman. She was even proposed for the role of Prime Minister, but the President refused to name her due to her husband's links to Bashar al-Assad.

8 See https://www.romania-insider.com/cncd-fine-romanian-president-hungarians.

9 See https://balkaninsight.com/2018/09/05/romanian-ruling-party-faces-criticism-over-nazi-statements-09-05-2018/.

political relevance since not only ethnic elites, but all kinds of other political entrepreneurs seek to capitalise on ethnic categories to garner support for themselves or to identify 'enemies' and scaremonger against them. However, the connection between the local expressions and lived experiences of ethnic relations and the instrumentalist categories of nationalist politics is not simple and straightforward, as Rogers Brubaker and his co-authors (Brubaker et al. 2006) have demonstrated in the case of Cluj-Napoca. Taking this insight further with a Polanyian twist, I will argue that ethnicity and historical patterns of ethnic relations embedded in the socio-economic sphere act as a shield for local interactions, deflecting (or at least filtering) politically motivated xenophobic arguments. It would be misleading to idealise the role of ethnicity in this social process. While one can see that the established patterns can serve as means of resistance to nationalistic scaremongering, the economy of embedded ethnic relations also perpetuates historical injustices and reproduces inequalities.

Therefore, it would be wrong to expect these historic forms of embedded ethnic relations to contribute to anything other than the re-assignment of the most vulnerable minorities to inferior positions, and these positions, in the case of Eastern European Roma, are in the margins, riven with negative ethnic prejudice, and even historically racialised. Even if arguably the most excluded ethnic category, Roma are not alone as targets of prejudice. A more recent population group who can be seen as displaced from the ethical ecology of Romanian society is the emerging Western diaspora. Migratory processes during the past decade have consolidated a new social category which can be defined by its new form of territorial arrangement and symbolic attachments. The emergence of the diaspora of 3–4 million Romanians within the wider EU over the past decades has generated a new socio-economic actor with a distinct political identity. The employment of this group is very diverse (with high numbers of medical doctors and nurses, students of all disciplines, skilled workers, and domestic care workers, builders and seasonal agricultural hands, etc.), but they are routinely portrayed in the Romanian public sphere as low-skilled workers seeking employment in low-class jobs abroad, thus turning the 'diaspora' into a rather stigmatised social identity. They live outside the reach of institutions (except for churches), and they often express deep discontent regarding mainstream domestic politics. The political attitudes of the diaspora first became an issue of public discussion during the two rounds of presidential elections in 2014. During the first round, thousands of Romanian citizens waited in long lines in front of the Romanian embassies in London, Berlin, Paris and the consulates in Munich, Turin and Barcelona. At the end of the day, many of them still remained on the streets and had not been able to vote. The two top candidates were Victor Ponta, the Prime Minister in office, who enjoyed the support of the territorially well-organised socialist party (PSD) governing Romania with a comfortable two-thirds coalition, and his challenger Klaus Iohannis, Mayor of the city of Sibiu, a much lesser-known politician with a German ethnic background (Transylvanian Saxon) supported by the Christian Liberal Alliance, a composite of his National Liberal Party, the Democratic Liberal Party, and the small Civic Alliance. As the first round of voting brought a rather comfortable 10% advantage for Victor Ponta (he obtained 40.4%), he and his party were looking forward to the second round with confidence.

The second round of voting had a similar outcome for 'the diaspora' whose many members would be denied their de facto right to vote. But the short period between the two rounds brought about a game-changing process. The Romanians abroad voted massively for Iohannis, but that brought in some 300,000 votes. The real change happened within the boundaries of Romania itself, and Iohannis ultimately doubled his supporters, totalling more than 6.28 million votes (54,4%)in the runoff. We could conclude from this example that migrants sent something else back home, along with their usual financial remittances, such that the friends and relatives of disenfranchised migrants voted in protest. The transnational transfer of attitudes and solidarity is complex: family ties, local identities, and ethno-national allegiance all play a role. Individuals are reconnected in intricate forms rather than simply being disembedded by migratory mobility. It is also clear that traditional forms of local ethnic interactions lose their force and relevance in migratory contexts. We can expect ideological and political messages to reach this segment of society even in the absence of traditional institutional channels. The diaspora continued to play a public role in the waves of anti-corruption protests during 2017–2019, culminating in a large 'diaspora at home' protest on 10 August 2018, which was violently dispersed by the Romanian

Gendarmerie. More recently, protest votes in the diaspora have taken a xenophobic turn: during the parliamentary election in December 2020 about 26% of Romanians abroad lent their support to a neo-fascist party (AUR) which has just entered Parliament (with 9%).

The preliminary conclusion from these observations is that ethnic categories have not lost their importance during the period discussed. The ethnic embeddedness of local economic ties remain a prominent social feature in Romania and the persistence and re-emergence of local ethnic categories can filter, diffuse, or deflect ideological and xenophobic messages that come from the higher echelons of politics. The existence of embedded historical ethnic divisions is a limiting condition rather than a factor that feeds xenophobic tendencies. Ethnic relations can stand for local forms of tolerance and civility, so turning local relations into more antagonistic, political relations not at all easy for politicians.[10] Moreover, the visible popular protest movements are very diverse, and therefore cannot simply be categorised as a reactionary countermovement. For example, the popular reaction against limiting the voting rights of Romanians abroad during the 2014 presidential election paralleled protests from liberal-minded, middle-class citizens against the hegemonic and cynical politics of the ruling socialist government.

In the following section I continue to present examples focused at the local level. I intend to show how local relations pose limiting conditions for outside interventions, including xenophobic messages. My focus will be on the ethnic Hungarian community, and its relationship with imaginary and real migrants, as well as the local Romani population in the new context.

Racialised Encounters with or without Migrants

During the summer of 2015 we conducted fieldwork in a Transylvanian village where Roma, Romanians and Hungarians were living. Our

---

10   The conspicuous popular absenteeism during the referendum, which was initiated by the Alliance for the Family in aid of a more exclusive redefinition of marriage as a 'union between a man and a woman' in the constitution, shows that anti-gay arguments failed to mobilise support, even if churches (with the exception of the Lutheran Church) endorsed and promoted the agenda and priests urged believers to vote.

research was focused on issues related to the recent mobility of the Roma. Local Hungarians discussed with approval the mobility of the local Roma and their return with goods and skills acquired abroad (see Toma, Tesăr, and Fosztó 2018). During our stay in the village in August 2015, locals, with increasing concern, followed the Hungarian media coverage of and commentary on the 'migration crisis', which was illustrated with abundant images of the refugees camping in front of the Keleti Railway station in Budapest. The locals noted that these migrants' parallels with Roma made them familiar and even likeable, although their arrival was very much framed as an 'invasion of migrants'. The images of the imaginary migrants grew darker as time passed.

Just one month later, the Hungarian government announced its intention to extend the border fence built to 'secure Europe' between Hungary and Serbia to include a portion of the Romanian-Hungarian border. The leader of the ethnic Hungarian party in Romania was quick to comment that this fence was not meant to separate Romanians from Hungarians and that the border would remain open for regular traffic. He added that the fence might even "be helpful for Romania", by discouraging migrants from planning to enter the EU though the country.[11] This xenophobic politics quickly found an audience, at least within the political sphere, and later in an increasing segment of the Hungarian-language media. The scaremongering against refugees gained new momentum when the government, led by Viktor Orbán, announced its intention in early 2016 to organise a referendum to block the allocation of refugees according to quotas proposed by the European Union. In line with the emerging anti-refugee campaign which followed the announcement, a local newspaper (*Székely Hírmondó*) reported on an 'incident' from a predominantly Hungarian town in Transylvania, Sfântu Gheorghe (Hu: Sepsiszentgyörgy). Reportedly, a dark-skinned male was spotted on the streets of the town and locals called the emergency number, scared of the 'migrant'. Other press outlets picked up the story, some of them criticising the anti-migrant campaign and mocking the Hungarian locals for their racism and fear on seeing a single black person (Balázsi-Pál 2016a). The online portal then published a correction with

---

11 https://www.maszol.ro/index.php/belfold/53061-kelemen-hunor-a-kerites-nem-a-romanokat-es-a-magyarokat-valasztja-el-egymastol.

a notice that the person who had called the emergency services had phoned the journalist up to say that there was indeed a refugee there, but nobody feared him, and that they had called emergency services because they were worried about the poor man, who admitted not to have any money, and that he hadn't eaten, and didn't have any shelter from the cold, mid-February night (Balázsi-Pál 2016b).

This sequence of events is illustrative of the different levels of interpretation and their multiplicity; while the first article (which has since been deleted) fell in line with the Orbán government's campaign, the second was critical of it, introducing the motive of 'racism'. The second article's commentary immediately called for a local refusal, and demands for clarification led to the third article. This sequence shows that far from there being a direct connection between political xenophobic messages and their local effects, encounters with real migrants might not immediately trigger the intended frightened reactions from citizens. The interpretive frames of the media were also reshaped as this story unfolded. The media campaign, originating from Hungary, reached and had an impact on the public sphere of the Hungarian-language press in Romania.

The process was evident once again in another incident (in August 2016), when a Hungarian-language county newspaper (*Háromszék*) was reporting on how locals celebrated the local feast in a small mountain village inhabited mainly by Hungarians, named Comandău (Hu: Komandó). The locality is situated high in the mountains at the eastern fringe of Transylvania, and its name derives from the term 'Grenzkommando', since it was founded as a border outpost under the Austro-Hungarian monarchy. As part of the village celebration, a dramatic scene about the 'migrant crisis' featuring schoolchildren was presented. A group of children hid in a small van as the "Syrian ice cream lorry" broke through the *Grenzkommando*, but was stopped by other children, who were acting as border guards. The 'illegal migrants' discovered in the van put up a fight, leading to a "spontaneous demonstration demanding Euros, women, and Germany". Finally, they were all loaded on to a train on the narrow-gauge railway (a symbol of the village's industrial heritage) and sent to "the Mutti", so local order was ultimately restored. This scene was most likely intended as a humorous social commentary, and was reported as such in the newspaper (Bokor

2016). It was obviously inspired by the anti-migrant media campaign from Hungary and made rather denigratory references to victims of human smuggling (the refrigerator lorry was a direct reference to a human smuggling tragedy that led to seventy-one deaths in 2015).[12] The event attracted harsh criticism from Transylvanian intellectuals and journalists for falling into the trap of a hate-mongering campaign, for the very questionable taste of the adults who had organised the whole thing, and for the irresponsibility of teachers putting their students (among them children of the local Roma playing the part of migrants) through the degrading scene (Magyari 2016; Parászka 2016; Szilágyi N. 2016). The paper that had published the original account (*Háromszék*) decided to block further public discussion, and warned against casting collective blame on the local community of Comandău (see Szilágyi N. 2016). Responses to the event were echoed in the media in Hungary but did not cross the language barrier into the Romanian press. Another xenophobic incident that garnered national media attention in Romania took place years later (January 2020) in Ditrău (Hu: Gyergyóditró), within the region inhabited by Szeklers. In the locality of about 5,000 the local bread factory decided to hire two bakers from Sri Lanka. A group of locals engaged in a heated discussion on social media, peppered with anti-immigrant hate speech and threats directed toward both the migrants and the owner of the bakery. Under the leadership of the local Catholic priest, these individuals mounted a protest movement and collected signatures against the idea of employing workers from abroad, which were handed in to the local council. Some argued that the racialised conflict overlapped with the exploitation of workers, since the bakery had been unable to find local employees to work in the same conditions, and therefore sought to recruit foreigners (Sipos 2020).

The event was extensively discussed in the press and an entry was even created on Wikipedia to summarise its details.[13] It became clear that similar instances of xenophobia against migrant workers had occurred in other regions of Romania, but in this case discontent with the appearance of foreign labourers was clearly articulated in terms of 'cultural' and

---

12   https://www.theguardian.com/world/2015/aug/28/more-than-70-dead-austria-migrant-truck-tragedy.

13   https://en.wikipedia.org/wiki/2020_Ditr%C4%83u_xenophobic_incident.

racial difference. The dispute potentially serves as an example of the potential for xenophobic arguments to be more controversial than the actual presence of disembedding economic forces. The 'Ditrău incident' turned into an emblem of the effects of xenophobic politics and racialised economic conflicts in Romania. Its occurrence in the context of the Hungarian local majority, which nevertheless forms a minority within the whole of Romania, revealed the dangers of exclusionary dynamics. There are an increasing number of voices among these ethnic Hungarians speaking against xenophobia, and one could conclude that diversity at different levels of society can reduce hate-mongering. Even certain individuals previously attracted to policies and ideas promoted by the Orbán government and the divisive political sphere of Hungary joined in to reject hate speech. Returning to the case of migrant and returning Roma presented at the beginning of this section, in our analysis of the field data we found that in most cases returnees are in a better situation (both in terms of skills, local ties, and finances) to negotiate their local repositioning within the socio-economic fabric. Strategies might differ, for instance in some cases these individuals conform with local social categories and cultural styles, while in other cases they contrast with them (Toma and Fosztó 2018). What seems to be rather widespread is the notion that the ethnic embeddedness of the local economy is not vanishing, even if its categories could be challenged by the new phenomena related to migration and return. The Roma could hardly escape from their position at the margins of local society, yet in spite of this, there are cases where we can witness social mobility that has reshaped the social and physical landscape of certain localities (Toma 2020). Better houses, more visible presence in the local public sphere, and new forms of exchange are slowly remodelling the age-old forms of exclusion. In the most positive cases, the new circumstances offer a reshaped embeddedness of the enhanced economic practices brought about by the new European mobility.

In Lieu of Conclusion: Refocus on the Local

At the beginning of this chapter I referred to a recent report of the European Union Agency for Fundamental Rights (FRA) and its appeal to make "a tangible difference to Roma people's lives" by public policy interventions. My intention in this text was to show that there are potentials for this transformation even if it is far from an easy task. I hope to demonstrate that anthropological analysis can contribute to this by bringing to the foreground the locally embedded nature of economic exchanges, and warning against the perils of pushing forward disembedding economic forces or transformative attempts, no matter if their origin is redistributive centrality or the state (as has been the case during most of the twentieth century in Romania) or the putatively impersonal logic of the market (as we witness increasingly during the past decades within Romania). In any case, lasting improvements to the social position of the vulnerable can only be achieved if the economic relations will be integrated and embedded into the local social life, which is most often marked by ethnic divisions. I argued that ethnicity in Transylvania, but more broadly in Romania, was historically, and remains today, a means of local embeddedness which maintains human categories and rules of interactions, and anchors local socio-economic exchanges. We should not view ethnic categories as representations exclusively dividing society, but should also see them as part of local social integration which can stand against the excesses of xenophobic attempts by centres of power. Ethnic relations in local communities can stand for local forms of tolerance and civility. Transforming these local relations into more antagonistic political forms is not always as easy as politicians engaged in nationalistic propaganda would wish. Policy interventions need to take account of the integrative and solidarity-generating aspects of ethnic and local identities. I also showed that Roma are rarely assigned advantageous positions by these local categories due to the ethnic and racial prejudices that they suffer.

So will these local relations offer shelter from increasingly xenophobic political messages and rising anti-Gypsyism from the media? Will it be possible, during a period where we see a general disembedding due to market forces, for local society to counteract the exclusionary tendencies? I am moderately optimistic and only hope that an embedded economy in local relations, categories, and interactions will enable a more general protection of human dignity, social rights, and solidarity. To make this happen, analysis and policies cannot continue to remain at the level of international organisations, and states must refocus on the local by taking account of the existing realities and potential on the ground.

References

Alexe, Anca. 2019. Spring Eurobarometer Shows Romanians Continue to Have Positive View of EU, but Most Don't Think Their Voice Counts in the Union. *Business Review. Where Romania Talks Business*, 25 April 2019, https://business-review.eu/news/spring-eurobarometer-shows-romanians-continue-to-have-positive-view-of-eu-but-most-dont-think-their-voice-counts-in-the-union-200069.

Balázsi-Pál, Előd. 2016a. Egy szinesbőrű férfi megáll az utcán Sepsiszentgyörgyön. Mi történeik? [A Person of Colour Stops on the Steet of Sfântu Gheorghe. What's Going On?]. Transidex, 2 November 2016, https://bpelod.transindex.ro/?cikk=1203&egy_szinesboru_ferfi_megall_az_utcan_sepsiszentgyorgyon._mi_tortenik.

Balázsi-Pál, Előd. 2016b. Mégis menekült járt Sepsin, és segítettek rajta [There Was Indeed a Refugee in Sfântu. And They Helped Him]. Transindex, 11 February 2016, https://bpelod.transindex.ro/?cikk=1205&megis_menekult_jart_sepsin_es_segitettek_rajta.

Beck, Sam. 1984. Ethnicity, Class, and Public Policy: Țiganii/Gypsies in Socialist Romania. In: Kot K. Shangriladze and Erica W. Townsend (eds). 1984. *Papers for the V. Congress of Southeast European Studies, Belgrade, September 1984*. Columbus, OH: Slavica Publishers, pp. 19–38.

Beck, Sam. 1985. The Romanian Gypsy Problem. In: Joanne Grumet (ed.) 1985. *Papers from the Fourth and Fifth Annual Meetings, Gypsy Lore Society, North American Chapter*. New York: Gypsy Lore Society, North American Chapter, pp. 100–109.

Beck, Sam. 1989. The Origins of Gypsy Slavery in Romania. *Dialectical Anthropology* 14 (1), 53–61.

Bokor, Gábor. 2016. Sikeres falunapok Kommandón. *Háromszék*, 8 August 2016, https://www.3szek.ro/load/cikk/94082/sikeres_falunapok_kommandon.

Brazzabeni, Micol, Manuela Ivone Cunha and Martin Fotta (eds). 2016. *Gypsy Economy. Romani Livelihoods and Notions of Worth in the 21th Century*. New York; Oxford: Berghahn Books.

Brubaker, Rogers, Margit Feischmidt, Jon Fox and Liana Grancea. 2006. *Nationalist Politics and Everyday Ethnicity in a Transylvanian Town*. Princeton: Princeton University Press.

Butoi, Ionuț. 2014. 'Cele două Românii': Originile și contextul unei formule controversate ['The Two Romanias': The Origins and the Context of a Controversial Formula]. *Sociologie Românească* 12 (1–2), 18–31.

Cercel, Cristian. 2019. *Romania and the Quest for European Identity. Philo-Germanism without Germans*. London: Routledge.

Fosztó, László. 2018. Was There a 'Gypsy Problem' in Socialist Romania. From Suppressing 'Nationalism' to Recognition of a National Minority. *Studia Universitatis Babeş-Bolyai Sociologia* 63 (2), 117–140. DOI: 10.2478/subbs-2018-0014

FRA. 2018. *A Persisting Concern: Anti-Gypsyism as a Barrier to Roma Inclusion.* Luxemburg: Publications Office of the European Union.

Gheorghe, Nicolae. 1983. Origins of Roma Slavery in the Romanian Principalities. *Roma* 7, 12–27.

Hann, Chris. 2009. Embedded Socialism? Land, Labor, and Money in Eastern Xinjiang. In: Chris Hann and Keith Hart (eds). 2009. *Market and Society: The Great Transformation Today.* Cambridge: Cambridge University Press, pp. 256–271.

Hann, Chris. 2019. *Repatriating Polanyi. Market Society in the Visegrád States.* Budapest ; New York: Central European University Press.

Hart, Keith. 2016. Afterword. In: Micol Brazzabeni, Manuela Ivone Cunha and Martin Fotta (eds). 2016. *Gypsy Economy. Romani Livelihoods and Notions of Worth in the 21th Century.* New York; Oxford: Berghahn Books, pp. 240–250.

Kligman, Gail and Katherine Verdery. 2011. *Peasants under Siege: The Collectivization of Romanian Agriculture, 1949–1962.* Princeton: Princeton University Press.

Ladányi, János and Iván Szelényi. 2006. *Patterns of Exclusion: Constructing Gypsy Ethnicity and the Making of an Underclass in Transitional Societies of Europe.* Boulder, CO; New York: East European Monographs: Distributed by Columbia University Press.

Magyari, Nándor László. 2016. Kommandó, végállomás? [Comandău, End of the Line?]. *Bukaresti Rádió*, 9 August 2016, https://www.bukarestiradio.ro/2016/08/09/kommando-vegallomas/.

Oltean, Ovidiu, Remus Gabriel Anghel and Christian Schuster (eds). 2017. *Reinvenând Germanitatea. Etnicizare, mobilitate şi împrumut cultural la marginea Europei* [Reinventing Germanity. Ethnicity, Mobility and Cultural Borrowing at the European Margins]. Tritonic: Bucharest.

Parászka, Boróka. 2016. Kommandó, a terápia [Comandău, the Therapy]. *Erdélyi Riport*, 10 August 2016, http://erdelyiriport.ro/publicisztika/kommando-a-terapia.

Polanyi, Karl. 1944. *The Great Transformation. The Political and Economic Origins of Our Time.* Boston: Beacon Press.

Sigona, Nando and Nidhi Trehan (eds). 2009. *Romani Politics in Contemporary Europe: Poverty, Ethnic Mobilization, and the Neoliberal Order.* London: Palgrave Macmillan UK.

Sipos, Zoltán. 2020. Anti-Migrants Hate Speech at Ditrău / Gyergyóditró to Hide a Case of Classic Exploitation. Átlátszó *Erdély*, 10 February 2020, https://

atlatszo.ro/en/english/anti-migrants-hate-speech-at-ditrau-gyergyoditro-to-hide-a-case-of-classic-exploitation/.

Stahl, Henri H. 1980. *Traditional Romanian Village Communities: The Transition from the Communal to the Capitalist Mode of Production in the Danube Region. Studies in Modern Capitalism.* Cambridge; New York: Cambridge University Press.

Stewart, Michael (ed.) 2012. *Gypsy 'Menace': Populism and the New Anti-Gypsy Politics.* London: Hurst Publishers.

Sándor, Szilágyi N. 2016. Én ember szeretnék maradni, ha nem nagy baj [I Would Like to Remain Human, if that is not too much bother]. *Magyar Szó*, 12 August 2016, https://maszol.ro/velemeny/Szilagyi-N-Sandor-En-ember-szeretnek-maradni-ha-nem-nagy-baj.

Toma, Stefánia. 2020. *The Microcosm of Migration and Return: Identity, Space and Home in Romania.* Trento: University of Trento, HOMInG Project Working Paper 9, https://erchoming.files.wordpress.com/2020/05/toma_wp_may-19_ba.pdf.

Toma, Stefánia and László Fosztó. 2018. Returnees and Their Neighbors: Migration of the Romanian Roma, Networks, Social Distance, and Local Development. *Szociológiai Szemle / Review of Sociology* 28 (4), 37–60, https://doi.org/10.51624/SzocSzemle.2018.4.2.

Toma, Stefánia, Cătălina Tesăr and László Fosztó. 2018. Romanian Roma at Home: Mobility Patterns, Migration Experiences, Networks, and Remittances. In: Yaron Matras and Daniele Viktor Leggio (eds). 2018. *Open Borders, Unlocked Cultures. Romanian Roma Migrants in Western Europe.* London: Routledge, pp. 57–82.

Verdery, Katherine. 1991. *National Ideology Under Socialism. Identity and Cultural Politics in Ceausescu's Romania.* Berkeley: University of California Press.

Vincze, Enikő, Norbert Petrovici, Cristina Raţ and Giovanni Picker (eds). 2019. *Racialized Labour in Romania. Spaces of Marginality at the Periphery of Global Capitalism.* Cham: Palgrave Macmillan, https://doi.org/10.1007/978-3-319-76273-9.

Yıldız, Can and Nicholas De Genova (eds). 2019. *Roma Migrants in the European Union: Un/Free Mobility.* New York; London: Routledge.

8. Post-Peasant Progressivism

On Liberal Tendencies in the Slovak Countryside[1]

Juraj Buzalka

This essay follows Chris Hann's long-term interest in peasants and their transformations in East-Central Europe. It complements Hann's perspective on the introduction of post-socialist liberalism in Hungary by presenting some arguments about socialist and post-socialist politics in Slovakia. While Chris Hann has pointed out in particular the consolidation of reactionary right-wing populism under the leadership of the national bourgeoisie as a consequence of the introduction of free-market liberalism and the reduction of the role of the state in providing social welfare for the Hungarian population, my Slovak examples show that we need to pay equal attention to the values represented in what I call post-peasant progressivism—a kind of autochthonous liberalism—as an important component of social and political emancipation, complementing reactionary post-peasant populism. In short, I argue that the progressive elements have often been overlooked by analyses of post-socialist populism. In what follows, I shall first present my reading of Chris Hann's critique of post-socialist liberalism. This will be followed by my understanding of populist developments in Slovakia and my own ethnography of progressivism from the perspective of the Slovak village and in relation to national politics. In the concluding section, I will reintegrate my argument that post-socialist populism has both reactionary and progressive moments.

---

1   This text benefited greatly from years-long discussions with László Fosztó and from the generous critiques of anonymous reviewers of this volume.

   https://doi.org/10.11647/OBP.0282.08

Populism and Transformations

Analysing the failure of the Polish state to collectivise the peasantry, Chris Hann (1985: 169) registered the persistence of peasantry and of a "peasant ethos" in rural, socialist south-east Poland. He also noticed similarities between the rural Solidarity movement of the 1980s and populist protests from before World War II. Hann was unsure as to what sort of populism could be preserved by modernised family farmers under state socialism, but he noticed in his "village without solidarity" that the only functioning community institution was the Roman Catholic Church. He wrote that "certainly the ethos has survived and peasants are united in their profound suspicion of the authorities," and "peasant religiosity remains at a high level, ensuring that the Catholic Church remains the major solidifying force in local communities and in the nation" (Hann 1985: 176). It seems already in his early works from the 1980s that Hann was considering populism especially as a reactionary manifestation of the agrarian past.

In one of his numerous articles on post-socialist populism, which I, for the purpose of this text, choose to be representative of his arguments on the rise of post-socialist populism, Chris Hann (2020) stresses that illiberal processes in rural East-Central Europe "are driven by the collapse of socialist embourgeoisement and the emergence of a new national bourgeoisie under peripheral capitalism." He claims that some of the moral responsibility for these developments lies with "the unwavering intellectual enthusiasts of abstract liberalism" (Hann 2020: 461). According to Hann, the major driving force behind this rise of illiberal populism is a specific version of market liberalism and neoliberalism. In his opinion, the vitality of liberal civil society—consisting of freedom of assembly, political pluralism and the rule of law—depends heavily on the political economy, for which the dismantling of the state was the most devastating development (Hann 2020: 461). As Hann argues, populists are against "civil society" or the "open society" exemplified in the liberal ideas of George Soros and all the NGOs supported by his network (Ibid.) In yet another argument, Hann (2020: 463) reiterates his analysis of the Polish village, arguing that the late state-socialist Solidarity movements against the workers' state cannot be seen only as a path of ascendance towards democracy. Lemkos and Ukrainians in south-eastern Poland in the 1980s, the minority autochthonous population in the region, suffering from dominant Polish nationalism, "preferred the securities and relative freedom they enjoyed under a weak socialist government to a social movement of the ascending Polish nationalists" (2020: 463). As Hann summarises, these undemocratic parameters of the Solidarity movement "were very far from promoting social tolerance and unlikely to serve the long-term interests of the working class" (Hann 2020: 463). He also points out (Ibid.) regarding post-1989 developments that "larger numbers of citizens found that some of their freedoms were constrained in new ways."

As Professor Hann further argues, one of the important deficiencies of post-socialist liberalism is intellectual elitism and the inability of liberal NGOs to go beyond the philosophy of governance based on cosmopolitan human rights and rule of law favouring individual private property. Some intellectuals whom Hann knew from late socialist Hungary "were able to socialise in pleasant cafés and obtain access to better material supplies through the astute use of their social and cultural capital" (Hann 2020: 462). Hann further argues that the new ideas of civil society not only created new elites, but that these interventions—at least in the case of Hungary—"were very short-term, leaving the local experts without any chance of building careers when the money ran out" (Hann 2020: 464). Western intellectuals promoting civil society in East-Central Europe had formed a "church" in Hann's opinion, in the sense that it became impossible to question the paradigm (Ibid. 464). In this new, post-Cold War ideology, civil society functioned to reproduce a civilisational divide and contributed to deep-rooted antinomies, in particular by accelerating economic marginalisation (for further discussion on civil society, see also Hann and Dunn 1996).

Hann also refers to the life and work of rural intellectuals. An emblematic figure of the village intellectual whom I found in my fieldsite near Przemyśl and whom Hann also knows well was Father Stanisław Bartminski. The Krasiczyn parish priest was known for his interest in political affairs in the whole of Poland, and his concerns about multicultural tolerance would easily fit into the definitions of civil society (Buzalka 2007: 140). Ferenc Erdei (1910–1971), the political representative of the policies of embourgeoisement in rural Hungary, who served as a communist Minister of Agriculture (1949–1953) and remained in the high echelons of power under the regime of János Kádár (1956–1988), has a special place in Hann's analyses. The emancipatory ideas of Erdei's work and thought were limited in pre-socialist Hungary, since "for Hungarian peasant families such as his own, it was blocked at a certain point by the dual class oppression of the Magyar gentry and aristocracy, who owned most of the land, and the Jews and German-speakers, who dominated the emerging capitalist economy of the cities" (Hann 2020: 465). As Hann stresses, "the principal opposition crystallised as a dichotomy between *népi* and *urbánus*, corresponding roughly to the countryside versus the city" (Ibid.). For narrowing the gap between the city and the country, state-socialist material embourgeoisement was particularly effective (Hann 2020: 475). Due to the crisis in the rural material economy after the collapse of state socialism, Hann argues, "the new populism is a response to renewed marginalisation under global capitalism" (Hann 2020: 479):

> The extreme nature of the Hungarian case today arises from the fact that the sense of precarity and relative deprivation is greater in a country where so many households, especially in the countryside and small towns, were engaged in dynamic accumulation in the last decades of socialism. (Ibid.)

The material reasons for the rise of Hungarian populism are obviously valid beyond the Hungarian case, notably in rural Slovakia. I have nevertheless argued (Buzalka 2015; 2020; 2021)—and I argue further in this paper—for a deeper historical analysis of the autochthonous sources of populism complementary to the arguments developed by Hann. Namely, I argue for the differentiation between various kinds of populist emancipatory projects in modern East-Central Europe, historical ones, but especially those developed in reaction to the state-socialist project. In most non-anthropological accounts, populism has been treated as an obstacle to the full development of liberal *civitas*, while most anthropologists see populism in a more positive light, stressing the embedded nature and community function of populism as a shield against the effects of large-scale transformations. I am nevertheless not aware of accounts that consider populism as a potentially progressive and even a liberal force in the context of post-socialism, similar in scope and influence to the tradition known in the American Midwest or some of the interwar agrarian movements in Eastern Europe.

My perspective, therefore, stresses the genuine progressive nature of some populist movements led by the liberal intelligentsia in Slovakia, who might be inadequately lumped into the category of market liberals. The reactionary populists, the 'conventional' post-socialist populists of the region, likewise represented by the elites, instead united former communist technocrats, post-socialist privatisers and nationalist intellectuals in Slovakia. I considered post-peasant populism as developing from a 'traditional' social structure, recalling the agrarian era on a societal scale, with large-scale transformations, such as socialism and post-socialism, contributing to the solidity of this structure, and what might be seen locally as a combination of identity narratives, collective memories and rural ideologies (Buzalka 2021: 22–23). While peasants were considered relics of an agrarian age who did not fit into the modernist discourse of socialism, at the same time, state-socialist economy and politics created large numbers of nominally modern citizens of materially advanced villages and cities who only slowly gave up their village identities and habits. I call these state-socialist people "post-peasants", using the term I first chose to characterise the religious-national populations in south-eastern Poland (Buzalka 2007). It can be argued that state socialism was—especially in its more advanced form in the 1970s and 1980s in countries like Hungary or Czechoslovakia—a populist regime *sui generis* promoting its own ideology, suspicious of urban culture and celebrating the folkish representations of "the people", in particular in its "actually existing" state-socialist form. The Czech sociologist Ivo Možný (1991) famously explained how families originally dispossessed of private property by communists in the 1950s in fact colonised the state in late socialism for their own benefit. In Slovakia, where the bulk of intellectuals came from the countryside, this was in contrast to the urbanised, state-socialist elites and working classes in the Czech lands as well as urban classes and societal awareness of national aristocracy in Poland and Hungary, where differentiation between the city and the country has been more intense.

In my article in the special volume dedicated to the Polanyian Double movement, initiated by Chris Hann (Buzalka 2021), I showed how countermovement emotions in the sense of Polanyi, whom Hann (2019) "repatriates" to the analyses of post socialism, can be successfully employed by reactionaries and by liberals, provided they can effectively mobilise key actors within Slovak society and mitigate the economic ideology of the free market. My focus was on leaders at the national level. In this article I follow a similar argument, complementing the societal perspective with a more detailed look at the role of populism in local politics. As Hann (2020: 478) writes about Hungary, "whereas the népi [national] movement in the interwar decades was concerned with the emancipation of the rural masses, the post-peasant populists [of the post-socialist period] resort to increasingly authoritarian means to consolidate the class power of a national bourgeoisie"; the situation in Slovakia might have been analysed differently.

The Slovak Republic was proclaimed on 1 January 1993 as one of the two successor states of the newly divided Czechoslovakia. As a state, Slovakia was founded on the progressive legacy of the nation-state of Czechs and Slovaks of the interwar period (1918–1938). While the urban Czech population dominated the former common state's industrial politics and economy, Slovak politics inherited most of its features in everyday politics from the agrarian Kingdom of Hungary. The initial exception was the narrow circles of the intelligentsia, born predominantly into Slovakia's Lutheran minority and with close ties to intellectual circles in Prague that sided with the progressive nation-building programme of President Tomáš Garrigue Masaryk (1850–1937). The growing Slovak elite, trained in the new Slovak universities after 1918, gradually came to demand national emancipation from the interwar republic.

The alternative—the predominantly Catholic political tradition— enjoyed major electoral support in the newly independent state. Formed around the "Father of the Nation ", the Catholic priest Andrej Hlinka (1864–1938), this national-conservative tradition was opposed to progressive ideas. In 1938, Hlinka's Slovak Peoples' Party became the only party representative of the Slovak Republic (1939–1945), where it established a nationalist autocracy with fascist tendencies as a vassal state of Nazi Germany. The ľudáks (the popular name for members of the Peoples' Party) considered the Slovak National Uprising of 1944 to be a war against the Slovaks' own state. The democrats and communists united in the fight against fascism and declared the major goal of the uprising to be the restoration of Czechoslovakia. After the elections of 1946, the democrats, the descendants of the agrarian party of the interwar period, were joined by Catholics who had not been compromised during the period of clerical fascism, and they won significantly over the communists. Due to the unitary nature of the state, however, Czech votes were decisive. The bold victory of the communists in the Czech lands made Czechoslovakia the only Eastern European country where the communists won in elections before introducing a dictatorship. Interpretations of the past that placed the Slovaks on the "good side" of post-war history, including the Slovak National Uprising, fell into the hands of communists. Throughout state socialism in Czechoslovakia, Slovak communists fought for a greater balance between the Czech and Slovak parts of the joint state. They finally achieved some bitter progress after the Warsaw Pact armies entered Czechoslovakia to suppress the Prague spring of 1968. The period of so-called normalisation lasted until 1989, and especially in Slovakia this meant the unprecedented development of the countryside and the advance of young Slovaks into higher positions in society and the economy. Nevertheless, this period required a compromise to be accepted with the rigid one-party regime established following the purges after 1968. It is they who became known as "Husák's children" (named after the General Secretary of the Communist Party and President Gustáv Husák, 1913–1991, an ethnic Slovak). This was the baby-boom generation that was born or came to adulthood during the normalisation period, who currently hold key positions in Slovakia.

Both reactionary and progressive forces in Slovakia after 1989 had to deal with this political legacy of a predominantly rural country. The bulk of Slovak post-peasants have been rural proletarians since the time of state socialism, as the successful collectivisation stripped Slovaks of their material independence. One can contrast this with the situation in Hungary, as presented by Hann in his book *Tázlár. A Village in Hungary* (1980). He refers to the rural households that pursued the private accumulation of consumer goods on a scale unknown elsewhere in the Soviet bloc. He argues that socialist policies and the populists in Hungary had somehow reached a compromise that was satisfactory to both sides, though he stresses that this did not mean that villagers were ever reconciled with socialist ideology. Instead, their values and world view remained populist-bourgeois. Although the rural proletarians in Slovakia lost most of their means and skills with regard to production for the market, they, too, retained an emotional and aesthetic attachment to the country. The market reformers legitimised their ideologies using this smallholders' nostalgia, but while Hungarian country people missed the privileges of their strata under Kádár's goulash-socialist economy, the people in Slovakia soon realised that the plots they inherited brought hardly any private revenues under the continuing dominance of the red barons in the privatised rural agricultural industry, just as they hardly used to bring any under normalisation, when the redistributive system and economic centralisation (the opposite to the Hungarian mixed economy) was feeding the country with very basic products. I present this Slovak case using my own personal story.

Post-socialist Memories

I grew up in the southern part of the district of Krupina, one of the mediaeval and the contemporary town centres to which most of the historical Hont county of the Hungarian Kingdom belongs. The handful of villages in the southern microregion of this district have also historically gravitated towards the agrarian town of Šahy (Ipolyság in Hungarian), which was a part of the Levice district. At the time of my childhood, this Slovak-Hungarian border town was home to eight thousand people—a dwindling Hungarian-speaking majority and a growing population of Slovaks. The town was surrounded by ethnically Hungarian villages, so the bilingual competence that I lacked was highly beneficial locally. In the 1970s and 1980s the southern parts of the Hont region were among the more prosperous agricultural parts of Czechoslovakia (a smaller part of the historical county, including the town of Nagymaros, facing the mediaeval castle of Visegrád on the opposite bank of the Danube, belonged to Hungary). Large-scale cooperative farming, along with some minor industry in the towns and numerous state jobs, provided employment for the local population. From 1969, Slovakia was a part of the so-called Czechoslovak Federation that comprised the Czechoslovak Socialist Republic. Slovakia was a subunit of the federation, a political appendix to the unitary state with limited autonomy. The areas of southern Slovakia were therefore marginal to the centres of power both within Slovakia as well as Czechoslovakia, as were the members of the Hungarian minority who inhabited the villages located to the south of mine. The Krupina subdistrict, to which my village Hontianske Moravce belonged, was subordinated to a larger district with its seat in the city of Zvolen, located fifty kilometres north of the village. Moravce was an ethnically Slovak village with a slowly shrinking Lutheran majority that was desperate to attract immigrants for its large, consolidated cooperative. The newcomers were very often poor, rural Catholics from the upper parts of the country. New socialist housing blocks were erected during my childhood to provide housing for this new population of rural proletarians, which was hesitantly but unavoidably accepted by the locals for the reason of basic prospects of growth, since the ageing locals had produced only a handful of offspring, who were themselves upwardly mobile and moving away to the urban centres. The late socialist period was therefore prosperous for my fellow villagers in an ambivalent way, as prosperity was weighed against the inflow of a new population considered as having a lower status and to whom the locals had been giving favour.

The change in power relations was visible during the perestroika period in the appointment of a new head of the cooperative—a communist of Catholic upbringing—who had immigrated from the populous village of Očová in central Slovakia, but who originally came from a region further to the north, considered historically very poor by the self-confident local post-peasants. The new head replaced the native heads of peasant descent who had been serving the cooperative for generations, since the hesitant introduction of collectivisation into the prosperous market-oriented village agriculture. The new mayor, the second major political figure in the village, was put into the office by the very late communist power holders. Although he was a newcomer to the village, he later won the first free election after 1989 and has remained in office ever since. I first noticed the existence of communist Czechoslovakia in the village daycare when my teacher, a young communist, complained to the authorities about being corrected by my father when she addressed him. He objected to being referred to as "comrade pastor" (*súdruh farár*). In elementary school I recall the desire to be a pioneer, a member of the communist youth organisation. The photos of President Gustáv Husák, the controversial symbol of the normalisation period that followed the suppression of the Prague Spring of 1968 by the Warsaw Pact armies, hung on the wall. I recall the communist coat of arms, which showed the Czech lion with flames on its chest as well as three hills, the communist-era symbol of Slovakia that replaced the older double cross associated with upper parts of the Hungarian Kingdom, which had been adopted for the Czechoslovak coat of arms in the interwar period. I also remember the exercises with gas masks and fake grenades and the long collective walks in nature that were supposed to prepare us for resilience in the case of a capitalist invasion. A cellar door in the former feudal mansion that had been altered to serve as the socialist healthcare centre was supposed to provide us with entry to a kind of military bunker, but it was always locked.

In 1988 the communist regime allowed the anniversary of the interwar Czechoslovakia to be commemorated (28 October was also a commemoration of the Czechoslovak Federation of 1960 and the day of nationalisation of 1945, which aimed to eliminate the "bourgeois" legacy of 28 October). This celebration indicated the continuing legacy of the First Republic, i.e. Czechoslovakia from 1918–1938, that the communist regime wished to suppress. The founders of the democratic republic also received more attention. These included Milan Rastislav Štefánik (1880–1919), whose tomb on the hill of Bradlo in western Slovakia was a pilgrimage site for thousands of families, including my own, and a sign of symbolic resistance against the regime. It seemed from the official ideology that Štefánik, the village-born son of a Lutheran pastor, a Paris based astronomer and a general in the French Army, almost did not exist for the socialist state. My grandfather, born in 1910, was a strong supporter of Czechoslovak democracy. He and his brother had experienced a hard childhood with their widowed peasant mother, until my grandfather received a proper parish in south-central Slovakia and married my grandmother, the daughter of a local teacher. My grandfather graduated in theology in Bratislava and managed to receive a so-called Masaryk stipend in order to study in Strasbourg. His activities behind the front lines led him to support the Slovak National Uprising undercover, aiming to serve for the restoration of Czechoslovakia. His rectory in the village of Stredné Plachtince, south-central Slovakia, was an important centre of political discussions. And his parish house continued to serve this purpose in his new workplace, too, as he was forced by the communist authorities to leave his parishioners for the village of Dunajská Lužná, near Bratislava, to which the people from Štefánik's native region under the hill of Bradlo—the strong guardians of the interwar Czechoslovak legacy—were resettled to replace the local Germans who were forced to leave as a consequence of the post-war peace agreements. My father (born in 1944) was a theology student when he took an active part in the 1968 demonstrations against the Soviet tanks. He met my mother, a student of economics, in one of the churches in Bratislava while he was practising his sermons.

My younger brother and I became children of normalisation; we belonged to a particularly strong cohort of youth born under the improving welfare conditions of late socialist Czechoslovakia based on the tacit agreement between the people and the authorities that if no civil protests were organised in the sense of a Prague Spring scenario—if people take refuge in the private sphere of their houses and gardens— then the regime would provide them with more welfare and consumer goods. I was born in Partizánske, my father's first rectory, in a city originally founded and built by the shoe factory industrialist, democrat and philanthropist of the interwar period, Tomáš Baťa, and originally named after him as Baťovany. The city is considered the only ideal industrial town in Slovakia, planned and built with a deep interest in workers' needs, thus representing an earlier, alternative industrialisation of an agrarian country under Czechoslovakia without the need for forced, disruptive, heavy industrialisation by the communists. I spent a lot of free time especially with my maternal grandmother, a pious peasant woman of central Slovakia who shared her stories about Czechoslovakia, World War II (including her fear of hungry Red Army soldiers) and especially the torturous collectivisation. She remembered voting for the Agrarian Party, which was preferred by Lutheran peasants in the Slovak part of Czechoslovakia, before the war. The Agrarian Party benefited from its coalition potential and usually opposed the policies of the reactionary Slovak Peoples' Party, which became the only recognised party in fascist Slovakia (1939–1945). The legacy of interwar Czechoslovakia was more vivid among the Slovak Protestant minority than among members of the Catholic majority. Biblical Czech served as a liturgical language for Slovak Lutherans since the Reformation, and the religious "democracy" among Protestants was often compared to the foundational myth of the Masaryk project. Masaryk had skilfully incorporated the anti-Catholic tradition from the Hussites, through Comenius's Protestant legacy, and the anti-aristocratic sentiments of the Lutherans, victims of Habsburg re-Catholicisation.

And the story of Slovak national awakeners, who were predominantly Protestant pastors and teachers, appealed directly to the peasant masses. This dominance of the rural intelligentsia not only set the tone for democratic mobilisation in Slovakia, with the central role of the rural intelligentsia, but also reproduced the confessional cleavage. The over-representation of Lutherans was also mirrored in the structures of the elites in the Czechoslovak Republic and contrasted to the Roman Catholic majority, whose church was part of the crown of Saint Stephen of pre-1918 Hungary. The resonances of confessional cleavage into Catholics and Protestants were still present in the Slovak National Uprising against the "Catholic" state and even survived state socialism, a system that was considered to be a communist-Lutheran *coup d'état* by many proponents of the Catholic tradition. The village of Hontianske Moravce, to which my father was invited as a pastor in 1978, was conservative in terms of values and habits, despite its having undergone deep collectivisation and infrastructural modernisation. My father to this day has very positive memories of his almost twenty years of service in the parish under state socialism. As his parishioners used to say, "if we live well, we want our priest to live well too!" The combination of cooperative or wage work in Šahy or Krupina and the work on one's own plot of land enabled the abundant consumption by locals, exceeding the regular availability of agricultural products to the urban population. Considering the frequency of goulash parties, the number of schnitzel per capita and the amount of wine consumed, late socialism is still remembered as a truly joyful period by the villagers, despite the actual situation not, in fact, being particularly bright.

After the tragedy in Chernobyl in 1986, my brother and I were forbidden by our parents to play outside. We were also not allowed to pick strawberries in the rectory garden. The problem for us was not that we were instructed not to speak about the catastrophe we had learned about from the "alien" Radio Free Europe ahead of the official announcement by the communist media; the major problem was how to tell our friends, the victims of communist authorities refusing to inform them about the danger, that we cannot go cycling with them despite the late spring sun being so high. The major compulsory events of my childhood were the May Day parades held in the district town of Krupina, which the pupils of the local school were driven to by the cooperative bus. The event meant quite serious partying for the villagers, especially after the official programme had ended. All of us wished to carry the Czechoslovak flag in the parade. The red Soviet flags were far less popular, and only our Roma classmates liked to carry them. Holding the flag helped the Roma feel that they belonged to the crowd, as they were usually segregated from us, the village boys. Despite significant improvements, the assimilation policies of the communist state underwent a significant crisis in the 1970s and 1980s (Scheffel and Mušinka 2019), which paved the way for further segregation after 1989, although nowadays virtually all the blame for Roma segregation is placed on the market transformation. My childhood idyll under late socialism was only interrupted by the investigation of my father by the secret police, based on several false accusations by his handful of local critics. Despite the curse of these openly atheist "parishioners", we were very lucky for the support of others who appealed to the authorities to defend their pastor. My father often worried about my career prospects due to our family's record, and he was positively surprised that I was accepted at the grammar school (*gymnázium*), which was considered an important prerequisite for university studies at that time. He nevertheless never dreamt of the humanities or social sciences, prominent subjects of propaganda, that I preferred, and he hoped at most for the ideology-free natural sciences, if I were allowed to enter the university at all, a genuine concern given our family's political unreliability.

I entered grammar school in September 1989 in Šahy. I was one of six students out of thirty-six who did not speak a word of Hungarian. My father perhaps thought that I would have a chance to learn Hungarian, a language his mother spoke well but that he was deprived of learning in his youth due to the unfavourable conditions for bilingualism under the nationalising communist post-war Slovakia (yet another argument against the responsibility for nationalism falling to post-socialist conditions). We had teachers who had moved to the town for the living quarters offered by the state, and I remember them all representing the first generation of intelligentsia growing up in villages. The mild climate and the vicinity of Budapest, eighty kilometres away and the capital of late socialist consumption, also played a role in attracting them. Throughout our studies—and earlier, while I was attending the music school in town—the Hungary across the border served as a symbol of the good life for people in normalisation Czechoslovakia, despite the long queues at the international border crossing. For us at the *gymnázium*, the Velvet Revolution took place suddenly. The teachers and especially the director, a wise Communist Party member, supported the change. We were allowed to attend the general strike of 27 November organised by the town's workers. The situation in Prague was high on the radar by that time and the visits of revolutionary leaders from Bratislava were welcomed. The young leaders brought information and hope, as had Hungarian television for those who spoke Hungarian. This optimistic period was quickly replaced by the gloomier prospects of economic reality. The economic transformation was accompanied by the new reactionary project of an independent Slovakia, in which former communists heavily invested. I particularly recall the visits of nationalist artists who travelled across the country provoking the representatives of the Hungarian minority, who were also experiencing the revival of their ethnic difference, not least thanks to the support from *anyaorszság* ("the mother country"). I remember in particular the figure of actress Eva Kristínová (1928–2020), the daughter of an officer who had suffered in fascist and communist jails, promoting Slovak independence. She saw no problem in putting her name next to the prominent figures of communist art, the new nationalists. At an event in the theatre hall she heavily criticised President Havel, the conscious follower of Masaryk's legacy. Obviously, she had not forgotten the myth of a thousand years of forced Magyarisation of the Slovaks.

The inhabitants of Štúrovo, a Hungarian-speaking town on the Danube some forty kilometres away that had been renamed after the leader of Slovak nineteenth-century nationalists with no ties to the town, wanted to return to the older name, Párkány. The actress argued that the city had an even more original Slavic name to which the current Hungarian-speaking inhabitants should return if they were dishonoured by the name of Štúr. The trick of her suggestion was that the old Slavic name of the fishermen's settlement was *Kokot*, a vulgar term used for *penis* in contemporary Slovak. The last day of December 1992, the day Czechoslovakia ceased to exist, I was at home. I think my parents were already in bed, because my father had a service to deliver the next morning. At a time when the television played only the Slovak part of the former common anthem there was silence in the village. I recall that the first positive patriotic blast came only ten years later, as a consequence of the Slovak ice hockey team's victory at the world championships in Goteborg.

By the time of my university studies in Bratislava in 1994–1999, my father had moved to another village. Since he had buried most of the dozens of parishioners who had thrown him a big welcoming party in the parish house garden in 1978, the demographic decline of Hontianske Moravce contributed very much to his decision. Some fifteen or so years after we left, I built a wine cellar in the neighbouring spa town that allowed me to reconnect with some of my old friends. The good life of the late socialist period and the hardships of post-socialist years were gone; the local situation had solidly improved as a consequence of Slovakia's entry into the European Union in 2004. The drive to the capital nowadays takes one hour and forty minutes thanks to the highway, which contrasts sharply with four or more hours under communism, when travel for more distant work was obviously far less pleasant. Of course, local services, public transport and regional job opportunities greatly declined after 1989 but who should have been serving, if demographics took the upper hand even before the introduction of the market? As my personal story shows, late socialism and post-socialism brought about ambivalent results when it comes to development. As I show in the following section, it would have sufficed to contrast these periods without considering the long-term effects of the historical legacies of the agrarian period that led to the post-peasant present via crucial communist transformation. Both structurally, when it comes to the role of rural intelligentsia, and symbolically, when it comes to the value of rural life, mobilisation can develop in two ways under transformation—towards greater reception of reactionarism as well as progressivism.

Post-socialist Progressivism

The previous sections referred to representatives of the old rural intelligentsia—especially priests and teachers—who on the one hand were the primary agents of popular emancipation and the introduction of reforms to the village and, on the other hand, of romantic nationalism as a part of reactionary populism. In order to illustrate this double role of the Slovak village intelligentsia, I provide below some personalities who might show the importance of my rural region for the progressive legacy of Slovakia. The cosmopolitan flavour comes from the life stories of people such as Ferdinand Daučík (1910–1986), the manager of several Spanish football clubs. A famous player in the Czechoslovak league and later the coach of the national team, he was born and grew up in

Šahy. After spending two years in communist prisons, he emigrated to Spain to become the coach of FC Barcelona. Another example is Juraj (Gyögy) Berczeller (1914–2008), in emigration known as George Best, who was a person responsible for the development of Slovak popular entertainment. He was a medical doctor, a piano tuner, a composer, a pianist-entertainer of operetta, jazz and light medley genre, who passed away in Australia. For ten years, from 1958 on, he was the resident pianist at the Tatra Revue Theatre in Bratislava, the key institution on the vibrant cultural scene of pre-1968 Bratislava.

The regional progressive tradition can be more appropriately demonstrated with the story of Ladislav Ballek (1941–2014), a leading and for many experts the best novelist of the second half of twentieth-century Slovak literature. His works were inspired by his youth in the region, in particular in Šahy and his native village of Terany, where his father served as a custom officer during the World War II period. Ballek enjoyed the image of a leftist progressive intellectual who in his positions of politician and diplomat supported the transition of the Communist Party into the democratic party emerging in the post-1989 period. His novels take inspiration from the agrarian town; they well illustrate the inter-ethnic relations and offer a critique of agrarian inequality, thus making his work truly progressive. The musician, composer, humourist, dramaturge, actor, columnist and promoter of the Internet in Slovakia, Jaroslav Filip (1949–2000), who had an extraordinary range of activities, was born and grew up in my own childhood village of Hontianske Moravce. He was one of the most prolific representatives of Bratislava café culture of the 1990s. His father, whom I had the chance to meet personally, was a teacher and director of the village school. Jaroslav Filip can be considered the court composer of the doyens of Slovak (urban) humour, Milan Lasica (1940-2021) and Július Satinský (1941-2002), who challenged in particular the boorishness and folklorist kitsch of Slovak patriots in their work. Their truly liberating and progressive humour and the songs composed by Filip based on their texts were distributed in a semi-legal form even among my friends in the village while the authors were banned from a full public appearance as a consequence of post-1968 normalisation. These figures can hardly be considered peasants, but their origins in agrarian regions and very often in peasant families, too, show how elites were recruited in Slovakia and how important the village was even for progressive projects. While the

Polish intelligentsia—both progressive and reactionary—comes from the large cities and its position is closely allied with the aristocracy, and while Budapest has always been a cradle of liberal cosmopolitanism differing sharply from the rest of Hungary, and while the Czechs, proletarians, entrepreneurs and intellectuals were all fairly urbanised back in the nineteenth century, the Slovak elites— both progressive and reactionary—originate in the village.

All the major political leaders of modern Slovakia were village-born, including the communist president of Czechoslovakia and one of the leaders of the Slovak National Uprising (1944) Gustáv Husák (1913–1991) and the popular leader of the Prague Spring Alexander Dubček (1921–1992). The "father of the nation", the Catholic priest and leader of the Slovak Peoples' Party Andrej Hlinka (1864–1938), and his follower Jozef Tiso (1887–1947), the president of the Slovak Republic under Nazi tutelage, who was hanged as a war criminal, grew up in a small town and village setting, respectively. The true village progressive of the interwar period was the Prime Minister of Czechoslovakia, Milan Hodža (1878–1944), the author of the *Federation in Central Europe* (1944), proposing the federation of Central European states united against the growing dangers of Germany and Russia, not least on the basis of their agrarian economies and cultures. In short, no member of the elite who claimed Slovak origin came from the ranks of the aristocracy, landowning or capitalist classes. The two contemporary intellectuals who might be representative of "café culture"—Ballek and Filip—were the creators and promoters of the progressive tradition, actively siding with the liberal-democratic camp against the nationalist reactionary of Vladimír Mečiar, the autocratic Prime Minister of Slovakia in 1990–1991 and 1994–1998, who is also a genuine Slovak villager by origin. It is true that villages like Hontianske Moravce managed to benefit from populist rule, and the countryside generally voted overwhelmingly for populists, but this support was not always for the benefit of the local people.

The head of the cooperative (and a member of parliament by the mid-1990s) and the mayor, both former communists, arranged state support for their cooperative as well as subsidies for village public projects using their ties to the populist party of Vladimír Mečiar in power. One of these projects was the resettlement of dozens of families from Ukraine who claimed Slovak origin. The two new blocks of flats were erected in the 1990s to offer immigrants housing, but the newcomers only slowly accommodated to the local customs. The only changes in the still demographically declining village now are a tiny Orthodox church, the communist House of Culture that was turned into a Roman Catholic prayer house, and the large Lutheran church which is ever emptier. The once flourishing private vineyards have been left to become overgrown by weeds; the old cooperative buildings are half-destroyed (the cooperative privatisers are only producing large-scale produce requiring fewer local jobs), and there are more and more houses for sale, despite the renovated mansion where I used to visit the dentist, new pavements along the district road, and the new highway some forty kilometres away that allows locals to commute faster for work to the big cities of Nitra and Bratislava, all built thanks to European Union subsidies. All of these developments remind of the progressive as well as reactionary potential of the rural social basis after 1989. This political significance of the conflict—that Hann in the case of Hungary locates as the conflict between pro-market liberal elites and reactionary, socially sensitive national populists—dominated over the market transformation. Liberal intellectuals I used to meet with were not blind supporters of the market's invisible hand. All of my teachers and intellectual friends—for example, literary historian Rudolf Chmel, who was the last Czechoslovak ambassador to Budapest, the Minister of Culture and later Vice-Prime Minister and served as the president of the Open Society Foundation in Slovakia, to mention the most prominent among them—came from a village or small-town setting. The most influential intellectual monthly *OS* (*Občianska spoločnosť*—"civil society"), established in 1997, aimed to oppose growing populist reactionary activities but at the same time to balance the ideological language of the economic reformers by discussing a fair and just society, democracy and human rights, which were not an invention of cosmopolitan elites but were newly questioned by the populist regime of the time (for more information about this period, see Buzalka 2019).

Although rural transformation was not a hot issue in these liberal circles, unfortunately, the rural origin of Slovak reactionism, to which the regime of that time subscribed, was heavily discussed by liberals as the major obstacle to development. The bulk of my student friends sided with the anti-Mečiar camp. Before the 1998 election that brought about a victory of a wide progressive coalition over reactionary populism, we participated in strikes against the attempts of the government to restrict university freedoms. My colleagues and I volunteered to observe the fairness of elections in our native villages in a situation where the ruling parties dominated the media, used sheer propaganda, and suppressed opposition, all signalling possible election fraud. More important for my generation was the deep international isolation that our country felt under the autocratic rule that sharply contrasted with the advancement of European integration in the neighbouring countries. Our weekend student trips to Prague were about enjoying the atmosphere of a European metropolis that our populist-dominated regime was lacking at that time. There were queues for visas to the United Kingdom in Bratislava but even "window shopping" to neighbouring Austria, which was very expensive for the average Slovak of that time, became complicated, as travellers faced more restrictions. Obviously, it would be a mistake to ignore the progressive tradition that existed well beyond the circles of the intelligentsia. I recorded several interviews with workers in Košice, eastern Slovakia, during my fieldwork in 2009 and 2010 (see, for example, Buzalka and Ferencová 2017). One retired steelworker in Košice explained to me the meaning of post-1989:

> I can buy the shoes I want and go to the mountains I prefer. That is freedom. It's not the hiking shoes or whatever one can buy now that wasn't available back then, but the opportunity to choose what one wanted to do with these purchases. It didn't work like this back then.

In the summer of 2019 I recorded the following discussion between two friends from south-central Slovakia. Zdenko (aged fifty-six), a bus driver, shared the opinion that the "communists robbed everybody of everything. Freedom, factories, craft services, and in 1953 all the money [the forced currency exchange was highly disadvantageous for ordinary savers]." Braňo (aged sixty-seven), a former truck driver, replied:

> The democrats stole everything that the communists left! The democrats sold us those flats that the communists gave us for free, along with the cooperatives, factories and so on, and they put the money in their private pockets. This is how they crushed the Slovak pride, the dignity of citizens, and then gave up our state sovereignty in favour of the European Union. How can I not side with the Communist Party when these crooks [the democrats] managed to fuck up everything?

Zdenko replied that privatised socialist flats were sold very advantageously by those who originally obtained them for a nominal price. And Braňo, himself the owner of a flat in a socialist block, which the villager Zdenko never possessed, continued:

> I just wanted to say that the housing problem was solved by the communists and that these flats were built in such a way that citizens could purchase them for a modest price. Now they are selling them for extraordinary prices. But housing is not a problem any longer thanks to the communists!

The value of socialist-era flats has increased enormously and those, especially from the country, who never received a socialist flat—such as Zdenko—felt the injustice of the argument generally held by followers of "communist nostalgia", such as Braňo. In contrast, many villagers suffered a serious loss in value of their spacious village properties built with official and unofficial socialist subsidies and the help of neighbours. Even when he got a decent job, Zdenko—like other villagers—found it impossible to buy a flat in the capital. Braňo, on the other hand, could not forget the privileges that people enjoyed simply by living in the countryside, combining domestic food production with relatively well-paid work in a factory. While Zdenko accepts the post-socialist reality, commutes to the capital and stays in a workers' hotel, going back to his house at the weekend just to cut the grass in his abandoned vegetable garden, Braňo, who has an adequate local job and whose property in the district capital has increased in value severalfold, criticises "the system" for destroying well-functioning communist housing policies. The voting preference of the two friends is also a matter of curiosity. While Braňo voted for the reactionaries, Zdenko has been a staunch supporter of moderate centrist politics since 1989. At first sight, the only difference is their family origin. Zdenko is the grandson of a small peasant and the son of socialist cooperative workers who remained moderately privileged in the socialist village. Braňo is the grandson of landless rural proletarians, whose numbers were high, especially on pre-socialist land estates of what is now southern Slovakia, and whose parents obtained flats in cooperative housing blocks built in the 1970s. The division into moderate centre-right progressive politics and reactionary post-communist nostalgia therefore does not neatly follow the cleavage into elites and the people, urbanites versus rural inhabitants in Slovakia, and it may not even fit the material inequalities or ways of life. As this essay argues, we should look at complementary expressions of progressive and reactionary politics across these divisions, as influenced by rural intellectuals. László Fosztó (this volume; see also Scheffel 2015 for eastern Slovakia) showed that ethnic tolerance and division in Romania has always been locally embedded, anchoring the local socioeconomic exchanges, and the eventual xenophobia coming from the nation-state politics might be efficiently calmed by the local relations and practices. To translate these efficient integrations back into national politics and policies is a role for intellectuals, especially if they originate or remain an inseparable part of local communities.

Liberal Ruralism

There was an urban movement of intellectuals in late socialist Slovakia who in the best tradition of the nineteenth-century intelligentsia assisted in "civilising" the villages. In the very late period of state socialism this movement emerged as expressions of environmental democracy and sustainability in the conditions of the devastating effects of heavy industrialisation that the communist regime was widely ignoring. The authors Petr Jehlička, Phillip Sarre and Juraj Podoba (2005) explicitly speak of a movement in Czechoslovakia, based principally on the assumptions of "liberal environmentalism". Mikuláš Huba, a geology professor, a former member of parliament and one of the leaders of the movement, characterised it as the articulation "of the vision for a new, democratic, more cultured and more ecological, healthier and prettier Slovakia". Eugen Gidl (1944–2021), a journalist, screenwriter and editor who was silenced during the normalisation period and after 1989 operated both in 'Public Against Violence', the major movement in Slovakia in 1989, and later, as an independent journalist, activist and one of the editors of the influential liberal 1990s journal *OS*—promoted positions that can be characterised as "left-liberal" and critical of the market transformation. The foundations of these critiques of bureaucratic centralism, which led to critiques of a similarly impersonal post-socialist market, lay in the period of late socialism around the publication of *Bratislava Nahlas* (Bratislava Aloud), published in 1987 as a sixty-page report covering problems ranging from environmental protection, quality of air, and disadvantageous Roma. This expert report, to which more than eighty authors from so-called grey zone—neither dissidents connected, for example, with Charter 77, nor fully loyal members of the communist state establishment—contributed, became the subject of important public discussion and a civic movement, along with the Catholic laity movement, exemplified by the "candle demonstration" for religious and civic freedoms on 28 March 1988, which was violently suppressed by the regime. Economic liberalism played no role in any of those autochthonous and influential Slovak political movements of late state socialism. As Gindl wrote twenty years after, the members of the environmental movement were

> [...] united by the green, and by that time ideological, ecological ethos, intimate relations with nature, and with material values of the past. They were looking for a room in which they could heal their attacked civic dignity, the major component of civic self-confidence [...] They managed to connect urban oversensitivity with the sensitivity of people with natural green empathy, the temporary country people [...] The break-outs of members to the countryside in search of folk blockhouses and hay-barns were not only escapes from the hostile reality [...] but they also cultivated a graceful egoism of self-renewal, able to bring a new vision of the world [...] Sociologists therefore called them positive deviants [...]

Not only Gindl, born in the town of Liptovský Mikuláš under the Tatra Mountains, but most other authors of the *Bratislava Aloud* manifesto, represented the solid political opposition at the time of the Velvet Revolution and several years since then. As Juraj Podoba (1998), himself a co-author of the report, argues, the green element played such a prominent role in the 1989 revolution that in Slovakia it could have been called the "green velvet revolution". One of the most visible symbols of the movement is the person of Ján Budaj, the leader of the November 1989 demonstrations, who since March 2021 has served as the Minister of Environment in the government of Igor Matovič and, since March 2021, in the government of Eduard Heger. As Juraj Podoba further refers to the period of nationalist politics in Slovakia of the 1990s, the marginalisation of environmental issues and the low profile of environmental policies in Slovakia was in sharp contrast with the high environmental concern and dynamic development of environmental institutions and laws in the late 1980s and early 1990s.

Podoba, using two case studies—the aluminium smelter in Žiar nad Hronom and the waterworks Gabčíkovo on the Danube—illustrates the changing attitudes of Slovak society regarding environmental issues during the post-socialist transition. He explains how environmentally harmful and previously unpopular symbols of the communist achievements against which the ecology-friendly resistance of the 1980s was targeted have been politically appropriated by populist reactionaries into symbols of achievement of the Slovak nation and independent Slovakia. To criticise these symbols as damaging the environment in the 1990s meant to criticise the Slovak nation. The victory of reactionary populism after the parliamentary elections of 1994, which brought the most illiberal post-1989 government of Vladimír Mečiar to power, was not fully caused by a defensive reaction of frustrated populations losing under market transformation. The reason that the Slovakia of 1990 differed in the intensity of reactionary politics vis-à-vis its Visegrad neighbours equally resulted from the underrepresentation of existing liberal forces in parliament due to their lack of strategic cooperation, not necessarily their lack of public support. As the political scientist Soňa Szomolányi (2019) argues, Slovakia's post-socialist development shows no strong evidence of path dependency on patterns of an essentially rural country, modernised according to the Soviet model. The decisive actors of November 1989 became liberal intellectuals, and they represented only a small minority. Despite having only minimal material and organisational resources, they showed what Szomolányi calls "value preparedness" (*hodnotovú pripravenosť*). The parliamentary form of government and the proportional electoral system were set up by liberal reformers and, unlike in neighbouring Poland and Hungary, these institutions represented a kind of insurance policy against authoritarian tendencies. As Szomolányi argues, the negotiated elite transition of Hungary and Poland might nowadays contradict the thesis of the most successful passage to democracy. Szomolányi's hypothesis is that it is citizens' participation in the process of political transformation—such as in November 1989, during the popular protests against the autocratic rule of Vladimír Mečiar in 1998 and for a decent Slovakia in 2018, following the killing of the journalist Ján Kuciak and consequent fall of the Prime Minister Róbert Fico—that plays the important role. Even in the case of the Solidarity movement in Poland, according to Szomolányi, the masses were not directly involved in the democratic settlement agreed between the communist and opposition elites, and the transition was only completed by the new non-communist constitution in 1997 (see Szomolányi 1999).

The Velvet Revolution of 1989 was led by liberal-minded intellectuals from the "grey zone"—i.e. not from among the communist dissidents like in the Czech lands—but critical professionals and intellectuals from established institutions, supported by members of the environmental movement and the dissident Catholic laity. Having a clear programme of democratic reforms, the members of this revolutionary generation had no solid plan for economic reform. On the contrary, post-communist and nationalist circles soon formed an alliance under the charismatic leadership of Vladimír Mečiar and gradually began to demand independence. The elections of 1994 allowed the autocratic Mečiar to form a government with a nationalist party and a small left-populist party. Mečiar's government successfully played with the legacy of the Slovak Republic from the World War II period, as well as with nostalgia for state socialism. This was the period of "wild privatisation", the aim of which was to create a "Slovak capitalist class". This goal was partly achieved through the state incurring an enormous level of debt. Popular political dissatisfaction nevertheless grew, and the elections of 1998 brought to power a genuine reform government which aimed to stabilise the economy and to catch up with Slovakia's neighbours through accession to the EU on 1 May 2004. Whether this makes Slovakia exceptional in a regional comparison is yet another question— the continual balance of reactionism and populism in 2021, if compared to the more reactionary regimes of Hungary under Viktor Orbán or Poland under Jarosław Kaczyński, favour the slight exception of the former Czechoslovakia. The argument in this paper nevertheless is that we need not lump all post-socialist populism together as representing reactionary politics. The progressive critiques of market liberalism—as I have shown above—also have indigenous origins.

Conclusion

This essay has offered a rather personal account of the role of populism in the development of post-socialist Slovakia. My goal was to engage with the productive ideas of Professor Chris Hann from the distance of almost twenty years since I wrote my doctoral thesis under his thorough supervision, for which I am enormously indebted. My major complementary account of his explanation of the rise of populism in Hungary was that we need to pay equal attention to the values represented in what I call the post-peasant progressivism—a kind of autochthonous liberalism—as an important component of social and political emancipation, complementing reactionary post-peasant populism. I argued that progressive elements have often been overlooked by analyses of post-socialist populism. Therefore, this humble critique represents a sort of academic maturing thanks to Hann's sharp, original and highly efficient intellectual stimulation. In summary, my perspective does not question Chris Hann's insistence on the importance of rural embourgeoisement during state socialism. This is only to complement his perspective on material economy with an account about post-peasant values mobilisation in Slovakia, which also remains deeply petty bourgeois but certainly does not need to be successfully mobilised by the narrow reactionary ideologies of populists like Vladimír Mečiar or Viktor Orbán only. With an ethnographic approach, we can show how the post-socialist countryside, with its populist roots, can also reveal progressive tendencies.

References

Buzalka, Juraj. 2015. The Political Lives of Dead Populists in Post-socialist Slovakia. In: Michal Kopeček and Piotr Wciślik (eds). 2015. *Liberal Democracy, Authoritarian Pasts and the Legacy of 1989. The Last Two Decades of Political Thought in East Central Europe*, Budapest: CEU Press, pp. 313–331.

Buzalka, Juraj. 2019. Co się stało z osią liberalnego konsensusu na Słowacji? (What Happened to the Axis of Liberal Consensus in Slovakia?). In: Magdalena Bogusławska, Anna Kobylińska and Sylwia Siedlecka (eds). 2019. *Zmiana ram: instytucje po 1989 roku w Europie Środkowej i na Balkanach*, Warszawa: Wydział Polonistyki Uniwersytetu Warszawskiego, pp. 53–72.

Buzalka, Juraj. 2020. *The Cultural Economy of Protest in Postsocialist European Union. Village Fascists and their Rivals*. London: Routledge.

Buzalka, Juraj. 2021. Village Fascists and Progressive Populists: Two Faces of the Countermovement in Slovakia. *Europe-Asia Studies* 73 (9), 1658–1682, https://doi.org/10.1080/09668136.2021.1978934.

Buzalka, Juraj and Michaela Ferencová. 2017. Workers and Populism in Slovakia. In: Victoria Goddard and Susana Narotzky (eds). 2017. *Work and Livelihood in Times of Crisis: History, Ethnography, Models*, London: Routledge, pp. 157–171.

László, Fosztó. 2022. Beyond Blue Eyes? Beyond Blue Eyes? Xenophobia on the Eastern Margins of the European Union. In: Juraj Buzalka and Agnieszka Pasieka (eds). 2022. *Anthropology of Transformation: From Europe to Asia and Back*. Cambridge: Open Book Publishers, pp. 155–178.

Hann, Chris. 1980. *Tázlár, a Village in Hungary*. Cambridge: Cambridge University Press.

Hann, Chris. 1985. *A Village without Solidarity: Polish Peasants in Years of Crisis*. New Haven, CT: Yale University Press.

Hann, Chris. 2018. Moral(ity and) Economy: Work, Workfare, and Fairness in Provincial Hungary. *European Journal of Sociology* 59 (2), 225–254, https:// doi.org/ 10.1017/S000397561700056X.

Hann, Chris. 2019. *Repatriating Polanyi: Market Society in the Visegrád States*. Budapest: CEU Press.

Hann, Chris. 2020. In search of civil society: From peasant populism to postpeasant illiberalism in provincial Hungary. *Social Science Information* 59 (3), 459–483, https://doi.org/10.1177/0539018420950189.

Hann, Chris and Dunn, Elizabeth (eds). 1996. *Civil Society: Challenging Western Models*. London: Routledge.

Jehlicka, Petr, Philip Sarre and Juraj Podoba. 1998. The Czech Environmental Movement's Knowledge Interests in the 1990s: Compatibility of Western Influences with pre-1989 Perspectives. *Environmental Politics* 14 (1), 64–82.

Možný, Ivo. 1991. *Proč tak snadno… Některé rodinné důvody sametové revoluce* (Why so easily… Some family reasons for the Velvet Revolution). SLON: Prague.

Podoba, Juraj. 1998. Rejecting Green Velvet: Transition, Environment and Nationalism in Slovakia. In: S. Baker and P. Jehlička (eds). 1998. *Dilemmas of Transition. The Environment, Democracy and Economic Reform in East Central Europe*, London; Portland, OR: Frank Cass, pp. 129–144.

Scheffel, David. 2015. Belonging and Domesticated Ethnicity in Veľký Šariš. *Romani Studies* 25 (2), 115–149, https://doi.org/10.3828/rs.2015.5.

Scheffel, David and Alexander Mušinka. 2019. "Third-class" Slovak Roma and Inclusion: Bricoleurs vs Social Engineers. *Anthropology Today* 35 (1), 17–21, https://doi.org/10.1111/1467-8322.12483.

Szomolányi, Soňa. 1999. November '89: Otvorenie prechodu a jeho aktéri na Slovensku. *Soudobé dějiny* VI (4), 421–442.

9. Swimming against the Tide

Right-wing Populism, Post-socialism and Beyond[1]

Agnieszka Pasieka

Introduction

"Why are we still discussing post-socialism?" was the question numerous scholars and commentators were asking, with annoyance, when the first decade of the twenty-first century was coming to an end. The fact that ten countries from the former Eastern bloc joined the European Union (in 2004) and that many of them were run by centrist governments which embraced neoliberal policies were to them sufficient proofs of the successful—and completed—transition. The most painful effects of the drastic reforms linked with the post-1989 "shock therapy" seemed to have been overcome and some incidents on the way to liberal democracy were treated merely as "hiccups along the way" or, rather, redefined through a linguistic equilibristic. Thus, millions of unemployed young Poles, Hungarians or Romanians who left for the "West" in search of employment, often well beyond their qualifications, were not to account for desperation but flexibility. Temporary political turmoils and low political participation meant that the Eastern European citizens were "still" learning democracy. And the growing share of foreign ownership in Eastern Europe was a sign of "successful" Europeanisation and "truly" open markets rather than of the power imbalance and the weakness of

1   I would like to thank Tatjana Thelen, Laszlo Foszto and the anonymous reviewers for their very helpful comments on this text; Rafal Rukat for research assistance; and my research participants for their willingness to talk to me. Fieldwork was funded by the Austrian Science Fund grant.

https://doi.org/10.11647/OBP.0282.09

local competitors. Authors of such enthusiastic claims seemed to have undergone their own "shock therapy" when a number of right-wing populists gained power in Eastern Europe. Importantly, they gained power after announcing that not only was it necessary to undo the ills of the transformation but also to bring *ordinary* people *real democratisation*. The question of post-socialism, and with it that of post-socialist victims/others/losers, once again returned to the fore.

Given his field of expertise and familiarity with numerous Eastern European contexts, it is far from surprising that Chris Hann has been vocal in the discussions on the recent developments, especially in Central-Eastern Europe. Even though right-wing populist (as well as far-right) parties have been on the rise across the continent, Central Eastern European societies became a target of particularly acute criticism for their unwillingness to welcome refugees during the so-called refugee crisis in 2015 and for supporting politicians who reached for xenophobic and Euro-sceptic rhetoric. Hann commented on these issues in a series of publications (2015; 2016; 2017), which can be succinctly described as imploring fellow intellectuals to take a more emphatic approach to the CEE, to recognise the profound disparities within Europe and to emphasise the post-socialist context. Later, he developed many of these thoughts in more extensive takes on populism, or rather on populisms, for instance when discussing the long road to populism (2019a; 2019b; 2019c) and populism's relation to civil society (2020). Most importantly, he demonstrated the importance of a *longue durée* perspective for the understanding of the current moment, making it clear that post-socialism was but one moment on the "road to populism."

Many of his arguments are in stark contrast with general feelings and tendencies, even those offered by anthropologists who admittedly are specialists in stating that "X is more complex" but who often forget about complexities when trying to understand their own societies, and especially when discussing concerns with which one cannot easily sympathise. Yet if we were to describe Hann's attitude as "swimming against the tide," we would need to emphasise that he has done it consistently. In the early 2000s, against the wave of enthusiasm for democratisation, he was analysing the growth of nationalist sentiments and exclusionary policies in the new democracies (e.g., Hann 1997; 1998). He persistently emphasised those social-economic aspects of transition, which were ignored by the bards of democratic progress across the EU, and he engaged critically with certain EU policies. Apart from drawing on his established research contacts in Hungary and Poland, he referred to the works of doctoral students who studied developments in the region (e.g. Buzalka 2008; Foszto 2009).

In short, the subjects Hann is tackling when grappling with the problem of populism and crisis of democracy reflect his attachment to a few themes that constitute *leitmotivs* in his scholarship. These are, among others, the questions of marginality and its different manifestations; broadly understood "East/West" dynamics; the relationship between morality and economy; property relations; and last but not least a critical engagement with the notion of "culture". Central among them is the idea of work: an idea that not only shaped the discussions on post-socialist developments (see, e.g., Buchowski 2018; Pine 1995; Ries 2009; Thelen 2006) but which constitute one of the key anthropological notions, as a lens through which to study social organisation, hierarchies, and gender relations, to name but a few.

Hann has engaged with the idea of work in numerous publications, most recently in an article chosen by the editors of this volume as a key reference (Hann 2018). Drawing on his long-term research in rural Hungary, Hann demonstrates that "work" has remained a central value among Hungarian villagers and as such is a target of political manipulation. Discussing contemporary developments, he shows that the villagers' deeply ingrained ideas of work have made them receptive to the xenophobic messages of the Hungarian government. Yet their responses need to be seen in a broader context than the usual recognition that lower classes see refugees as economic migrants, and hence as competitors for already scarce resources. The arguments of Tazlar's inhabitants are related to the idea of fairness—fairness in relation to work opportunities (i.e., among local people who lack resources to go to work abroad and the newcomers' resources), fairness among the European states (i.e., rich Germany vis-à-vis poorer CEE countries), as well as fairness in terms of provision of support and use of resources (i.e., the allowances received by the Hungarian workforce and by migrant-newcomers) (Hann 2018: 246). Hann further uses these examples to argue in favour of an approach which recognises the entanglement between the moral and the material dimensions of the economy (Ibid.: 251).

In this contribution, I draw on Hann's reflections on work, moral and ethical concerns, to discuss a case study of a Polish far-right youth movement, called 'Polish Labour'. Inspired by Hann's scholarship, I demonstrate the centrality of the notion of work in their agenda. I ask to what extent the perception of work—that is, what 'good work' means or who has the right to work—can be said to constitute a yardstick which the movements' members use to make judgements about other, sometimes seemingly unrelated, issues. Like Hann, I try to approach their often-despicable views as an anthropologist should, that is by providing a broader context of their actions and claims and trying to understand them without expiating them and paying attention to the language I use. To put it differently, I want to demonstrate that describing someone as "receptive to xenophobic messages" rather than a "xenophobe" is not a question of relativism, but an attempt at understanding.

Right-wing Populism and a (Missing) Anthropological Perspective

Literature on right-wing populism in Europe is abundant and, as a result of recent developments, it has been growing very quickly. Rather unsurprisingly, political scientists and political sociologists dominate in discussions on the subject (for widely quoted studies, see, e.g. Mudde 2007; Muller 2016; Brubaker 2017). What is also rather unsurprising if we consider the parameters of the broader discussion is the fact that right-wing populism is often discussed in parallel with the far right and neo-nationalism (if not treated synonymously with them), rather than in the context of left-wing populism. This tendency has two problematic outcomes. First, carelessly throwing adjectives at quite varied political phenomena precludes the possibility of understanding what is actually at stake and understanding the difference between political phenomena as different as the Polish Law and Justice party, the German Alternative fur Deutschland party, and the American Tea Party movement. (A careful scrutiny of differences would of course allow us to identify similarities, too—see, e.g., Samet and Schiller 2017). Related to that is the fact that the term "populism" seems to operate mainly as an invective, as a deeply-charged term which simply denotes an opponent and consequently loses its analytical quality (Comaroff 2009). Second, this reluctance to situate right-wing populism within a broader context of populist politics precludes the understanding of the important economic basis of populism which links its left-wing and right-wing variations, as it links its historical and present-day manifestations. It also prevents us from recognising the strategic use of populist rhetorical tropes and agendas by politicians representing different fractions; consider, for example, Italy, where three rather different politicians, Matteo Salvini, Matteo Renzi and Beppe Grillo, can all be said to embody populist features (see Loperfido 2018).

Anthropology has the potential to address these shortcomings. Indeed, many anthropologists discussed the growth of populist sentiments in the context of globalisation and neoliberalisation as early as a decade or two ago, before commentators would use the notion of "populism" to explain the successes of Trump, Orban or Farage (see, e.g., Gingrich and Banks 2006; Kalb and Halmai 2011; Comaroff 2009). An important comparative lens may be found in studies of populism in Latin America and India (e.g. Albro 2000; Hawkins 2010; Hansen 2001). As Hann has argued, a broader—temporarily and geographically— context is necessary to understand what we are observing today.

Still, while it is clear that more anthropological works on populism are needed, in order to provide in-depth empirical evidence, it is still not recognised widely enough that such studies and such knowledge have implications for anthropology *at large*. The first is the recognition of populist currents within anthropology itself (Hann 2017; Mazzarella 2019); and that this somewhat inherent populist stance cannot but affect the ways we interact with our interlocutors and fellow scholars within the field. The second is the acknowledgement of the persistent hierarchies of knowledge. Wary of the problem of Eurocentrism (and at times even Western-Europe-centrism), anthropologists are in the position to demonstrate a more complex political background of current political debates. To show that, as Paula Chakravartty and Skirupa Roy (2017: 4074) point out, "[t]he current scholarly interest in the topic of populism reflects the familiar Eurocentric practice of granting world-historical significance and generalizability to a phenomenon only when it occurs in Europe and North America—hence, the 'global age of populism' is pronounced to be upon us only after the election of Donald Trump to the U.S. presidency in November 2016."

In light of the above premises, anthropologists seem to be best positioned to deliberate (and take seriously) ideas on economy and society that our interlocutors engage with in their everyday lives, including alternative socio-political scenarios they put forward. This means opening up the discussion on populism, rather than closing it off by assuming populism to be just an "accident" on the way. In the following, I am offering a glimpse of one such socio-political project which, although quite marginal, can be said to account for increasingly widespread sentiments. My analysis complicates widespread analyses of populism by demonstrating that in our research into participants' accounts and experiences, the line between criticising "the system" and blaming "the others" is often blurred.

Polish Labour

The material I am drawing on here comes from my ethnographic project on the European far-right youth (Pasieka 2020; 2021; 2022; forthcoming). One of the project's aims is to demonstrate the diversity of personal trajectories of the activists dubbed "far-right" as well as the organisational agendas. The project problematises the very term "far right" in that it points to the socialist component in activists' agendas and their embrace of what are perceived as "traditionally" left-wing agendas and modes of action. In emphasising this, I do not mean to repeat the well-worn cliché about the blurred boundaries between left and right or to question the fact that numerous far-right actors continue to promote hardcore neoliberal policies. On the contrary, the project shows that rather than "blurring" the left/right distinction, my research participants purposefully emphasise the "left" components—in the main anti-capitalist sentiments—and strongly accentuate what makes them different from the neo-liberal right.

One such group is Polish Labour [*Praca Polska*, hereafter: PP] founded in 2017 by Krystian, a former member of the oldest Polish far-right organisation, National Radical Camp. Within the last four years, Kristian has managed to gather several dozens of activists and establish structures in several Polish cities. At the moment, the movement is composed of several dozen people. Krystian and his girlfriend, Maria, likewise a former member of the National Radical Camp, are the leading figures. Both are in their early twenties and combine studies with work.

PP shares with other radical nationalist organisations the belief in a sovereign nation-state, criticism of the EU and the US, and a rejection of foreign capital. Nation, in their view, has an ethnic basis, and migration to Poland and Europe is to be stopped. What makes them stand out among similar organisations is a very detailed programme of social economy, which includes advocating for progressive taxation, availability of social housing, widespread workers' unions, and a reformed labour code. Even though the PP members do not remember socialism, they advocate correcting the mistakes of the transformation era. For example, they consider it vital to address the problem of regional marginalisation by restoring bus and train connections (removed in the post-socialist era due to their presumed unprofitability) and to support the mining industry. Some of their claims appear contradictory, if you consider, for instance, their emphasis on environment-friendly policies and care for nature along with the necessity to build nuclear energy and bring back heavy industry. Other policies, instead, may appear progressive in comparison with the kindred groups, in that PP promotes religiously neutral policies and widely available nurseries and daycare which would allow both mothers and parents in general to work.

PP promotes these ideas and puts them into practice through three forms of activism: "Social Campaigns"—which could also be labeled "informative campaigns"; "Events"—usually one-day-long conferences and fund-raising events; and "Library"—publication and promotion of contemporary and historical works on national and social questions, such as Kazimierz Dagnan and Engelbert Pernerstorfer.[2] Tech-savvy, they successfully use social media to promote their activities. Most of their conferences and lectures are streamed online. They put a strong emphasis on the design and aesthetics, making sure the materials produced are of high quality, eye-catching and different from "typical" nationalist propaganda materials. Their logo includes a simple graphic of an ant and in their promotional materials they rarely reach for national symbols.

---

2   Dagnan (1891–1986) was a Polish politician and creator of a national socialist party in the interwar era. He argued in favor of non-Marxist socialism. Pernerstorfer (1850–1918) was an Austrian social democrat and journalist.

When I met with Krystian for the first time in a Warsaw café I quickly realised my unpreparedness: I had not read Piketty's *Capital in the Twenty-First Century* (2013), to which he was just re-listening as an audiobook. He noticed that I felt embarrassed and in order to cheer me up he said something like "Oh, don't worry, you specialise in ethnic minorities and religious pluralism," which made me realise *he* was well prepared for our conversation. As it turned out, before meeting me he spent a good few hours reading my freely available publications, especially those related to my doctoral project (Pasieka 2015). Knowing what my views were, he did not try to hide or tone down his statements.

This was clear in particular in relation to an issue that constituted the key subject of my earlier work: the plight of ethnic minorities in Poland (especially Ukrainian minorities) and the politics of multiculturalism. Krystian devoted a lot of time to this question, openly stating his opposition to a foreign labour force, which had drastically increased in Poland in recent years (1.5 million Ukrainians in 2019; a quadruple increase on the previous five years). Yet whereas other nationalist groups I have been studying tend to talk about the national government's actions or "EU" politics, he would emphasise that *"capitalists* bring immigrants."

He justified his objection to migrant workers on several grounds. The first was a recognition that he shares with Tazlar villagers (and numerous other people in Europe and beyond) that migrants lead to competition and wage dumping, hence, they are not beneficial for the local (Polish) population. The second was the fact that the situation was not beneficial for Ukrainians: they were underpaid in Poland and often worked in scandalous conditions. On a different occasion, he stated that "Ukrainians are less and less satisfied with the work in Poland. Poles treat them as serfs [*jak chłopow pańszczyźnianych*]." The employers were eager to employ them because they had to be more subordinate and dependent on them. In order to raise Ukrainians' awareness of this issue, PP created a poster targeting Ukrainian workers and informing them about the minimum wage in Poland, with the aim of making them realise that they were underpaid. The third reason was that by leaving Ukraine, migrants—usually young and skilled people—were slowing down the process of change in and transformation of their own society. As a consequence, they were also aborting the process of global change.

"Anticapitalism needs to be global," says Krystian, "Ukrainians need to do it [act against capitalism] at home."[3]

Generally, ethnic diversity does not go hand-in-hand with class/workers' solidarity, Krystian claimed. He would corroborate this claim with examples from history, among them the case of Austro-Hungary discussed by Pernerstorfer. "In a factory, some sort of borderland comes into being," he said, concluding that there was no place for national commissions within workers' unions. He grinned when pronouncing the word "borderland," as if to say: "yes, I did read your stuff on minorities in Poland and know all this terminology". He was ironic at times, but throughout most of the conversation he was clearly and straightforwardly outlining their programme. If I objected to his claims, he never adopted a defensive tone but simply explained his position in the context of their broader agenda.

Krystian emphasises that their movement is only making its first steps and that they need to start as a sort of think-tank. "We need to arm activists with economic arguments," he says. "We need to *economise nationalism* [zekonomizować nacjonalizm]." This is why, even though the organisation aims to express the interests of the working class, it is mostly represented by students now. He describes its profile as *"inteligencko-pracowniczy"* (of intelligentsia and workers)—a notion that brings to mind the discourse that was prominent in the discussions on the Polish anti-communist regime activism (see Kubik 1994). Krystian claims that PP attracts two kinds of people: those with high cultural capital and a positivist attitude, and workers or union members. What unites them is the belief in "reformism" and in a paced (step-by-step) revolution.

The audience of the events organised by PP supports this claim. One recent PP conference took place in Katowice, a mid-size town in the Silesia region, in a small venue rented for the occasion. Among the audience were university students and graduates as well as a few young men who seemed to have just left a football stadium. PP organises such events quite frequently, each time choosing a specific leading theme. The

---

3   Due to the ongoing Russian aggression on Ukraine, the situation and basic number of Ukrainian workers in Poland has rapidly changed recently. It is too early to make any conclusive statements.

Katowice event was devoted to the situation of workers in the Silesia region.

The first part of the meeting was composed of a few short lectures. Among the issues discussed was the situation of Polish miners and the history of the national-socialist movement in Upper Silesia from the nineteenth century until the World War II. Krystian, who gave a talk on the latter issue, emphasised that the Silesians fought for values similar to those that PP represents: that is, they fought for better working conditions and they strove to defend Polish identity. When asked by the audience how much the historical dimension mattered, he said that PP could learn political pragmatism and realism from their forebears.

The second part took the form of a workshop, the aim of which was to discuss potential cooperation partners for PP. Activists and guests created a circle to facilitate the exchange of ideas and to emphasise the horizontal nature of the movement. The first group of potential partners discussed were entrepreneurs to whom PP wanted to reach out. A specific goal would be to make them sensitive to the issue of workers' rights as well as the benefits for the national economy: paying taxes in Poland and employing ethnic Poles.

The second group targeted as potential collaborators were local representatives of the governing right-wing populist party, Law and Justice. In emphasising their wish to cooperate with local party members, the speakers assumed these individuals to be less corrupt than high-level politicians and more genuinely concerned about everyday matters. Some activists objected, emphasising that cooperation could be difficult due to PiS politicians' clerical outlook. Others challenged those claims, in turn asking their opponents not to exaggerate the role of religious matters when it came to cooperation in other fields. Taking the floor, Krystian emphasised that what mattered more were PiS views on "social questions." Generally, however, he believes that the PP agenda evokes much more interest among left-leaning people, especially those who do not feel represented by the parties dubbed left-wing but in fact preoccupied only with issues of "sexuality" (i.e. gay rights, transgender rights, etc.). One of his mates added that yet another obsession of such groups is "anti-fascism". Instead of tackling economic issues and real problems, they sit at university conferences and ponder whether something counts as fascism or not. Krystian proposed, however, to at least try to establish cooperation with those students studying economics.

Yet another activist spoke up about a potential alliance with football fans, in what appeared to be an inclusive gesture towards some of the guests. In trying to engage them in the discussion, Krystian asked the guests to say something about the social/class background of football fans. They confirmed that most of them were working class. However, they did not seem keen to engage in discussion; instead, they eagerly took part in the martial arts training that concluded the conference.

Work and Populism, Work of Populism

Many of the activities carried out by PP might just as well be found among left-wing groups. They offer free-of-charge school tutorial for children from needy families and legal advice in the domain of labour law, social assistance, or house rentals. What PP activists do and claim is centred on the idea of work and on the plights of working people, and what prompted many of them to act were precisely different work experiences. Asked about his reasons for leaving the National Radical Camp and establishing a new group, Krystian says: "Well, I got onto the job market—and realised something had to be done."

Krystian's rationale is far from unique. Similar discourses and forms of activism have been common for numerous social movements across Europe; those movements which combine nationalist, exclusionary rhetoric with a vision of a socialist state and some sort of "welfare chauvinism." Hogar Social in Spain, Casa Pound in Italy, early Golden Dawn in Greece—all of them offer a radical critique of the status quo. Operating at times (only) as movements and at times as political parties, they emphasise their role as carriers of a new political message and new forms of activism, including attempts to colonise the previously left-wing political terrain. They talk about the needs and voices of average people, betrayal of the elites, and abandonment of the working-class by left-wing parties. Does this make them "populists"?

Krystian is eager to offer an answer to this question. In discussing the Polish case, he says that the ruling party, Law and Justice, won the 2015 elections thanks to a generous social programme and promises of redistribution but has by now abandoned strictly populist claims centred around social issues. However, their initially generous social spending awoke societal aspirations, especially among what he calls the "*klasa ludowa*"—"popular class." And this is where movements like his step in. "The demons like us come now," he says with an ironic smile. It would be stupid, he observes, not to embrace the opportunity and try to fill the existing gap and to put forward their view of a nationalist-socialist order.

In talking about the aspirations of the "popular class", Krystian at the same time sheds light on the trajectories of the PP members. The young people who support movements as PP members are not necessarily unemployed, nor have they been forced to accept any job offer available. More commonly they are underemployed—they have jobs beneath their real qualifications, whether in their home country or as seasonal migrants in Western countries. Many of them are fed up with being second-class workers in foreign firms and resent the working conditions offered, for example, by multinational corporations in Poland. They realise the discrepancy of earnings in their home country and in Germany, France or the UK.

Is there anything unique for the post-socialist context about such activism and such claims? PP activists' peers in Southern Europe invoke a very similar vocabulary, complaining about exploitation by the West and brain drain. Like Hungarians and Poles, they complain about their state being reduced to "a new state of peripheral dependency" (Hann 2019b). Across Europe, young people talk about unfulfilled promises and a lack of perspectives. We could hear similar rhetoric expressed by Hann's interlocutors (2018).

It is thus perhaps not about uniqueness, but about the relative weight of promises that the youth in post-socialist Europe have at the back of their minds when assessing today's situation. The "happily ever after" narrative of post-1989 development, and the political-economic mechanisms that accompanied it, were particularly consequential in shaping both expectations and opportunities. Thus, rather than being seen as an odd case—as incubators of populism (Hann 2017) and regions inhabited by nationalists and xenophobes—Eastern Europe is an important, comparative case whose analysis sheds light on a much broader terrain.

Conclusion

In a recent analysis of civil society and populism, Hann observes that his research participants in rural Hungary vote for Orban not because they became "rabid nationalists" but "because no other party has made a comparable effort to speak to their concerns, following a generation of postsocialist insecurity in which they have been systematically marginalized at the expense of a new national bourgeoisie" (2020: 479). Indeed, the incapacity to reach voters is an argument that has been made often by those who have tried to explain the shifting sympathies—the growing support for far-right and right-wing populism in the European cities' peripheries, the predominantly working-class areas, and the popularity of liberal, left-wing ideologies in the bourgeois city centres—whether in Slovakia, Italy or the UK. In Poland, even scholars have begun to admit that the language of the left has become so impenetrable and obsessed with political correctness that they are stressed about their own vocabulary being not *en vogue* (Matyja 2020; see also Loperfido 2018).

Hann further quotes data provided by Piketty to demonstrate persistent inequalities between Western and Eastern Europe. The young founder of PP would likely welcome reference to Piketty, as he would agree with the importance of language. He might be a student and a self-acclaimed think-tank founder but he works at the reception desk in a hardware store. "I meet *these people* everyday," he says, by "these people" meaning the underpaid construction workers (Ukrainian and Polish) and industry employees. "These people" are at the same time the people he aims to reach through the PP agenda, through the posters which inform them that an employer is obliged to provide an employee with water, as well as those which warn against a wave of migrant workers from Belarus.

Statements of this sort clearly demonstrate that a genuine preoccupation with the plight of the working-class, as well as a consideration of work as a key value may go hand in hand with exclusionary rhetoric. It would be simplistic to see the latter only as the result of economic conditions, just as it would be paternalistic to "expiate" Eastern European xenophobic rhetoric, which comes to the fore once their beloved working-class members have a foreign passport.

It would equally be simplistic to romanticise the new generation of activist-volunteers who dig up the Marxist language of capitalist exploitation but turn a blind eye to the fact that they use this language to perform exclusion. Hann's work prompts us to do something else: he reminds us that this exclusionary rhetoric linked with the (imagined or real) competition on the job market needs to be situated in a wider context of deep-seated ideas and values, including moral ideas—which may include both local constructions of community and universal human strivings. In talking about a populist tradition within anthropology, he rightly observes that anthropology specialises in the study of persisting sociocultural traits, not only change but also continuity (Hann 2017). The problem of populism, as analysed by him, is thus a very good illustration of critical anthropological issues: the tension between certain universal patterns and local specificities, and specifically between the conflict produced by neoliberal economies and the different expressions of "countermovement."

Seen in this light, it may seem that what we are facing today is not even a mis-understanding of populism—its causes, its appeal, its main actors—but a refusal to engage with it. We note here yet another analogy with the discussions on post-socialism: although anthropologists have talked about the complexity of the post-socialist transformation (and especially its "less bright" sides), since the early 1990s, it took quite some time until their insights were acknowledged. Commenting upon his recent (and yet another) critical engagement with the "export" of Western civil society to Eastern Europe, Hann expressed that he is embarrassed he keeps making this point all over again, and has been for over thirty years now (Hann, private communication). Apparently, swimming against the tide requires not only skill but also endurance.

References

Albro, Robert. 2000. The Populist Chola: Cultural Mediation and the Political Imagination in Quillacollo, Bolivia. *Journal of Latin American Anthropology* 5 (2), 30–88, https://doi.org/10.1525/jlca.2000.5.2.30.

Brubaker, Rogers. 2017. Between nationalism and civilizationism: the European populist moment in comparative perspective. *Ethnic and Racial Studies* 40 (8) 1191–1226, https://doi.org/10.1080/01419870.2017.1294700.

Buchowski, Michał. 2018. *Czyściec: antropologia neoliberalnego postsocjalizmu.* Poznań: Wydawnictwo Naukowe Uniwersytetu im. Adama Mickiewicza.

Buzalka, Juraj. 2008. *Nation and Religion. The Politics of Commemoration in South-East Poland.* Berlin: Lit-Verlag.

Chakravartty, Paula and Srirupa Ro (eds). 2017. Mediatized Populisms: Interasian Lineages. *International Journal of Communication (Special Issue)* 11, 4073–4092, https://ijoc.org/index.php/ijoc/article/view/6703/2157.

Comaroff, Jean. 2011. Populism and Late Liberalism: A Special Affinity? *The ANNALS of the American Academy of Political and Social Science* 637 (1), 99–111, https://doi.org/10.1177/0002716211406079.

Fosztó, László. 2009. *Ritual Revitalisation after Socialism: Community, Personhood, and Conversion among Roma in a Transylvanian Village.* Munster: Lit-Verlag.

Gingrich, A. and M. Banks. 2006. *Neo-nationalism in Europe & Beyond. Perspectives from Social Anthropology.* New York; Oxford: Berghahn Books.

Hann, Chris. 1997. The Nation-State, Religion, and Uncivil Society: Two Perspectives from the Periphery. *Daedalus* 126 (2), 27–45.

Hann, Chris. 1998. Postsocialist Nationalism: Rediscovering the Past in Southeast Poland. *Slavic Review* 57 (4), 840–863, https://doi.org/10.2307/2501049.

Hann, Chris. 2015. The fragility of Europe's Willkommenskultur. *Anthropology Today* 31 (6), 1–2, https://doi.org/10.1111/1467-8322.12208.

Hann, Chris. 2016. Overheated underdogs: civilizational analysis and migration on the Danube-Tisza interfluve. *History and Anthropology* 27 (5), 602–616, https://doi.org/10.1080/02757206.2016.1219353.

Hann, Chris. 2017. Whose moods? Anthropologists in a Bubble. Comment on Borneman, John, and Parvis Ghassem-Fachandi "The concept of *Stimmung*: from indifference to xenophobia in Germany's refugee crisis". *Hau: Journal of Ethnographic Theory* 7 (3), 147–151, https://www.journals.uchicago.edu/doi/pdfplus/10.14318/hau7.3.009.

Hann, Chris. 2019a. The road to populism. *Global Dialogue* 9, October 25, https://globaldialogue.isa-sociology.org/the-road-to-populism/.

Hann, Chris. 2019b. Anthropology and populism. *Anthropology Today* 35 (1), 1–2, https://doi.org/10.1111/1467-8322.12479.

Hann, Chris. 2019c. Talk during plenary session "Populist persusations," DGSKA Conference, Konstanz, October 2, 2019

Hann, Chris. 2020. In search of civil society: from peasant populism to postpeasant illiberalism in provincial Hungary. *Social Science Information,* 59 (3), 459–483, https://doi.org/10.1177/0539018420950189.

Hansen, Thomas. 2001. *Wages of Violence: Naming and Identity in Postcolonial Bombay.* Princeton; Oxford: Princeton University Press, https://doi.org/10.2307/j.ctv346nsw.

Hawkins, Kirk. 2010. Who Mobilizes? Participatory Democracy in Chávez's Bolivarian Revolution. *Latin American Politics and Society* 52 (3), 31–66, https://doi.org/10.1111/j.1548-2456.2010.00089.x.

Kalb, Don and Halmai Gábor, (eds). 2011. *Headlines of Nation, Subtexts of Class. Working Class Populism and the Return of the Repressed in Neoliberal Europe.* New York; Oxford: Berghahn Books.

Loperfido, Giacomo. 2018. What Can Anthropology Say about Populism? *Anthropology News* 59 (3), e240-e243, https://doi.org/10.1111/AN.801.

Matyja, Rafał. 2020. Matyja: Lewica mogłaby być partią udanej transformacji sektora publicznego. *Krytyka Polityczna*, 22 July, https://krytykapolityczna.pl/kraj/lewica-partia-udanej-transformacji-sektor-publiczny-rafal-matyja/.

Mazzarella, William. 2019. The Anthropology of Populism: Beyond the Liberal Settlement. *Annual Review of Anthropology* 48 (1), 45–60, https://doi.org/10.1146/annurev-anthro-102218-011412.

Mudde, Cas. 2007. *Populist Radical Right Parties in Europe.* Cambridge: Cambridge University Press, https://doi.org/10.1017/CBO9780511492037.

Müller, Jan-Werner. 2016. *What Is Populism?* Philadelphia: University of Pennsylvania Press, https://doi.org/10.9783/9780812293784.

Pasieka, Agnieszka. 2015. *Hierarchy and Pluralism. Living Religious Difference in Catholic Poland.* New York: Palgrave Macmillan, https://doi.org/10.1057/9781137482860.

Pine, Francis. 1995. Kinship, Work and the State in Post-socialist Rural Poland. *Cambridge Anthropology* 18, 47–58.

Ries, Nancy. 2009. Potato Ontology: Surviving Postsocialism in Russia. *Cultural Anthropology* 24 (2), 181–212, https://doi.org/10.1111/j.1548-1360.2009.01129.x.

Samet, Robert and Naomi Schiller. 2017. All Populisms Are Not Created Equal. *Anthropology News* 58, e63-e70, https://doi.org/10.1111/AN.432.

Thelen, Tatjana. 2006. Experiences of Devaluation: Work, Gender and Identity in eastern Germany. *Working paper, Max Planck Institut für ethnologischen Forschung* No. 85, Halle/Saale, https://www.eth.mpg.de/cms/en/publications/working_papers/wp0085.

10. *Transoceania*

Connecting the World beyond Eurasia[1]

Edyta Roszko

Introduction

As a child, I often sat and stared at a yellow-grey stone carving that had pride of place atop the heavy wooden wardrobe at the house of my late paternal grandparents in Białystok—a city in north-eastern Poland. The carving was peculiar—two connected vessels interlaced with galloping deer, blooming flowers, and monkeys, both seated and climbing. My father told me that he remembered the carving ensconced in that exact place on the wardrobe as far back as his own childhood. My grandmother (born in 1913) told me that the piece had been in her family for generations. It had been brought to Białystok from Ekaterinoslav (present-day Dnipro, in central Ukraine)—a territory historically contested by the Russian (1721–1917) and Ottoman Empires (1299–1922) and the Polish–Lithuanian Commonwealth (1569–1795)— where she was born and where her father ran the Tsar's stables. Like many Poles who lived in the Russian Empire at the turn of the twentieth century, her father had found his way into the imperial administration and secured a position that guaranteed a good livelihood for his family. But he had a keen survival instinct and sensed the Bolshevik Revolution looming on the horizon. My grandmother was a few years old when her

---

1   In researching and writing this article I have received funding from the European Research Council (ERC) under the European Union's Horizon 2020 research and innovation programme (Grant agreement No. 802223 *Transoceanic Fishers: Multiple Mobilities in and out of the South China Sea*—TransOcean—ERC-2018- StG).

https://doi.org/10.11647/OBP.0282.10

father decided to leave Ekaterinoslav for Białystok. He sold whatever he could and left the rest of his property behind, taking only a few valuables: some gold Russian rubles, jewellery, kilims and artwork. My grandmother did not know how her family had acquired the stone carving; all she knew was that it came "from somewhere in the East, from Siberia". Years later, when my profession as an anthropologist brought me to Taiwan and southern China for ethnographic research, I encountered scenic and floral motifs in Chinese works of art that I recognised as similar to the carving on my grandmother's wardrobe. Later, I learned that my grandmother's double vase was a Chinese calligraphy inkpot and brush holder carved from soapstone, most likely in one of the early nineteenth-century Qing dynasty imperial workshops in the coastal province of Fujian or Zhenjiang. My family probably came into possession of this decorative piece through the overland trade route linking Harbin—where many Poles worked—to Europe via the Eurasian landmass.

I bring up this family heirloom because it serves as an illustration of the interactions and circulations that have connected Europe and Asia through the mobility of people ever since the time of the old Silk Road. More recent interactions brought chinoiserie objects—including the one on my great-grandparents' wardrobe—into European homes in the eighteenth and ninetieth centuries. The chinoiserie fashion admittedly represented the rather superficial and orientalised vision of the 'Far East' that had begun to form in the European imagination after Vasco da Gama's discovery of the direct sea route to India and the consequent increased access to China through expanding European trade with Asia. This vignette is not so much intended to point out the European fascination with the East, but to open up my discussion of connectivity between Europe and Asia, which has much deeper historical roots than Vasco da Gama's maritime expedition to India or the modest Chinese soapstone carving at the house of my grandparents might suggest. This chapter is about such connectivities, but extends beyond them to a non-Eurasian and non-Eurocentric history of long-term interactions which continue to co-define the world we inhabit today.

Historians tend to characterise societies in terms of empires, geographers in terms of continents and nation-states, and anthropologists in terms of specific localities and cultures. Trained in British social anthropology, Chris Hann, who conducted his ethnographic research in socialist and post-socialist Eastern Europe and various parts of the Turkic-speaking world, took a different route: he used his knowledge of specific places and cultures to rethink the European continent and the so-called European civilisation from a *longue durée* perspective. Hann shifted his attention from the historically modern cartographic classifications that divide Asia and Europe into two separate continents and culturally distinct civilisations to the persistent connectivities and commonalities across the entire landmass known as *Eurasia*. But for Hann, 'Eurasia' is much more than a continent *per se*. Rather, it is a "'supra continental' unity forged over the past three millennia" that expanded from "its core civilizations to include more and more non agrarian penumbra regions, where quite different forms of civilization developed" (Hann 2016: 2). The concept of Eurasia thus offers a perspective that seeks to escape the binary of Europe and the rest of the world—the West and the rest—and rejects the "a priori existence of Europe and Asia as distinct continents" (Hann 2018b: 17; Hann 2018a; Goody 2010; see also Lieberman 2003).

It was only in the early modern period that Europe carved itself out from the Eurasian landmass as a separate continent, making it the only continent completely connected by land to another continent (Lewis and Wigen 1997: 28–31; Salemink forthcoming). Oscar Salemink (forthcoming) argues that, historically speaking, the idea of Europe emerged through the collection, circulation, classification and exhibition of objects from places outside of Europe—Africa, Asia and the Americas—in the museums and curiosity cabinets of the early modern period, when Europe rose to world dominance. At the same time, the museums and curiosity cabinets constituted the very space where the *representations* of the racialised, non-European worlds were developed in the name of European science and "objective truth" (Gregory 1994). Hann developed his concept of Eurasia to go beyond this kind of Eurocentrism, which envisioned Europe as a unique and distinct continent and as the pinnacle of civilisation vis-à-vis all the others. Nevertheless, when he published his clearest and most definitive exposé of his Eurasia concept in the pages of *Current Anthropology*, some commentators accused him of simply offering yet another type of universalist ethnocentrism that continues to obscure the intellectual and technological contributions that Africa, Oceania and the Americas have made to Eurasia (Hann 2016: 10–20). Hann himself admits that his emphasis on Eurasia implies a concentration on agrarian empires and, thus, on terrestrial connections, thereby overlooking the important maritime connectivities across the Indian Ocean and other seas. To correct this terrestrial bias, he notes that we need more thorough engagement with the Indian Ocean, including the Swahili coast of East Africa and the southern shores of the Mediterranean (Hann 2018b: 17).

This chapter is not intended to be another discussion of the utility of Hann's concept of Eurasia, but an attempt to take his *longue durée* optic to pose new questions about what non-Eurasian histories of globalisation have to "contribute to wider historical conversations [...] without abandoning the particularism of the ethnographer" (Hann 2017: 227). Hann observes that the prevailing present-centric approach in social science tends to look at historically "shallow temporalities" of the modern globalised world, rarely extending beyond the reach of the memory of elderly informants. To remedy the lack of any serious scrutiny of the present as a historical outcome, Hann advocates engaging with world history and contextualising ethnographic data "with regard to long-term patterns of socio-cultural resilience and transformation" (Hann 2017: 226–227). At the same time, he warns that even global history is too often trapped in Eurocentric narratives and Western geographical imaginaries that have become hegemonic on a universal scale, something that is imaginatively captured in Michel-Rolph Trouillot's concept of North Atlantic universals (2002). As a former student of Chris Hann, I started my anthropological endeavours with a localised focus on religious practices among coastal communities in central Vietnam, but moved on to global competitions over resources, starting with the South China Sea and gradually expanding outward. Consequently, I find myself closer than ever to Hann's injunction to combine ethnography with deep history and even archaeology—a point I will develop later. I agree with Hann that it is important to destabilise Western narratives of modernity grounded in a European continental pedigree, but I also believe that engaging with global history from the perspective of the sea and archipelagos might be a way to add depth and complexity to the terrestrial bias in his narrative of Eurasian historical connectivities (Trouillot 2002; Gilroy 1993; DeLoughrey 2007). While I take inspiration from Hann's concept of Eurasia and his focus on interconnectedness and commonalities within Eurasia, I wish to pose a different question: What can we learn about long-term exchanges and interactions if we turn to the ocean instead of the Eurasian landmass as the basis for an alternative global history? To answer this question, I address sea-borne oceanic connectivity *before*, *during* and *after* the age of European expansion and supremacy, and embrace the discovery that all seas and oceans are in fact a single global ocean.

Following the *Ocean Literacy Framework*, which defines 'the ocean' as "one interconnected circulation system powered by wind, tides, the force of the Earth's rotation (Coriolis effect), the Sun, and water density differences", I conceive of all the planet's oceans as a single ocean with many ocean basins, including the Atlantic, Indian, Pacific, Southern and Arctic. Taking the singularity of the globally interconnected ocean instead of the Eurasian continent as a starting point, I propose, in parallel to Eurasia, the concept of *Transoceania* to foreground the Atlantic, Indian, and Pacific basins and the peoples who navigate them and have always been mobile. In doing so, I extend the continental and ocean worlds beyond territorially bounded empires, nation-states and inward-looking national histories. Transoceania thus is not a place, but a spatio-temporal construct that captures people's marine and maritime mobilities in past and present, thereby connecting vernacular geographies and histories that straddle both ocean basins and continents. I do not claim by any means that this is new. Gustavo Lins Ribeiro, in his response to Hann's concept of Eurasia, offers the example of the tight wooden world of the sailing ship, where labour flows of "sailors, pirates, and slaves disseminated ideas of freedom and societies without state, class division, and exploitation across the Atlantic in a triangle formed by Africa, the Americas and Europe, influencing Northern radical imaginaries" (Ribeiro in Hann 2016: 17; Rediker 1987; Linebaugh and Rediker 2000; Taylor 1988; Gilroy 1993). In *The Graves of Tarim*, Engseng Ho (2006) brilliantly narrates the "local cosmopolitanism" of Hadrami Yemen migrants who settled down in Arabia, India and Southeast Asia, becoming locals while remaining cosmopolitans with their connections across the sea. Drawing on history, archaeology and geography, Burkhard Schnepel and Edward Alpers (2018) trace the connections and interactions between small islands in the Indian Ocean, where migrant histories of labour, slavery and cosmopolitanisms traverse littoral empires and nation-states.

The transoceanic perspective thus helps us to avoid a Eurocentric "territorial trap" (Agnew 1994) and to recover subaltern historiographies which would otherwise remain concealed. By attending to these subaltern historiographies not from the terrestrial core of the continent but from its ragged edges—coasts, islands and archipelagos—we are able to chart the hidden contours of vernacular geographies that contest the linear perspective of Eurasian chronological history and rigid modern claims of bounded territory, ethnicity and nationality. The next part of this chapter turns precisely to these ragged edges connected not by the lines of modern cartography, but by human mobility.

Mobile Maritime Peoples, not Empires

Jack Goody aptly pointed out the arrogance of Europeans who tend to think of themselves as having first "'discovered' and 'explored' the world" (Goody 2010: 60). Indeed, in geography lessons in high school, most of us learned that Christopher Columbus and Vasco da Gama were those who discovered 'new continents' and opened the ocean to European trade and colonisation, but we learn almost nothing about those who left no written records of their voyages. But these ancient mariners who sailed their outrigger canoes and dhows by the stars, clouds and waves in the open ocean left other evidence that modern science is recovering and interpreting, albeit on a steep learning curve. Linguistic, ethnographic, genetic and bio-archaeological findings suggest that neither the fifteenth-century European explorers nor their famous antecedent—the Ming-era admiral Zheng He, who reached the East African Coast at the beginning of the fifteenth century—had a monopoly on transoceanic voyages (Goody 2010: 60; see also Wade 2005; Sen 2016). The inventors of long-distance navigation were Austronesian-speaking seafarers who probably originated in what today is southern China or Taiwan and now populate most of insular Southeast Asia and the Pacific. More than five millennia ago they started the most extraordinary series of voyages of discovery and settlement in all of human history (Roszko 2021a: 297; Dening 2007).

Over the next thousand years, they spread south through the Philippines to Sulawesi, the Moluccas, northern Borneo and eastern Java. Two thousand years ago they sailed from Southeast Asia as far as

Madagascar in the Indian Ocean and Easter Island in the Pacific Ocean (Crowther et al. 2016). Aotearoa, now known as New Zealand, was probably the land they settled last, arriving there around 1300 CE. This was not a single wave of migration, but a staggered series of voyages that took place in stages. For example, while it is known that Madagascar is populated by Austronesian speakers, new archaeobotanical evidence suggests that Austronesians settled in mainland Africa and the Comoros archipelago before they translocated to Madagascar (Crowther et al. 2016: 6639). Navigating oceans and seas was not just a matter of contacting new people, but more often a matter of renewing already existing ties and networks (Tagliacozzo 2009: 114). There are accounts indicating that during the first millennium and a half of the Common Era, peoples from the Indonesian archipelago still retained commercial contact with Madagascar (Reid 2015: 64). When the first generation of Portuguese travellers arrived in Madagascar in the mid-1500s, they also encountered the memory of this long-ago travel and connection with Southeast Asian people described as from "Jawa" (Reid 2015: 64). To this day, across the Indonesian archipelago, the Malayo-Austronesian term *merantau*—referring to travel and diasporic connectivity—persists both in practice and in narrative (Salazar 2016). Anthropologists also argue that a pre-thirteenth-century trade route plied by Austronesians (most likely Malagasy) might have extended from Madagascar to southern Arabia via the Swahili coast. The archaeobotanical record, which includes plants collected in Madagascar and on the coast of the East African mainland (Crowther et al. 2016), is complemented by Ibn al-Mujawir's early thirteenth-century account of the western and southern areas of the Arabian Peninsula, which provides some clues about the mobility and networks of Austronesian speakers. On his journey to Aden around 1230, Ibn al-Mujawir noted that people from "al Qumr"—which is present-day Madagascar—travelled between the island of Kilwa (off the coast of what is now Tanzania), Mogadishu and Aden using outrigger canoes, which suggests their Austronesian origins (Fleisher et al. 2015: 107; Smith 2008).

Anthropologists speculate that these mariners might have paid regular visits to the old port of Sharma (in what is now Yemen) and other southern Arabian ports, and it is even possible that east-African traders and other maritime labourers travelled aboard Austronesian vessels and Arabo-Persian ships (Fleisher et al. 2015: 107). Other botanical evidence links Southeast Asians with Polynesian peoples, but some anthropologists have long argued that Polynesians might also have some Native American ancestry, pointing to the existence of crops native to the Americas in Polynesia (Ioannidis et al. 2020). Furthermore, the recent analysis of genome-wide variation in individuals from islands across the Pacific provides indisputable genetic evidence of prehistoric contact between Polynesians and South Americans more than a millennium ago (Ioannidis et al. 2020). While some archaeologists argue that South Americans reached eastern Polynesia, bringing their native crops, stoneworking skills and certain cults with them, the question of whether it was Polynesians who sailed east to South America and back or South Americans who sailed west remains open (Wallin 2020: 1). Both possibilities seem to fit the genetic data (Ioannidis et al. 2020). In tracing the human history of the ocean and its connectivity, we should not forget about expeditions made by groups of Amerindian mariners who ventured far beyond the continental mainland to reach the Caribbean islands about 4000 BCE. In northern Europe, the Vikings sailed across the north Atlantic between the eighth and eleventh centuries, reaching Iceland, Greenland and Newfoundland to the west, as far south as North Africa and the Mediterranean, and as far east as Russia (Kiev), Constantinople and the Middle East (Brink 2008). These European Vikings find their parallel in the Cham seafarers of early Southeast Asia. Much as the Cham—an Austronesian-speaking seafaring group in what is now central Vietnam—never formed a unified kingdom and drew on ethnically diverse maritime peoples to mount their naval attacks (Hall 2011: 80; Hardy and Nguyễn Tien Đông 2019), so the Vikings' maritime raids were made by seafaring warriors hailing not only from Scandinavia, but from other places as well. A recent genetic study shows that Vikings who originated in what today is Sweden did not form a singular 'Viking world', but actually constituted multiple worlds with a large proportion of Southern European and Asian ancestry, thereby demonstrating large-scale connectivity facilitated by sea-borne mobility (Margaryan et al. 2020).

The Indian writer and trained anthropologist Amitav Ghosh confessed that he yearns "for a certain kind of universalism—not a universalism merely of principles and philosophy, but one of face-to-face encounters, of everyday experience" (2009: 37). Ghosh connected this kind of yearning, "the affinity for strangers", to the spirit of the Non-Aligned Movement—a forum of so-called developing states that sought to navigate a world divided during the Cold War and which was characterised by the ethos of decolonisation and "deep historical roots and powerful cultural resonances". In the field of culture, Ghosh (2009: 37–38) says this kind of xenophilia "represented an attempt to restore and recommence the exchanges and conversations that had been interrupted by the long centuries of European imperial dominance" but that had, in reality, never ceased. As I have indicated, these exchanges and conversations stretch back to the ancient mariners who navigated the Indian and Pacific oceans and the Caribbean, but they also extend to the commerce and communications that once linked Yemen and China, Indonesia and East Africa, India and the Middle East (Ghosh 2009: 37–38), as I discuss in the next section.

The Ocean Worlds

It was historians rather than anthropologists who turned to the oceans and seas as a unit of analysis in mapping the kind of universalism that builds on long-standing sea-borne interactions and exchanges. The best example of that approach is Fernand Braudel's (1972) seminal work on the 'Mediterranean World' and the rise of civilisations, which drew on the fragmented geographies of peninsulas and seas and their connection to hinterlands. From a Braudelian perspective, the Roman Empire was terrestrial, but it was also and above all a maritime empire entirely centred on the Mediterranean, which formed the geographic core of the empire. In fact, the Mediterranean Sea was so important to the Romans that they referred to it simply as *Mare Nostrum* ('Our Sea'). In this connection it is worth remembering that the British Empire was a maritime empire consisting of non-contiguous territories connected by transoceanic shipping. More importantly, Braudel's panoramic view of the Mediterranean as a unifying and integrating entity gave new impetus to scholars—including Goody—to shift their focus from the scale of the nation to a broader regional perspective (Roszko 2021a: 304). For example, scholars such as Anthony Reid (1988; 1993; 1999), Denys Lombard (2007) and Heather Sutherland (2003) looked at the

Mediterranean as a model for understanding Southeast Asia. According to this model, China and Southeast Asia are connected across the South China Sea, which integrates them geographically and economically (Sutherland 2003). Anthony Reid proposed the concept of the 'Malay World'—a reference to ancient polities and cultural zones that extended beyond the present-day borders of nation-states—to emphasise the significance of maritime trading connections and networks spanning the Southeast Asia region and southern China (Reid 1988; 1993; 1999; 2004). Gwyn Campbell (2019) went even further, championing the idea of the 'Indian Ocean World', which encompasses the Malay World, China, Africa, and the Middle East through multi-layered connections, whether genetic, botanical, technological, cultural or economic. Recently, tracing the mobility of seafarers, slaves, soldiers, migrants, labourers and convicts who moved around, between and across polities, colonies and empires, Clare Anderson (2012) brought the "subaltern lives in the Indian Ocean World" to our attention. By triangulating the transnational archives of penal colonies and prisons with ethnography, Anderson was able to bring the richness of these sea-borne histories against and "along the archival grain" (see also Stoler 2009). The Mediterranean analogy thus liberated scholars from the straitjacket of "political borders", opening a new avenue for the exploration of connections and borrowings, continuity and change beyond the rigid national, regional or continental frames (Sutherland 2003; see also Lewis and Wigen 1997).[2]

Drawing on Braudel's work on the Mediterranean, Goody (2010: 111–112) argued that capitalism was not the invention of one country or one region, but an aspect of merchant economies that emerged in the Bronze Age. Mediterranean historian David Abulafia (2019: xx) takes this strain of thought further, arguing that the history of long-distance travel across the seas and the ocean is the history of people willing to take risks, including the reinvestment of their resources in search of

---

2   Despite the fact that Europe's geopolitical centrality declined with the emergence of maritime seafaring across the Atlantic, the Mediterranean remained a zone of connection between European powers and their North African colonies and dominions until the independence of Algeria in 1962. In the present time, the Mediterranean is no longer a zone of connection in the Braudelian sense; rather, it has become a militarised border zone separating Africa and the Middle East from Europe. The issue of the Mediterranean Sea emerging as a "'political border", however, is beyond the scope of this chapter.

profit and wealth. Using present-day concepts, he suggests that we could probably call them early capitalists. Abulafi (2019: xxi) continues, becoming visible at the very start of the Indian Ocean trade, in the cities of Bronze Age Mesopotamia, and throughout the following centuries. We are thus dealing not with the 'European miracle', but rather with interacting economies, cultures and systems of knowledge that mutually influenced each other for thousands of years (Goody 2010: 112). In this vein, the world's oldest transoceanic long-distance trade—which created the Indian Ocean World—was tied not to empires or states, but to old diasporas that straddle regions and continents (Hofmeyr 2010: 722). Much of the travel was motivated by religious communities that, for a variety of reasons, often established overseas diasporas. Over time, these diasporas interacted with empires, expanding their diasporic networks—Jewish, Zoroastrian, Buddhist, Christian, Muslim—thereby directly feeding into forms of indigenous capitalism that produced the long-term trajectories leading to today's Asian economic success (Hofmeyr 2010: 722). From a *longue durée* perspective, when the Europeans intruded on the scene of the old inter-Asian trading and banking system of the Indian Ocean, they encountered organised groups of Chinese, Indian and Jewish bankers who maintained long-distance credit networks connecting several countries (Ray 1995: 553).

Historian Rajat Kanta Ray brilliantly shows that the encounter between the European transnational systems of credit and trade and those of the Indian Ocean world was much more complex than the unilateral expansion of the Western "capitalist world economy" that is presented in standard historical accounts. According to Ray (1995: 552–553), "[t]he transition from fixed book credits and unregistered loans to the world of mobile credits operating through negotiable instruments had taken place in Asia long before the arrival of the Europeans". While it is true that modern Asian enterprises are the product of quick adaptation to the new realities of international trade introduced by Europeans, their current success remains deeply rooted in old "Asian maritime and monetary activities going back to a dim past" (Ray 1995: 553). The "European miracle", with its supposed progression from antiquity via feudalism to bourgeois capitalism (Goody 2010: 112), thus dissolves in the old Indian Ocean trade routes and diasporic networks that once connected the Indus civilisation to

Mesopotamia and East Africa and Yemen to Malaysia, just to mention a few examples. Sumerians, Harrapans, Hadrami Yemenis, Gujaratis, Tamils, Buginese, Cham, Malays, Jews, Armenians and Muslims—they all participated for millennia in trade beyond the state. Abulafia (2019: xx) is right when he says that we cannot understand the "European presence around the shores of the oceans" in the fifteenth century without "taking into account the less well-documented activities of non-European merchants and sailors, some of whom were indigenous to the lands in which they lived, others of whom formed part of widespread diasporas". Hann goes even further, asserting that even the narrative of fifteenth-century mercantile capitalism is already so thoroughly situated within the Europeanist paradigm that it would be misleading to take it as a starting point in our understanding of the social relations of the capitalist mode of production, which should be traced back to the urban revolution of Bronze Age Eurasia (Hann 2018b: 27; but cf. Moore 2015; 2016). As Engseng Ho reminds us, the Europeans—Portuguese, Dutch and English—"were strange new traders who brought their states with them" and "created militarised trading-post empires in the Indian Ocean, following Venetian and Genoese precedents in the Mediterranean" (Ho 2006: xxi). Indeed, the age of European supremacy and the ideas Europeans brought to new places initiated a tectonic shift in how the world was imagined, mapped and governed, but it was still a world characterised by the movements of many different tectonic plates.

Transoceania: From Terrestrial Divides to the Singularity and Connectedness of the Ocean

When the anthropologist-turned-journalist Ian Urbina interviewed Vietnamese fishermen who fished without legal permission in other countries' waters, they turned out to be fairly "ocean literate persons", able to explain that "there aren't many oceans; there's just one" (Urbina 2019: 408). Indeed, as noted earlier in the chapter, according to the *Ocean Literacy Guide* there is only one ocean, which covers approximately seventy percent of Earth's surface.[3] However, the fishermen's point regarding

---

3   See 'Ocean Literacy: The Essential Principles and Fundamental Concepts of Ocean Sciences for Learners of All Ages', Version 2, March 2013, http://www.coexploration. org/oceanliteracy/documents/OceanLitChart.pdf.

the singularity of the ocean was not as much about the *functioning* of the ocean as it was about the *connectedness* of the ocean, which has for centuries supported navigation and trade. Environmental historian John Gillis (2018: 109) reminds us that, prior to the nineteenth century, world maps and our geographical vocabulary had focused on a series of distinct points rather than on lines. Harbours, estuaries, headlands, peninsulas and islands were used for navigation purposes and were of great strategic importance to the rise and fall of maritime empires. From the nineteenth century onward, however, we can observe a reverse trend, with lines gaining new importance while the significance of old geographical points along the shore faded. In the nineteenth century, the trading post empires evolved into terrestrial colonial states, with the coast defining one or more of their most significant boundaries (Gillis 2018: 110). Once the islands and littoral were projected as discrete lines on the cartographic grid, the coast and its diverse landforms became the property of the state and, subsequently, of private owners (Gillis 2018: 109–112).

The reconfiguration of the coast from a permeable and fluid zone of contact to a fixed national boundary facilitated the emergence of the Exclusive Economic Zone (EEZ) regime, promulgated from 1982 onwards, which gives states sovereign rights to the exploration of all resources within 200 nautical miles of their coastal shores. As the new regime became widely accepted and globalised, most countries with significant coastlines enclosed or sought to enclose and nationalise their ocean spaces within the maritime borders of the new EEZs. In other words, EEZs allow coastal countries to extend their territorial sovereignty and, in some cases, to claim as their exclusive state property high seas or open sea areas that until the late twentieth century had been zones of connection and resource commons. In the post-Brexit naval stand-off around the Channel Islands, the UK's policy of 'taking back control' of the national waters and France's claims on the basis of 'long-standing traditional fishing grounds' lay bare how historically modern the invention of maritime sovereignty is, incompatible with traditional fishing rights in what until the passage of the United Nations Convention on the Law of the Sea (UNCLOS) in 1982 had been regarded as 'the high seas'. The territorial dispute between China and a number of ASEAN countries and Taiwan over sovereignty in the South China Sea is another case in point where the high seas and remote reefs that have historically been used by ethnically diverse seafarers are imagined by claimant states as their national territory (Roszko 2015). Today, the long-standing connectivity and interactions in the sea create a sort of "territorial anxiety predicated on a historically recent understanding of territoriality as a constituent of state-spatial thinking represented and produced through cartographic technologies" (Roszko 2017: 22; see also Elden 2009; 2013). This could happen because the early twentieth century's concept of homogeneous, bounded space in the form of the nation-state replaced non-Western imperial understandings of unbounded space and territory (Callahan 2009: 141, 146).

Consequently, the old transoceanic circulations had to be appropriated and domesticated by the projection of historically modern concepts such as sovereignty, EEZs and Grotius's idea of *mare liberum* ('freedom of the seas'). Lewis and Wigen (1997: 198) remind us in their excellent analysis that neither continents nor world regions nor modern territorial concepts are timeless entities; they are contingent outcomes of historical processes. They are the result of Western geographical imaginaries that became hegemonic through analytical frameworks such as the "Black Atlantic" (Gilroy 1993) and "North Atlantic universals" (Trouillot 2002). As the categories of vernacular, European, land-based imaginaries were universalised, the resulting universals were, in turn, re-vernacularised, thereby erasing local histories.

An Emergent Thalassography
of Transoceanic Connections

Thus far in this chapter I have sought to foreground the sea-borne connectivity and history *on* the ocean and seas, not just *of* the ocean (see Pearson 2003: 9). Proposing the concept of Transoceania, I have argued that transoceanic connections can help us challenge what Michel-Rolph Trouillot (2002: 220) labelled "particulars" or "chunks of human history" that have been turned into historical standards, not to describe the world, but to offer certain normative visions of it. These standards can blind us to other vernacular geographies and histories. The question then arises: How can anthropologists retrieve mobile sea-borne and sea-oriented livelihoods and histories from the hegemonic and universalised visions of the world that we have access to? The answer, Hann (2017: 227) tells us, is by embracing "the particularism of the ethnographer". Obviously, mobile maritime actors such as fishers, slaves, seafarers, traders and pirates are not easily pinned down within the static geographical and political frames of continents, empires and nation-states. Yet a larger conception of interconnected oceanic worlds helps us to situate the spatial context within which these various forms of floating labour intersect, coexist, interact, collaborate, compete and influence each other across temporal scales (see Gilroy 1993; Hoskins and Nguyen 2014).

An ethnographic approach—one that traces the recent past through the accounts of people recorded in the present—could help connect the dots between spatially distant places and temporally disparate events, practices and people (Roszko 2020: 22–23). Rather than following them on the sea (which can be quite difficult to accomplish), anthropologists can try to grasp the constellations of networks, practices and encounters that are taking place at the edges of water bodies and on the land at specific on-shore nodal points (see Ho 2006; Roszko 2017; Schnepel 2019). In this sense, the empirical and analytical fields are mobile, multi-sited, relational, ongoing and, at the same time, oriented towards the historically deep connections and patterns that underpin people's present-day practices. It appears that the Indian Ocean has attracted the most attention among historians as a "transnational and oceanic" unit of analysis and method (Hofmayer 2012), as a zone of "transregional connections" (Ho 2004), or as "connectivity in motion" (Schnepel and Alpers 2019). This trend has been followed by social scientists, who have adopted a new paradigm of 'transpacific connections' that forge diasporas ("displaced people") and transnationalism ("movement of people and capital across national borders") across the Pacific (Hoskins and Nguyen 2014; see also Roszko 2021a). In my own work on the South China Sea, I have developed a specific form of what I call an *emergent thalassography of transoceanic connections*, in reference to connections that are discontinuous and unstable, but sometimes coalesce around a single, localised ethnographic space that is, at the same time, rarely fixed in one place.

Expanding Peter Miller's (2013: 16) definition of thalassography as "sea-based history-writing that focuses on connectivity, networks and individuals" (see also Vink 2007; Steinberg 2013; 2014), I understand thalassography as the historically informed, vernacular-based geography-*cum*-methodology for researching mobile maritime actors' practices in transoceanic spaces. Based on a combination of historical, ethnographic and documentary methods, thalassography as the historical and vernacular geography of the sea helps to identify sea-oriented people's experience-based, vernacular knowledge of diverse aspects of the ocean. For the floating labour—seafarers, fishers, poachers, smugglers, militia and pirates—the sea is not just a wide surface, but an ever-changing seascape made up of sea features, sites and histories; memories of fortunes, disasters and daily survival; the transgression of bodily, physical and geographical limits; and state regulations and borders. The comparative analysis of life histories, oral traditions, enduring customs, logbooks, maps, graphic representations of territory, and technological changes in maritime and marine practices can help us uncover the ways in which these various labourers interact with ocean spaces, illuminating larger processes that would otherwise remain obscure (see Feldman 2011; see also Hofmeyer 2012; Roszko 2021b; Vink 2007; Steinberg 2014). However, without engaging in deep history and archaeology and without contextualising our ethnographic data, this thalassography methodology still only amounts to historically "shallow temporalities", to use Hann's term (2017: 226). I share his conviction that we should not limit ourselves to "ethnographies in the neoliberal present" (Hann 2016: 7) and that anthropology and archaeology together can provide us with a more complete story about humankind. In my own research, I have found it particularly fruitful to collaborate with archaeologists and historians to trace the various connections at different temporal and spatial scales in order to develop an analytical model of what Hann (2017a: 227) called "long-term patterns of socio-cultural resilience and transformation" of (in my case) coastal communities.

Over the years, bridging different historical periods, countries and regions, I have developed insights into fishers as mobile maritime actors who capitalise on long-standing historical patterns of interconnected marine and maritime mobilities in pursuit of livelihoods (see Roszko 2021b). For example, my ethnographic research and collaboration with archaeologists and historians on a number of islands in the South China Sea uncovered ancient Cham wells as vital sources of freshwater close to the shore. In the past, these wells enabled seafaring, trade and the development of fisheries, making the islands on which the wells were located part of an important network of freshwater sources not only for Cham, but also for Malay, Arab, Persian and other sailors throughout the first two millennia CE. The maritime and marine knowledge of the seascape and the skills accumulated by fishers-*cum*-seafarers during their past ventures have not vanished; they have been passed down through generations and applied to new ventures, whether it is the smuggling of goods or people, poaching or piracy (Roszko 2021b). With the rise of nation-states, the maritime routes expanded and changed and the fluid ethnic identities hardened, but the deeper structures of "local cosmopolitanism" (Ho 2006) underlying "sea work" remain stubbornly persistent down through the generations, if not centuries. Engaging archaeology along with ethnography in recording subaltern transoceanic histories offers an approach that shifts our focus away from unitary models such as national histories and area studies, as well as from colonial histories of expansion, towards more fluid transoceanic connections that span various ocean-based worlds and build on long-standing patterns of movement among peoples who have always been mobile.

Conclusion

Let me briefly return to the opening vignette and the Chinese soapstone carving. My father and grandparents had no idea that the carving was Chinese; all they knew was that it came from the 'East'. It is possible that earlier generations of my paternal grandmother's family were more aware of the object's origins, but this knowledge was lost over time. This chapter is an attempt to recover forgotten, or perhaps more precisely, neglected exchanges and interactions that go far beyond the Eurasian continent. They might start on land and extend far into the ocean worlds, or *vice versa*. By taking Chris Hann's *longue durée* approach, I have shown that the Indian Ocean is the site of some of the oldest trade routes and is one of the earliest connective seas in history in terms of how it was used and navigated by humans. Passage over its waters dates back at least five thousand years, to the time when trade in the Red Sea began. Michael Pearson says that "[b]y comparison, the Atlantic is 1,000 years old, if one takes account of the Viking voyages, while the whole Atlantic is just over 500 years old. The Pacific has seen long-distance voyaging for at most 2,000 years, though nowhere near the density of communication as that over the Indian Ocean" (Pearson 2003: 3). Although the Pacific is the largest of the ocean basins, European geographers claim that it had no name until Europeans baptised it the *Mare Pacificum* ('the Peaceful Sea'). But to the Polynesian seafarers who arrived long before Europeans, "the Pacific's awesome vastness was minimised somewhat by its ten thousand islands, many grouped into archipelagos, which felt to their inhabitants something like watery mainlands, connected rather than separated by water" (Gillis 2012: 45). In the Polynesian navigators' view, the Pacific was the sea of connected islands that represented their common heritage generated by transoceanic voyages, and not a series of isolated islands in the distant ocean (Hau'ofa 2008). Lewis and Wigen (1997: 199) argue that only a sea-centred perspective can reveal these complex connections and exchanges, which come in sometimes unexpected configurations that differ from those that the static constructs of continents might imply.

If Eurasia brings to the fore "unity-in-civilizational-diversity of the Old World" and shatters the myth of Europe as the superior continent (Hann 2016: 1), the analytical construct of Transoceania connects the various ocean and sea worlds, offering a deterritorialised view of competing universalisms beyond the Eurasian supercontinent. Such universalism is not based on European hegemonic visions of the world, but on everyday encounters and interactions through seafaring, fisheries, trade, piracy and slavery (Hofmeyr 2010; 2012; DeLoughrey 2007). It is the ocean rather than the land that makes visible other, vernacular geographies and histories that allow for transregional, comparative and subaltern approaches (Burton et al. 2013). Transoceania is thus a spatio-temporal construct, encompassing both non-Eurasian and Eurasian navigators and mutually constituted by vernacular geographies of continents and ocean worlds. It is not defined by the Bronze Revolution or by the age of European dominance, but by the vernacular histories and practices of mobile peoples. Transoceania's subaltern seafaring histories are grounded not in solid archaeological remnants preserved on the continents; rather, they flow and drift on the scraps and fragments of extant genetic, botanical, linguistic and ethnographic evidence. Transoceania emerges from the discontinuous and wavering landforms in the great singular ocean, rising in the guise of what Antonio Benítez-Rojo (1996) poetically calls "the repeating island"—of languages, ethnicities and traditions—that gives shape to complex, non-linear and fragmented transoceanic genealogies and connectivities. These transoceanic connectivities and genealogies do not exclude continents; to the contrary, they connect continents but—turning European hegemony on its head—tie them more closely to the rhythms of the sea tides and the monsoons. In the end, the connectivities afforded by the geographic constructs of Eurasia and Transoceania have historically intersected and still, to this day, mutually depend on one another.

References

Abulafia, David. 2019. *The Boundless Sea: A Human History of the Oceans*. Oxford: Oxford University Press.

Agnew, John. 1994. The Territorial Trap: The Geographical Assumptions of International relations theory. Review of International Political Economy 1 (1), 53–80, https://doi.org/10.1080/09692299408434268.

Anderson, Clare. 2012. *Subaltern Lives: Biographies of Colonialism in the Indian Ocean World, 1790–1920*. Cambridge: Cambridge University Press.

Benítez-Rojo, Antonio. 1996. *The Repeating Island: The Caribbean and the Postmodern Perspective*. Durham and London: Duke University Press.

Braudel, Fernand. 1972. *The Mediterranean and the Mediterranean World in the Age of Philip II*. New York: Harper Collins Publishers.

Brink, Stefan (ed.). 2008. *The Viking World*. New York: Routledge.

Burton, Antoinette, Madhavi Kale, Isabel Hofmeyr, Clare Anderson, Christopher J. Lee, and Nile Green. 2013. Sea Tracks and Trails: Indian Ocean Worlds as Method. *History Compass* 11 (7), 497–502, https://doi.org/10.1111/hic3.12060.

Callahan, William A. 2009. The Cartography of National Humiliation and the Emergence of China's Geobody. *Public Culture* 21 (1), 141–173, https://doi.org/10.1215/08992363-2008-024.

Campbell, Gwyn. 2019. *Africa and the Indian Ocean World from Early Times to Circa 1900* (New Approaches to African History). Cambridge: Cambridge University Press, https://doi.org/10.1017/9781139028769.

Crowther, Alison, Leilani Lukas, Richard Helm, Mark Horton, Ceri Shipton, Henry T. Wright, Sarah Walshaw, Matthew Pawlowicz, Chental Radimilahy, Katerina Douka, Llorenc Picornell-Gelabert, Dorian Q. Fuller and Nicole L. Boivin. 2016. Ancient Crops Provide First Archaeological signature of the westward Austronesian expansion. *PNAS* 113(24), 6635–6640, https://doi. org/10.1073/pnas.1522714113.

DeLoughrey, Elisabeth. M. 2007. *Routes and Roots: Navigating Caribbean and Pacific Island Literature*. Honolulu: University of Hawai'i Press.

Dening, Greg. 2007. Sea People of the West. *Geographical Review* 97(2), 288–301, https://doi.org/10.1111/j.1931-0846.2007.tb00404.x.

Elden, Stuart. 2009. *Terror and Territory: The Spatial Extent of Sovereignty*. Minneapolis: University of Minnesota Press.

Elden, Stuart. 2013. *The Birth of Territory*. Chicago, IL: University of Chicago Press.

Feldman, Gregory. 2011. If Ethnography is More than Participant-Observation, then The Relations are More than Connections: The Case of Nonlocal Ethnography in a World of Apparatuses. *Anthropological Theory* 11(4), 375–395, https://doi.org/10.1177/1463499611429904.

Fleisher, J., P. Lane, A. LaViolette, M. Horton, E. Pollard, E. Quintana Morales, T. Vernet, A. Christie and S. Wynne-Jones. 2015. When did the Swahili Become Maritime? *American Anthropologist* 117 (1), 100–115, https://doi. org/10.1111/aman.12171.

Ghosh, Amitav. 2009. Confessions of a Xenophile. *Chimurenga* 14, 35–41.

Gilroy, Paul. 1993. *The Black Atlantic: Modernity and Double Consciousness*. London; New York: Verso.

Gillis, John R. 2012. *The Human Shore: Seacoasts in History*. Chicago and London: University of Chicago Press.

Gillis, John R. 2018. The Changing Nature of Ocean Boundaries. In: R. F. Buschmann and L. Nolde (eds). 2018. *The World's Oceans: Geography, History and Environment*. ABC: CLIO, LLC, pp. 110–114.

Goody, Jack. 2010. *The Eurasian Miracle*. Cambridge and Malden: Polity.

Gregory, Derek. 1994. *Geographical Imagination*. Cambridge, MA: Blackwell Publishers.

Hardy, Andrew and Nguyễn Tien Đông. 2019. The People of Champa: Evidence for a New Hypothesis from the Landscape History of Quảng Ngãi. In: Arlo Griffiths, Andrew Hardy and Geoff Wade (eds), 2019. *Champa: Territories and Networks of a Southeast Asian Kingdom*, Paris: École française d'Extrême-Orient, pp. 121–143.

Hall, Kenneth R. 2011. *A History of Early Southeast Asia: Maritime Trade and Societal Development, 100–1500*. Plymouth: Rowman and Littlefield Publishers, INC.

Hann Chris. 2016. A Concept of Eurasia. *Current Anthropology* 57 (1), 1–27, https://doi.org/10.1086/684625.

Hann, Chris. 2017. Long Live Eurasian Civ! Towards a New Confluence of Anthropology and World History. *Zeitschrift für Ethnologie* 142(2), 225–244.

Hann, Chris. 2018a. Preface: Recognizing Eurasia. *Comparativ. Zeitschrift für Globalgeschichte und vergleichende Gesellschaftsforschung* 28 (4), 7–13.

Hann, Chris. 2018b. Eurasian Dynamics: From Agrarian Axiality to the Connectivities of the Capitalocene. *Comparativ. Zeitschrift für Globalgeschichte und vergleichende Gesellschaftsforschung* 28 (4), 14–27.

Ho, Engseng. 2004. Empire through Diasporic Eyes: A View from the Other Boat. *Comparative Studies in Society and History* 46, 210–245.

Ho, Engseng. 2006. *The Graves of Tarim: Genealogy and Mobility across the Indian Ocean.* Berkley, CA; London: University of California Press.

Hofmeyr, Isabel. 2010. Universalizing the Indian Ocean. *PMLA* 125(3), 721–729.

Hofmeyr, Isabel. 2012. The Complicating Sea: The Indian Ocean as Method. *Comparative Studies of South Asia, Africa and the Middle East* 32 (3), 584–590, https://doi.org/10.1215/1089201X-1891579.

Hoskins, Janet. and Viet Thanh Nguyen (eds). 2014. *Transpacific Studies: Framing an Emerging Field.* Honolulu: University of Hawai'i Press.

Hau'ofa, Epeli. 2008. *We Are the Ocean: Selected Works.* Honolulu: University of Hawai'i Press.

Ioannidis, A.G., J. Blanco-Portillo, K. Sandoval, et al. 2020. Native American gene flow into Polynesia predating Easter Island settlement. *Nature* 583, 572–577, https://doi-org.ep.fjernadgang.kb.dk/10.1038/s41586-020-2487-2.

Lieberman, Victor. 2003. *Strange Parallels, c. 800–1830.* Cambridge: Cambridge University Press.

Linebaugh, Peter and Marcus Rediker. 2000. *The Many-Headed Hydra: Sailors, Slaves, Commoners, and the Hidden History of the Revolutionary Atlantic.* Boston: Beacon Press.

Lewis, Martin and Karen E. Wigen. 1997. *The Myth of Continents: A Critique of Metageography.* Berkley, CA; London: University of California Press.

Lombard, Denys. 2007. Another 'Mediterranean' in Southeast Asia. *Chinese Southern Diaspora Studies*, 1, 3–9.

Margaryan, A., D.J. Lawson, M. Sikora, et al. Population Genomics of the Viking World. 2020. *Nature* 585, 390–396, https://doi.org/10.1038/s41586-020-2688-8.

Miller, Peter N. (ed.) 2013. *The Sea: Thalassography and Historiography.* Ann Arbor: University of Michigan Press.

Moore, Jason W. 2015. *Capitalism in the Web of Life: Ecology and the Accumulation of Capital.* London: Verso.

Moore, Jason W. (ed). 2016. *Anthropocene or Capitalocene? Nature, History, and the Crisis of Capitalism.* Oakland: PM Press.

Pearson, Michael. 2003. *The Indian Ocean*. London; New York: Routledge Taylor and Francis Group.

Rediker, Marcus. 1987. *Between the Devil and the Deep Blue Sea: Merchant, Seamen, Pirates, and the Anglo-American Maritime World, 1700–1750*. New York: Cambridge University Press.

Ray, Rajat Kanta. 1995. The Age of European Domination: The Rise of the Bazaar, 1800–1914. *Modern Asian Studies* 29 (3), 449–554.

Reid, Anthony. 1988. *Southeast Asia in the Age of Commerce 1450–1680 (Vol. 1: The Lands Below the Winds)*. New Haven: Yale University Press.

Reid, Anthony. 1993. *Southeast Asia in the Age of Commerce 1450–1680 (Vol. 2: Expansion and Crisis)*. New Haven: Yale University Press.

Reid, Anthony. 1999. *Charting the Shape of Early Modern Southeast Asia*. Chiang Mai: Silkworm Books.

Reid, Anthony. 2004. Understanding Melayu (Malay) as a Source of Diverse Modern Identities. *Journal of Southeast Asian Studies* 32 (3), 295–313, https://doi.org./10.1017/S0022463401000157.

Reid, Anthony. 2015. A History of Southeast Asia: Critical Crossroads. Malden, MA: Wiley Blackwell.

Roszko, Edyta. 2015. Maritime Territorialisation as Performance of Sovereignty and Nationhood in the South China Sea. *Nations and Nationalism* 21 (2), 230–249, https://doi.org/10.1111/nana.12094.

Roszko, Edyta. 2017. Fishermen and Territorial Anxieties in China and Vietnam: Narratives of the South China Sea beyond the Nation frame, *Cross-Currents: East Asian History and Culture Review* 6 (1), 20–51, https://doi.org/10.1177/0891241618758854.

Roszko, Edyta. 2020 [2021]. *Fishers, Monk and Cadres: Navigating State, Religion and the South China Sea in Central Vietnam*. Copenhagen and Honolulu: Nordic Institute of Asian Studies (NIAS) Press and University of Hawai'i Press, http://hdl.handle.net/10125/76750.

Roszko. Edyta. 2021a. Maritime Anthropology. In: Lene Pedersen and Lisa Cliggett (eds). 2021. *The Sage Handbook of Cultural Anthropology*, London: Sage Publication Ltd, pp. 297–315.

Roszko, Edyta. 2021b. Navigating Seas, Markets, and Sovereignties: Fishers and Occupational Slippage in the South China Sea. *Anthropological Quarterly* 94 (4), 639–668, https://doi.org/10.1353/anq.2021.0046.

Salemink, Oscar. Forthcoming. Introduction: Global Art in Local Art Worlds and the Global Hierarchy of Value. In: Oscar Salemink, Amélia Siegel Corrêa, Jens Sejrup and Vibe Nielsen (eds). *Global Art in Local Art Worlds: De-centering and Re-centering Europe in the Global Hierarchy of Value*, London: Routledge.

Index

Africa ix, 223–230, 232
age cohort 98–100
al-Mujawir, Ibn 227
ambient faith 63, 67. *See also* Eastern Orthodox Christianity
anarchy 121
archipelagos 224, 226–227, 238
Asia ix, xvi–xvii, xx, xxii–xxiii, 51, 54–56, 64–70, 105, 107, 112–113, 122, 222–223, 225–228, 230–231
atheism viii, 51–52, 56, 60, 62, 65, 99, 137, 191
Atlantic Ocean 224–225, 228, 230, 234, 237
Austronesia 226–228

belonging xvii, 13, 27–30, 40–42, 55, 57, 61, 63, 65–69, 122, 139, 143, 156
Benda-Beckmann, Franz and Keebet von 29, 39
Berdahl, Daphne 139
Black Atlantic 234
Braudel, Fernand 229–230
Bronze Age 230–232
Bulgaria vii, 28, 106

Casanova, Jose 56
Catholicism viii, xv, xxiii, 39–40, 43, 46, 66, 91, 173, 180, 184, 187, 189–190, 195–196, 200, 202
  Catholic Church 39, 43, 46, 180
Central and Eastern Europe (CEE) xii–xiii, xv, xvii, xx, xxii–xxiii, 1, 3, 5, 6, 17, 49, 51, 54–55, 66–68, 70, 158, 206–207. *See also* Eastern Europe
Central Asia ix, xvii, xx, xxii–xxiii, 51, 54–55, 64–70, 105, 107
Christianity viii, xiii, xv, xvii, 52, 58, 63–66, 68, 70, 83, 85–90, 92–93, 96, 149–150, 169, 231. *See also* Catholicism; *See also* Eastern Orthodox Christianity
  anthropology of Christianity xv, 52, 64–65, 83, 85–86
civilisation 53, 68, 93, 156, 181, 199, 223, 231
civility 27, 35, 44, 53–55, 58–61, 63–65, 67, 70–71, 170, 175
  local civility 170, 175
  uncivility 35
civil religion xvii, xxii, 51–53, 55–58, 69–70
civil society 52–53, 58, 180–181, 196, 206, 217–218
class ix, 13, 69, 94, 107–108, 123, 133–135, 142, 168, 170, 181–182, 184, 202, 213, 215–217, 225
  class boundaries 123
  class "harmony" 123
  class interests 107
  class sensibilities 108
  middle class 69, 108, 123, 125, 133–134, 170. *See also* middle strata
  popular class 216
  working class 133–134, 142, 181, 213, 215, 217

colonisation 183, 215, 226
compromise 109, 116, 185
    historic compromise 109
    Soviet-era compromise 109, 116
conflict 27, 36–37, 46, 58, 63, 65, 88, 96, 99, 173, 196, 218
    ethnic conflict viii, 25
    post-secular conflict 58
    property conflict 45. *See also* property: property relations
connectivity 222, 225, 227–228, 234–235
continents xvi, xix, 206, 222–226, 228, 230–231, 234–235, 237–239
conversion vii, 54, 60–61, 70
conviviality 35, 45, 47
corruption ix, 14–15, 43, 45, 114–115, 119, 121, 123–124, 166, 169, 214
countermovement 107, 126, 147, 170, 183, 218
Croatia viii, xvii, xxii, 25–46
Croats 26, 30–32, 34–36, 38–39, 41, 43–47
Czechoslovakia 183–193, 195–196, 199, 202

Eastern Europe viii–ix, xi, xix–xx, 5, 156, 158, 165, 168, 182, 185, 205–206, 216–218, 223. *See also* Central and Eastern Europe (CEE)
    vis-à-vis Western Europe 57, 60, 65, 87, 90, 160, 207, 223
Eastern Orthodox Christianity viii, xiii, xv, 39–41, 57–58, 63–68, 70, 81–100, 196. *See also* ambient faith; *See also* Old Believers; *See also* Orthodoxy: priestless Orthodoxy
economy viii, xi, xiii–xviii, 4–6, 9, 12, 17, 26–31, 36–39, 41, 45–47, 59–60, 64–66, 70, 81–86, 89–90, 95, 97–100, 105–112, 114–117, 120–126, 131–134, 136–141, 143–144, 146–150, 156, 158–161, 164–165, 167–168, 170, 174–175, 180–186, 192, 195–196, 202–203, 206–210, 213–214, 216–218, 230–231
    economic prosperity 83
    shortage economy 140–141
Engler, Wolfgang 142

ethnicity vii, xv–xvi, xviii, xx, 12, 25–26, 43, 45, 47, 61, 65–66, 68, 70, 83, 87, 158–160, 162–171, 174–175, 185, 192, 194, 199, 211–214, 226, 237, 239. *See also* conflict: ethnic conflict; *See also* nationalism: ethno-nationalism; *See also* nationality: ethno-nationality; *See also* solidarity: inter-ethnic solidarity
    embedded ethnicity 158, 161, 165, 168
ethnocentrism xv, 53, 85, 87, 90, 223
Eurasia xii–xiii, xvi, xix, xxiv, 105, 107, 221–226, 232, 237–239
European Union vii–viii, ix, 6, 8, 23–24, 27, 42–45, 47, 71, 94, 107, 155–158, 160, 162, 165, 168, 171, 174, 193, 196–197, 202, 205, 207, 211–212

fascism vii, 122–123, 138, 141, 170, 184, 189, 192, 214

GDR (German Democratic Republic) xx, 136–143
gender viii, 59, 81, 83–84, 98–100, 144, 207
generations xii–xiv, xix–xx, 28, 31, 33–34, 42, 47, 66, 82, 84, 98–99, 114, 122, 156, 163, 185, 187, 191, 197, 202, 217–218, 221, 227, 237
Goody, Jack xvi, 223, 226, 229–231
Gramsci, Antonio
    Gramscian 122
grassroots activism xi, xxiii, 111, 114, 116
Gypsies 159, 164, 167. *See also* Roma (Romani)
    anti-Gypsyism xviii, 157–159, 167, 175

Habermas, Jürgen 53, 56
Hann, Chris xii–xxv, 2, 5, 25, 28–29, 35, 39–40, 42, 52–58, 61, 64–65, 70–71, 83, 85–87, 89, 105–107, 124, 126, 132, 148–150, 158–159, 179–185, 196, 202–203, 206–209, 216–218, 222–225, 232, 235–238
hegemony 87, 107–108, 122–123, 156, 170, 224, 234, 238–239
heterotopia 44
Ho, Engseng 225, 232, 235, 237

home xx, 25, 27, 30, 32, 34, 40, 43, 67, 69, 82, 156–157, 159–161, 169, 186, 192, 213, 216, 222

hope xx, 39, 43–44, 88, 133, 162, 175, 191–192

housing
  houses xxiv, 10, 25–26, 28–41, 43–44, 46–47, 82, 114, 117, 132, 174, 188–189, 193, 196, 198, 215, 221–222
  housing property xvii, 25, 27–30, 32, 35–38
  housing relations 25, 27–29, 32. *See also* property: property relations
  socially owned 30, 37–38

Hungary xiii–xiv, xviii, xxiii, 12, 68, 106–107, 110, 126, 149–150, 152, 160–163, 165–167, 170–174, 179, 181–187, 190–192, 195–196, 201–202, 205, 207, 213, 216–217

identity ix, xv–xvii, xix, 12–13, 15–16, 27, 31, 55, 59, 62, 65, 67–70, 83–84, 87, 92–94, 98–100, 136, 150, 162, 164, 168–169, 175, 183, 214, 237
  ethno-national identity 55, 65, 67, 69. *See also* nationality: ethno-nationality
  national identity 55, 65, 67–69, 87, 150

ideology 5, 29, 38, 60, 70, 92–93, 118, 123, 132, 135–137, 141–143, 149, 151, 161–162, 166, 169–170, 181, 183–185, 188, 191, 196, 200, 203, 217

Indian Ocean 224–225, 227, 230–232, 235, 237–238

intelligentsia/intellectuals 53, 162, 173, 181–184, 190–191, 193–197, 199, 201–202, 206, 213

international organisations ix, 36–38, 45, 175

Islam 57, 62–64, 66–67, 69, 87, 107, 111, 113–115, 167, 231

islands 225–228, 233, 236–239

Italy
  southern Italy xvi, 1, 3, 5–8, 10–11, 13, 15, 17, 23

labour vii, 46, 55, 83, 94, 99, 105–106, 111, 120, 131, 134, 136, 138, 141, 143, 145, 148–150, 167, 196, 211–212, 225, 235–236. *See also* work
  industrial labour vii, 131
  labourers 120, 136, 156, 173, 227, 230, 236. *See also* work: workers

liberalism xi, xviii, xxii, 179–181, 200, 202–203

livelihood struggle 122, 125

longue-durée perspective xi

Luehrmann, Sonja 57, 59–61

middle strata 108, 110, 112, 114–116, 124–126. *See also* class: middle class

migration vii, 25, 45, 94, 111, 117–118, 148, 156, 159, 162, 165, 171, 174, 211,
  economic migration 207
  migrants 150, 156, 163, 169–173, 207, 212, 216, 225, 230
  mobility 6, 133, 156, 158, 160, 169, 171, 174, 222, 226–228, 230
  maritime mobilities 225, 236

modernisation 54, 57, 71, 89, 109, 125, 161–162, 180, 190, 201

modernity xi, xv–xvii, 2–3, 28, 44, 51–54, 56–57, 60, 70, 84–85, 89–90, 93–94, 100, 134, 224

nationalism vii, xv, xvii, 27, 30, 36, 39, 45–47, 52, 61, 63, 65, 68–69, 71, 111, 132, 135, 142, 159, 168, 181, 183–184, 191–193, 195, 200, 202, 206, 208, 211–213, 215–217. *See also* identity: national identity
  ethno-nationalism xv, xvii, 27, 30, 39, 52, 61. *See also* identity: ethno-national identity; *See also* religion: ethno-national religious knot

nationality 27, 71, 93, 113, 159, 226
  ethno-nationality 27. *See also* identity: ethno-national identity

neoliberalism 27, 35, 37–38, 45–46, 106–107, 112, 145, 149, 160, 180, 218, 236
  neoliberalisation 209
  neoliberal policies xii, 27, 46, 205, 210

North Atlantic universals 234

oceans ix, xix, 225–230, 232–234, 236–238. *See also* Indian Ocean; *See also* Pacific Ocean
Old Believers 81–82, 84, 91–92, 94–100
Orthodoxy. *See* Eastern Orthodox Christianity
  priestless Orthodoxy 82–84, 91–92, 96, 100

Pacific Ocean 227
peasants xviii, xxiii, 14, 68–69, 93, 99, 134, 136, 142, 161, 164, 179, 180, 182–185, 187–190, 193–194, 198, 203. *See also* populism: post-peasant populism
perestroika 98, 110, 115, 187
Poland vii–ix, xiv, xviii, xxii–xxiii, 40, 57–58, 68, 91, 94, 180–181, 183, 195, 201–202, 205, 207–208, 210–217, 221–222
Polanyi, Karl xiv, xvi, 106–107, 126, 148, 158–159, 161, 165, 167–168, 183
politics vii–ix, xi–xv, xvii–xviii, 2, 6–7, 9, 12–13, 15–16, 28–29, 37–38, 43, 45–46, 51–57, 59, 61–64, 66, 68–71, 84, 88–90, 92–93, 95–96, 100, 107–111, 114–116, 119–120, 122–123, 125–126, 135, 142, 148–149, 155–161, 165–172, 174–175, 179–181, 183–188, 191, 195–196, 198–203, 205, 207–210, 212, 214–217, 230, 235
  politics of differentiation 61–63
populism xi, xvi, xviii–xix, xxiii, 68–69, 71, 107–108, 110, 126, 149, 158, 179–180, 182–185, 193, 195–197, 201–203, 206–210, 214–218
  post-peasant populism xviii, xxiii, 68–69, 179, 183, 203
post-secularity. *See* secularism: post-secularity
post-socialism. *See* socialism: post-socialism
private sector 113, 124–125
privatisation 30–31, 37–39, 45, 57, 112, 119, 143, 160, 183, 186, 196–197, 202

deprivatisation of religion xxiii, 51, 56
progressivism xviii, 179, 193, 203
propaganda 118, 136, 175, 191, 197, 211
property xvii, 25, 27–38, 40, 43, 45–46, 61, 94, 96, 181, 183, 198, 207, 222, 233
  private property xvii, 35, 37–38, 46, 181, 183
  property relations viii–xix, 25, 27–29, 35, 39, 49, 207. *See also* conflict: property conflict; *See also* housing: housing relations
protest 97, 114–115, 117, 142, 144–147, 151, 166, 169–170, 173, 180, 189, 201
Protestantism xv, xxii, 56–57, 65, 70, 83–87, 90–91, 132–134, 137–138, 142–143, 147, 189–190
  Protestant ethic 84, 86, 132–133, 137–138, 142
public sector 113–114, 121, 123–125

reactionarism xviii, 107, 170, 179–180, 183, 185, 189, 192–193, 195–196, 198–199, 201–203
religion vii–ix, xii–xiii, xv–xvii, xix, xxii–xxiii, 13, 15, 39–40, 51–71, 81–88, 90, 92, 94–100, 114–115, 137, 143, 161, 183, 189, 200, 212, 214, 224, 231. *See also* civil religion
  anthropologies of religion 60
  ethno-national religious knot 67, 69
  religious authority viii, 92, 97, 100
  religious revivals xvii, 51, 56, 59, 70
ritual viii–ix, xxii, 10, 31, 59, 62, 67, 82, 95–96, 98–99, 163
  ritual practice 99
Romania vii, 28, 60, 68, 84, 88, 155–156, 158–166, 168–175, 199, 205
Roma (Romani) vii, 150, 156–160, 164–168, 170–171, 173–175, 191, 199. *See also* Gypsies
ruralism vii, xviii, 1, 6, 12–13, 28–29, 58, 68, 83, 99, 106–107, 111–114, 150, 161–162, 164, 166, 180–187, 190, 193, 196, 198–199, 201, 203, 207, 217
  rural communities vii, 106, 112
  rural transformation 162

Scott, James 105, 148
seafarers xix, 226, 228, 230, 234–238
secularism viii, 51–67, 70–71, 84, 89, 111, 114, 138, 143
  post-secularity 51, 53–54, 56–58, 63
  post-Soviet secularism 63, 68
  Soviet secularism 57, 70
Serbia 26, 33, 35, 37, 45, 171
Serbs 26, 30–32, 34–47
shock therapy 110, 143, 205–206
Slovakia xviii, xxii, 6–15, 17, 21, 23, 28, 179, 182–203, 217
socialism vii–viii, xi–xx, xxii–xxiii, 5–9, 11–12, 14, 25, 27–30, 32, 35, 37–40, 42, 44–46, 51–68, 70–71, 98, 105–107, 112, 119, 126, 131–132, 135, 137–139, 143, 149–151, 156, 159–163, 167, 169–170, 179–191, 193, 197–203, 205–207, 210–211, 214–216, 218, 223
  post-socialism viii, xi–xiv, xvi–xx, xxii–xxiii, 6–7, 9, 12, 14, 25, 27–28, 30, 32, 38–40, 46, 51, 53–62, 64–67, 70–71, 105–106, 112, 119, 126, 161, 179–181, 183–184, 186, 191, 193, 198–199, 201–203, 206–207, 211, 216, 223
    post-socialist transformation xi, xiii–xiv, xvii, xxiii, 6–7, 9, 12, 28, 30, 56, 60, 70, 218
social security vii, xvii, 27, 29, 39, 45
solidarity 1, 47, 58, 138, 160, 169, 175, 180, 213
  inter-ethnic solidarity 47
Soviet Union (USSR) xiii, 52, 65, 71, 109–110, 113, 122
Szeklerland 162–163, 165
Szeklers 173

Taylor, Charles 53, 57, 225
thalassography 234–236
Thompson, Edward P. 105, 108, 148
Transoceania xix, 221, 225–226, 229, 231–232, 234–239

Treuhandanstalt 143
trust xvi, 1–17, 23, 45, 106, 139, 155

unemployment xviii, 35, 38, 41, 132, 143–147, 150–151, 162, 205, 216

values xiv, xviii, 5–6, 11, 16–17, 27, 29, 35, 42, 46, 58–59, 66, 68, 95, 105–108, 110, 126, 132, 137–138, 147–151, 179, 185, 190, 200, 203, 214, 218
villages xiv, xxiv, 6–7, 9–10, 12–14, 32, 37, 41, 44, 46, 81–82, 91, 95–98, 100, 117–120, 160–161, 164, 170–172, 179–181, 183, 186–188, 190–199
  villagers 8–10, 12–14, 41, 120, 162, 185, 187, 190, 195, 198, 207, 212

Wanner, Catherine 57, 61, 63, 66–68
Washington Consensus 110
welfare state 134
work ix, xii–xv, xvii–xxi, xxiii–xxv, 6, 9–10, 28–29, 33–34, 51–62, 64–65, 70, 82, 86, 94, 97–99, 106–107, 110–112, 116, 118–119, 121–126, 131–151, 156, 158–159, 165, 173, 181–182, 190, 193–194, 196–198, 207–208, 211–212, 215, 217–218, 229–230, 235, 237. *See also* labour
  workers 30, 66, 81, 98, 109, 112–113, 119, 123, 131–135, 137–142, 144–145, 147–151, 168, 173, 180, 189, 192, 197–198, 211–214, 216–217. *See also* labour: labourers
workfare xiii, 106–107, 126, 149
workplaces xvii, 27–28, 30, 38, 123–124, 139, 143, 150, 188
  socialist workplace 139, 143, 150

xenophilia 229
xenophobia xviii, 155, 158–160, 166–168, 170–175, 199, 206–208, 216–217

Yugoslavia viii, 29–30, 45

About the Team

Alessandra Tosi was the managing editor for this book.

Melissa Purkiss performed the copy-editing and proofreading.

Katy Saunders designed the cover. The cover was produced in InDesign using the Fontin font.

Melissa Purkiss and Luca Baffa typeset the book in InDesign and produced the paperback and hardback editions. The text font is Tex Gyre Pagella; the heading font is Californian FB.

Luca produced the EPUB, AZW3, PDF, HTML, and XML editions — the conversion is performed with open source software such as pandoc (https://pandoc.org/) created by John MacFarlane and other tools freely available on our GitHub page (https://github.com/OpenBookPublishers).

This book need not end here...

Share

All our books—including the one you have just read—are free to access online so that students, researchers and members of the public who can't afford a printed edition will have access to the same ideas. This title will be accessed online by hundreds of readers each month across the globe: why not share the link so that someone you know is one of them?

This book and additional content is available at:

https://doi.org/10.11647/OBP.0282

Donate

Open Book Publishers is an award-winning, scholar-led, not-for-profit press making knowledge freely available one book at a time. We don't charge authors to publish with us: instead, our work is supported by our library members and by donations from people who believe that research shouldn't be locked behind paywalls.

Why not join them in freeing knowledge by supporting us: https://www.openbookpublishers.com/support-us

Like Open Book Publishers

Follow @OpenBookPublish

Read more at the Open Book Publishers **BLOG**

You may also be interested in:

Lifestyle in Siberia and the Russian North

Joachim Otto Habeck

https://doi.org/10.11647/obp.0171

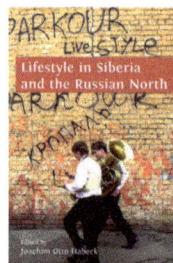

Mobilities, Boundaries, and Travelling Ideas
Rethinking Translocality Beyond Central Asia and the Caucasus

Manja Stephan-Emmrich and Philipp Schröder (eds.)

https://doi.org/10.11647/obp.0114

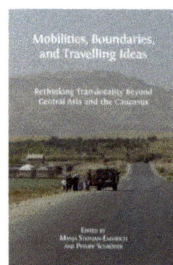

Life Histories of Etnos Theory in Russia and Beyond

David G. Anderson, Dmitry V. Arzyutov, Sergei S. Alymov (eds.)

https://doi.org/10.11647/obp.0150

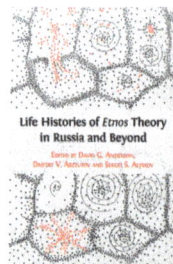